BREAKTHROUGH

Also by Ruth Maxwell
The Booze Battle

BREAKTHROUGH

*What To Do
When Alcoholism
or Chemical
Dependency Hits
Close To Home*

RUTH MAXWELL

Ballantine Books • New York

All rights reserved under International and Pan-American Copyright Conventions. Published in the United States by Ballantine Books, a division of Random House, Inc., New York, and simultaneously in Canada by Random House of Canada Limited, Toronto.

Library of Congress Cataloging in Publication Data

Maxwell, Ruth, 1933–
 Breakthrough: what to do when alcoholism or
 chemical dependency hits close to home

 Bibliography: p. 273
 Includes index
 1. Alcoholics—Rehabilitation—United States,
2. Alcoholics—United States—Family relationships,
I. Title.
HV5279.M29 1986   362.2′92   85-90871
ISBN: 0-345-31956-7

Manufactured in the United States of America
Design by Holly Johnson

First Edition: September 1986
10 9 8 7 6 5 4 3 2 1

In memory of
　　　　Rebecca McLaren Maxwell
　　　　　　for giving me life

In gratitude to
　　　　Grace Baker Maxwell
　　　　　　for nurturing me
　　　　　　　　and
　　　　Robert Grove Maxwell
　　　　　　for big footsteps

Contents

Contents

Acknowledgments

I have many people to thank:

Joëlle Delbourgo, my editor, whose ideas are reflected throughout, and especially for getting me started and keeping me going.

Sharlyn Carter for her enthusiasm and assistance throughout, and especially for her suggestion that I write the book in the same order that I work with clients.

Lothar Gidro-Frank, M.D., for his enthusiasm and assistance throughout, and especially for his advice on the sections dealing with defenses.

Kathy Collins, whose tears as she typed made me believe I was on the right track, and especially for providing sanity in my nonwriting work life.

Judi, Rachel, and Dan, for once again putting up with a writing mom, and especially for their love and nurturing.

Rick Hernandez and Susan Robards, for their enthusiasm, and especially for believing in me.

Colleagues from whom I have learned, Bob de Veer, Gordon Bohl, Vernon Johnson, Ann Smith, Doris Krupnick, Carol Kitman, Bob Aylmer, David Treadway, as well as those whose writings are mentioned in the book.

And most especially all the families and chemically dependent persons with whom I have worked, who have given as much, if not more, than they have received.

BREAKTHROUGH

I

You're Not Crazy

If you are living with someone who is harmfully involved with alcohol or drugs, you may be questioning your own sanity. *You're not crazy. You may feel shattered, but you are not crazy.*

Look at some of the rules of your household. Rules set by the alcohol- or drug-dependent person, the most disturbed person in your family. Rules strengthened by the very fact they're rarely articulated. Rules that are inhuman. Rules that would make *anyone* feel crazy.

Rule number one. *The alcohol- or drug-dependent person is the most important person in the family.* His needs and wants matter the most, while yours matter little, if at all. This rule, set forth by behavior more than words, clearly states that the chemically dependent person can do whatever he wishes whenever he wishes, and that you exist to serve him.

Rule number two. *The alcohol- or drug-dependent person is always right; you are always wrong.* No matter what you do, you never win, not for long.

Rule number three. *His alcohol or drug use is not the primary problem.* This rule, set forth by both words and actions, clearly states that outside circumstances and people, especially you, are at fault not, God forbid, his alcohol or drug use. Therefore, it is your responsibility to shape up and avoid talking to anyone about his chemical use.

No wonder you're feeling crazy!

If you find you are following these rules, you might also be making his use of alcohol or drugs your primary concern. If so, you are concentrating on the wrong problem and causing more problems.

If you concentrate on his drinking or drug use, you are destined to try to get him to cut down or stop altogether, to figure out why he's using or drinking so much, and to alter his life so he can alter his chemical use. As a result, you'll give him exactly what he needs in order to do more of what you do not want him to do. In turn, you'll become even more shattered, more terribly traumatized, while he'll get sicker.

It will serve you better to concern yourself primarily with his deteriorating personality—his increasing mental and emotional mismanagement. There is hope—for both of you. Once you understand what lies behind his irrational behavior, you will be able to help both yourself and him, even if he does not want help.

I gave a paper on motivating unmotivated alcohol- and drug-dependent persons last year in Athens at the international conference on addictions and was nearly booed out of the room. I described various means for getting the alcohol- or drug-dependent person into treatment, some of which are performed behind his back, and all of which are often dependent upon determining addiction from the data of the family rather than the chemical-dependent person. My audience was composed largely of psychiatrists from Europe and Scandinavia, and they were shocked. Coming from backgrounds deeply steeped in traditional psychiatric wisdom, they firmly believed that people cannot be treated unless they are motivated for treatment. They considered it unethical to operate behind a person's back. But they were outright flabbergasted to hear that we were determining addiction without seeing the addicted person.

How many of you, like my European colleagues, believe that you can't help an alcoholic or drug addict until he wants help—until he "hits bottom"? How many of you believe there's something wrong about going behind a person's back? How many of you believe the alcoholic or drug addict has to be examined by someone else in order to be diagnosed? All of you perhaps. Yet, none of the above is true.

When alcoholics and drug addicts hit bottom, they reach that moment in time when they gain sufficient insight into their condition to become willing to do something about it. You do not have to wait for the alcohol- or drug-dependent person to do so. Counting on an outside circumstance—job loss, a drunk driving charge, holes in his nostrils, an enlarged liver, whatever—to increase his insight is risky business. What is "bottom" for one may not be "bottom" for another. Then, too, he may be killed or incarcerated before hitting bottom. I will describe various things you can do to create a "bottom" for him, to increase his insight into his condition so that he becomes willing to change. Many of the steps I'll describe are open and aboveboard. But in case they are not effective, I'll also talk about steps you can take behind his back that are almost sure to work. I'll also tell you how you can determine if alcoholism or drug addiction is present so you can help him earlier in the disease process, when he is most treatable.

Before going further, let's clarify two matters: gender and alcoholism versus drug addiction/dependency.

Neither sex is immune, both become addicted to alcohol and drugs, perhaps in equal numbers. To emphasize addiction of both sexes and to avoid the awkwardness of (s)he, I'll do as baby doctors do when they write books these days. Unless describing specific persons, I'll alternate genders, case by case. Because adolescents are also not immune, when I speak generally, what I say will apply to youths as well as adults.

Alcohol in any beverage form—beer, wine, or liquor—is a

central nervous system depressant and, as such, is a drug—a powerful drug capable of altering our thinking, feeling, and behavior. Persons addicted to alcohol and persons addicted to other mood-altering, mind-changing drugs that act upon the central nervous system, such as marijuana, cocaine, heroin, other narcotics, sedatives, and tranquilizers, have more *in common* than they have *in difference.* For all practical purposes, any differences between alcohol addiction and other drug addictions do not make a difference. The addiction phenomenon is the same, regardless of the addicting agent, be it a liquid, solid, or gas; used alone or in combination; legal or illegal; socially acceptable or unacceptable. The truth is, the brain could care less!

The addiction picture is changing in the United States. We don't see as many "pure" alcoholics as in the past. Nor do we see "pure" cocaine, heroin, or marijuana addicts. Today, most persons who become addicted, especially those under forty, use more than one chemical and many are addicted to more than one chemical. Even if they are not multiple-drug addicted, they readily substitute other drugs when their drug of choice—alcohol, for example, or cocaine—is no longer used or is not available; thus the addiction progresses on relentlessly.

The terms *addiction* and *dependency* mean the same thing. In the past, many people believed that dependency had to do with a psychological need for the drug while addiction had to do with a physiological need. Today we know the psychological dependency is simply an earlier phase of addiction, thus, I'll use the terms *addiction* and *dependency* synonymously. A person psychologically dependent is no less addicted; as with mid-stage pregnancy, the addiction just doesn't show as much.

I'll use the term *chemical dependency* frequently throughout the book, incorporating all phases of addiction as well as the phenomenon of addiction, which is the same no matter what the addicting agent. Thus, when speaking of the alcoholic or drug addict, I'll use the terms *dependent* or *chemically dependent person.*

To highlight the incredible intertwining that occurs between the dependent and his loved ones, I'll use the term *co-dependent* when speaking of his spouse, lover, parent, or child. The term *co-dependency* will represent the family members' maladaptive responses to chemical dependency.

Chemical dependency is an illness—a primary illness with its own set of symptoms and its own progressive stages. Chemical dependency is not a moral issue, nor is it a symptom of something else. Even if they should desire, people do not deliberately become addicted; nor, even though they may ardently wish to, do they prevent it. Addiction to alcohol, cocaine, heroin, and all the other drugs has something to do with the chemical itself. Certain drugs, such as cocaine and heroin, have a very high addiction potential, causing addiction in most users, while alcohol has a lower addiction potential, causing addiction in about 10 percent of users. Then, too, addiction has something to do with time and dose factors; and it certainly has to do with genetic factors. While I will discuss causes of addiction in more detail as we move on, the fact remains that we do not know of any one cause but can assume that many factors go into the creation of this formidably progressive and clearly describable illness.

Chemical dependency is a tyranny of the highest order. The alcohol- or drug-dependent person is governed totally by the forces of his addiction, and in turn he governs others totally. He becomes an awesome tyrant. His irrational behavior is very specific and so powerful that it alters the thoughts, feelings, and behavior of others.

None of us, without specific knowledge and help, has protection against this kind of behavior in the person to whom we've given our love and trust. If repeatedly blamed and raged at, all of us will feel guilty, and our fear will compel us to keep peace at any price. If repeatedly embarrassed, scorned, and provoked, all of us will cringe in shame or fly off into rages of our own. If faced daily with arrogance and grossly distorted perceptions, all of us will feel inadequate and begin to question our own sanity.

It is only when we understand what lies behind his irrational but powerful behavior that we can remain intact ourselves and be helpful to the chemically dependent person. Without this understanding, his behavior will destroy our integrity; it will invade our boundaries and cause us to become unwell.

Under the onslaughts of the tyranny of chemical dependency, family members do well just to survive. They may believe they have not coped well, but they have in fact responded with enormous courage. They may feel they have failed, but in reality they have been fighting a battle for their personhood, if not their life. Under the circumstances it is a wonder they are in one piece.

Spouses, lovers, parents, and children often believe they've had no choice in their response to the chemically dependent person, and they're so right. The cards have been stacked against them. Not only is the dependent's behavior irrational, the illness of chemical dependency is different from other illnesses in several ways.

First, its onset is subtle, and before the co-dependents can see it, they are in it. They use protective measures to adapt and these measures then begin to have a momentum of their own; using them calls for their further use. As a result, co-dependents enter into maladaptive responses to an illness they can't see and, by the time they can see it, they are trapped by their own responses.

Initially and for quite some time, the dependent's illness is sporadic; crises are followed by lengthy periods of peace, which lead members of the family to believe that life has returned to normal and that they had little reason for their concerns. Because of its subtle onset and its sporadic nature, co-dependents cannot grasp the magnitude of the illness and are unable to see that the illness is present during times of peace as well as times of crisis. Instead, remembering the way life used to be, they live from crisis to crisis, fully expecting a permanent return to the normality of the past seemingly promised by each period of peace. It would be far easier for the family to get a handle on the illness without those deceiving peaceful periods.

Most illnesses are diagnosed fairly early; consequently people know what they're up against and treatment can be sought. Chemical dependency presents clearly diagnosable *physical* symptoms only in its late stage. Without physical symptoms, many health professionals feel they cannot make an accurate diagnosis in the earlier stages. Such an argument, rather than carrying weight, measures the inadequacy of these professionals' addiction education. Chemical dependency can be diagnosed early and should be, as it is most treatable in its earlier stages. But because few health professionals know enough about the illness to detect it, chemically dependent persons and their families are forced into the use of home remedies for years. Chemical dependency is the third leading killer in the United States. Late diagnoses and resort to home remedies in the place of early treatment are a national disgrace and a personal tragedy for millions.

Chemical dependency is different from other illnesses because it bears a stigma. Chemical dependency is commonly perceived as a self-induced condition, rather than the illness it really is. I often think that Betty Ford has done as much as any person or professional group to help society perceive chemical dependency as a treatable illness, rather than a shameful moral issue. Plotting behind her back, Betty's family intervened upon her illness, and Betty accepted treatment. In her recovery she formed a treatment center to help others. Rather than hiding behind a conspiracy of silence, she gracefully acknowledged her own illness. How shameful can chemical dependency be if she has it? Still, the stigma remains; out of their shame and fear of condemnation, chemically dependent persons and their families are forced to keep the problem hidden. Thus, they are not able to seek or receive the help they need in a timely fashion.

I will describe the underlying forces of addiction, so that you can better meet the dependent's needs as well as your own. But learning how to be truly helpful and how to remain intact depends first upon understanding that the chemically dependent person is powerless, unable to consistently control his chemical use. I can write a million books and talk until I'm blue in the face, and nothing will help until you see and accept that he has lost control of his chemical use, which means there is absolutely nothing you can do to help him apply that which he doesn't have. Loss of control is certainly the problem but, as you will see, control is in no way the solution.

Mostly I will address the deterioration and rebuilding of the personality, matters of the head and heart, in both the chemically dependent person and his loved ones. We'll follow two families as they break through the tyranny of chemical dependency, and we'll meet briefly with many others as well.

We'll begin with Susan as she first seeks help for her husband's chemical dependency. She's been trying to get him to cut down or stop using cocaine and alcohol for over eight years, and she's more than a little shattered as a result. But she doesn't stay shattered for long. As soon as she begins to see what lies behind Jeff's crazy behavior, she is able to put herself back together again. Within weeks, she is able to get Jeff to agree to enter treatment, but because he is incredibly stubborn, to say the least, she has to go to considerable lengths to secure his compliance. Jeff fights his treatment every step of the way, but gets the message in spite of himself. You will see that the treatment of chemical dependency addresses the problem of uncontrolled chemical use, but that it concentrates mostly on mental and emotional mismanagement and management. Susan and their oldest son, Alan, much to their consternation, find that their treatment concentrates on their maladaptive responses and not on Jeff's illness.

Along the way you'll meet Jim and his family. Poor Jim. For a while it seemed like his whole life was falling apart. No sooner had he come to me for help for his elderly mother, a very proper lady who passed out drunk in the beauty parlor, than his "happy" fifteen-year-old daughter told him she was depressed and concerned about her marijuana use. Jim was already worried about his oldest daughter, who smoked pot and drank alcohol on weekends and was no longer doing very well in school. For Jim, a perfectionist who demanded great things from himself and others, it was all a bit too much. His father had died of alcoholism when Jim was a teenager. The last thing Jim wanted or expected was to find addiction in both his mother and one of his children. He couldn't understand why they had not learned their lesson.

Finally, we will follow both Susan's and Jim's families as they face and overcome their problems. Like Susan, Jim, and so many others, you also can help yourself and your dependent loved one, so that you *both* can break through the tyranny of chemical dependency. But you will need help. This illness is far too malignant for anyone to handle alone. Fortunately, help exists.

Al-Anon, (Pill-Anon, and Narc-Anon), the self-help organizations for families of alcoholics and drug-addicted persons, is available in most communities; as is Parents Anonymous, for parents of chemically dependent adolescents; and Alateen, for children of alcoholic parents. Adult Children of Alcoholics (COA) self-help groups also exist and are of great value for helping adults resolve problems stemming from parental alcoholism. All of these organizations are designed to help the family members help themselves.

Alcoholics Anonymous (AA), for alcoholics, also exists in communities throughout the United States, as does Narcotics Anonymous (NA), for other drug-dependent persons.

These self-help groups are incredibly powerful sources of help. It's irrelevant whether or not you *like* attending meetings of these organizations, though in time you no doubt will, if not immediately. Think about this for a moment. Do you *like* going to the dentist? Who *likes* treatment? It's your *need* for help that has relevance, and little else. These organizations are listed in the telephone directory.

There are both out-patient and residential chemical dependency centers in several areas of the United States, where both families and chemically dependent persons can receive assistance in evaluation and intervention as well as treatment. These centers are listed in telephone directories under alcohol, drug, or chemical dependency services or under hospitals.

I will relate the experiences of everyone you will meet drawing from interviews with them while they were in counseling with me. I've changed their names and every other tangible characteristic while, to the best of my ability, I have remained true to their regression into illness and their progression into wellness, to matters of the head and heart, and to actions they have taken.

I believe that illness does not diminish in any way the inherent value of a human being. I have experienced the illness of which I write, and I am well today because I was accepted, cared for, and loved, even though ill. My concern as I introduce you to the people I've accepted, cared for, and loved is that I will not do justice to their personhood, to their courage, strengths, and many other special intangible characteristics. They have been meaningful and dear to me; I hope they will be to you.

In essence, we'll be looking at a tyranny and how to break through that tyranny. First we'll see *what is*, then *what can be*. Let's meet Susan. She hardly has her coat off before she nearly blasts us out of my office.

2

Susan

Susan was late for her first appointment and full of apologies. "I'm sorry. I don't know what happened to me. I've been on this street hundreds of times, and I just couldn't find it this morning. Isn't that stupid? I'm very sorry; I just can't seem to do anything right," she said, looking flustered and unable to get herself or her belongings into any kind of settled arrangement on the sofa in my office. Having chosen not to leave her coat in the waiting room, she had it over her shoulders, but it kept sliding down her back. Her cigarettes fell to the floor; she couldn't find her lighter, and her datebook, bulging with papers, looked as if it were about to pop the encircling rubber bands. Locating her lighter, Susan continued reaching around inside her purse as if she needed something more before she could speak. Then, apparently unable to find whatever it was that she wanted, she gave up her search, sat on the edge of her seat and said, "This is really silly; I'm sorry I'm so late."

"You're here, Susan; that's what counts," I replied, hoping

to reassure her. "We have plenty of time, so you don't have to rush." But Susan remained perched on the edge of the sofa, amidst all her belongings, prepared for flight. She reminded me of one of those little birds that collects pieces of colorful cloth, tinfoil, pretty feathers, and whatever else it can find for its nest—except Susan didn't seem all that comfortable in the nest she had made for herself on the edge of the sofa.

"Oh, but I can't believe I got lost. I just can't imagine what happened; it seems like I can't even think properly. I don't even know if I should be here," she said, remaining perched on the edge of her seat.

"This is where you should be, Susan. When you called, you said you were concerned about your husband's drinking, and that's why I'm here, to help you with those concerns . . ."

"But I don't even know if Jeff's an alcoholic," she interrupted. "He keeps saying he isn't, and maybe he really isn't. He goes to work every day . . . why, he's never even late for work, so I'm just not sure. Oh, I'm so confused."

"You have every reason to feel confused. Drinking problems cause confusion," I said, but before I could continue Susan was once again searching frantically in her purse. Finally, she pulled forth a packet of snapshots and thrust them at me. The top picture was of a man slumped on a sofa, arms akimbo, legs stretched out before him, beer cans lined up on the table alongside him, his head back, mouth open, apparently passed out. Knowing that I didn't need to see pictures, I returned the packet to Susan, who was by then fumbling with a tape recorder. Before I could say a word, loud shouts filled my office— a man and woman haranguing each other at the top of their voices. Susan had found the on button but now couldn't seem to locate the volume control. My flighty little bird was brewing up quite a storm, all within the first five minutes of our meeting.

I got up, walked over to Susan, picked up the tape recorder, turned it off, picked up her pocketbook, replaced both the recorder and the pictures, put her pocketbook down, and walked back to my chair. "Susan, are you going to stay?" I asked. "You look as if you are about to fly away at any moment. We have plenty of time, and we need to talk. Please, sit back, get comfortable, and leave your purse alone. I don't need anything more than your words. Your husband may not believe you when you tell him he has a drinking problem, but I am going to believe every word you say. So forget all that stuff and tell me about what's happening in your life right now. It seems as if it's been very painful."

"It's been horrible," she answered, sitting back in the sofa slightly more at ease. "I can't stand one more minute of it. He drinks every night and it's terrible. He doesn't remember what he says—he rambles and argues—and he makes me feel as if there's something wrong with me. It probably is my fault. Jeff's a wonderful person and I really love him. I just wish he wouldn't drink so much, but no matter what I say, he won't listen."

"That must be very frustrating," I said.

"Everything he does is frustrating. My whole life is frustrating," she replied.

"I'd like a clearer picture of what your life is like right now, Susan. Tell me about last night. Describe your evening from the time Jeff arrived home."

Susan said that she could never be sure of what time Jeff would arrive home, that several times a month he would call to say that he'd be late and then arrive home at two or three in the morning, so drunk he could barely climb the stairs. Most other evenings he'd arrive home anywhere between eight and ten.

"What happens then? Do you serve him dinner?" I asked.

"Yes, and it's not just a simple meal. Jeff's a fussy eater and he expects at least three courses."

"Do you like cooking a full meal that late in the evening?" I asked.

"Well, I guess I'd like it better a little earlier, but I really don't mind."

"Okay, let's go back to last night. What was your evening like?"

"Oh, I don't know," she answered vaguely. "Every evening ends up in an argument. No matter what I say, he starts arguing or telling me everything's my fault . . . and maybe it is. All day long I plan exactly what I'm going to say to Jeff that evening. I even rehearse *how* I'm going to talk to him, but it doesn't help. Nothing I do is right."

"That must be very difficult for you . . . to try so hard and always fail."

"It is . . . it really is. But he's a wonderful person."

"Susan, it would be natural for you to be feeling some disloyalty, as if you shouldn't be talking about Jeff. Is that how you're feeling?"

"That's exactly how I'm feeling," she replied quickly. "I keep thinking he's such a wonderful person, how can I be saying these horrible things about him . . . behind his back. Jeff's a very private person."

"And I'd almost guarantee that his drinking is the number-one forbidden topic, is that right?" I asked.

"Yes," she chuckled, much more at ease. "It certainly is."

"Well, in order to determine the extent of Jeff's problem, I'm going to need to hear more about his drinking. Is it going to be okay with you to break that 'no talk' rule of his?"

"Yes, I've had it. I just can't stand it anymore. What do you want to know?"

"First, I'd like a clearer picture of your life right now, then I'd like some history of when the troubles started. But let's start with last night. What time did Jeff get home? Had he been drinking? What did he do when he got home? What did you do—that kind of thing."

"It was horrible, it's always horrible. Oh, I'm sorry, what did you ask? I'm not answering your question, am I?"

"That's all right, Susan. I know it's difficult for you to concentrate right now. What I'd like to know, if you feel up to it, is specifically what happened last night."

"It's okay, I'm feeling better. Jeff got home a little after nine and he *had* been drinking. He drinks every evening after work. When he got home, he fixed a drink first thing and then started a fire in the fireplace, like he always does. Then he sat down to read the newspaper.

"I had planned veal chops with sweet peppers and vinegar and, as you probably know, they have to be timed very carefully, so I had to disturb Jeff to ask him when he'd like to eat. He told me to leave him alone, that he wanted to relax. But I didn't know what to do. I had the chops but didn't dare cook them in case he didn't want to eat, but I was afraid not to cook them in case he did. So I had to interrupt him again, and he got so mad that he followed me into the kitchen and started yelling at me. Then he picked up a bowl of fruit and threw it across the room. The apples flew all over the place and chips of glass got in the veal. It was terrible. Then he stomped out of the kitchen saying that I was a lousy wife . . . that I'm always getting in his way. Oh, I can't take it. I really can't take any more."

"I can certainly see why," I replied. "Susan, I want to depart from last night for just a moment. Do you have children?"

Susan then reported that they had three sons, Alan nearly eleven, Tad eight, and Scotty five. She said that she always made sure the boys were in bed by eight each evening. "You have no idea what happens if they're up when Jeff gets home."

"What happens?"

"Oh, goodness, anything and everything—you name it and he does it. He yells at them or spends three hours lecturing them about their homework. Or he keeps them up all hours rambling on about his childhood or the wars in Central America. Anything's possible, but usually what happens is that one of the kids will say something he doesn't like, then he lines them up and lets them have it. He lines us all up . . ."

"Does he ever hit any of you?" I asked.

"No, never. He's never hit the kids. Jeff's a wonderful father. He works very hard to provide for them. No, he's never hit them. He really loves them."

"Has he ever hit you?" I asked.

"Well, yes, he did hit me once," Susan replied hesitantly. At my urging, she said that the month before Jeff had pushed her up against a wall and punched her in the face with his fists. When Susan screamed, their oldest son, Alan, came running into the kitchen and tried to stop Jeff. In response, Jeff picked Alan up and threw him across the kitchen and then stormed out of the house, leaving them bruised and in tears. Susan was indignant in manner as she described this scene, but in no other way revealed any of her feelings. When I commented on how disturbing this assault must have been, she again ignored her feelings and said, "He didn't even remember it the next morning. He told me I was imagining things. He does that all the time, and I can't *stand* it. I don't know who to believe anymore. I think maybe I *am* imagining things and yet I know they happen."

"No wonder you're feeling confused—a little crazy even," I said.

"Not a *little* crazy! *Very* crazy, that's how I feel most of the time," Susan answered.

"Susan, I'm going to tell you something very important. *You* are not crazy. If Jeff's an alcoholic, *he's* crazy, but *you aren't.* You are terribly traumatized, but not crazy; but you look right now as if you don't believe me; is that true?"

"How can he be crazy? He works! He holds an important position in his company. He's a regional manager. You should see him when he leaves the house in the morning. He looks terrific—all dressed up, neat as a pin, smiling like nothing was wrong. I feel like I'm crazy to even *think* he's crazy."

"Yes," I smiled. "I can understand that. I'm often amazed at how good alcoholics can look, but I've got news for you, they're still crazy. Let's get back to last night. You wanted to know a simple thing like when to cook the veal chops and Jeff followed you into the kitchen in some kind of snit. What happened after that?"

"Oh, he just ranted on about how I'm always on his back, always making his life difficult. I said something about wishing he wouldn't drink so much and then he shouted at me, saying as long as he's working and doesn't have hangovers, that he's not an alcoholic. He told me he has a *wife* problem, not a *drinking* problem.

"Anyway, then he went back into the den, drank some more and fell asleep in front of the T.V. He never did have his dinner—that's the way it is most evenings," Susan reported. "He gets drunk, passes out in front of the television set, and then stumbles up to bed some time in the middle of the night. I usually end up throwing his dinner in the garbage."

"That's not a very pretty picture of a life, is it, Susan?" I gently asked.

"No, it isn't. It's a terrible life," she replied softly.

"But you've given me a *clear* picture. I feel like I have a good idea of what you're going through right now, and that will help me, so I can help you. But first I need more information. I need some of the history of when this all started. If you're up to it, we can do that now, or we can wait for your next appointment. Which would you prefer?"

"Oh, I'd rather get it over with," Susan replied, and she then described some of the history of her life with Jeff, beginning with their freshman year in college when they first started dating.

Jeff drank heavily at that time, especially on weekends, but Susan wasn't really worried, as most of their friends drank as much or more. Susan didn't like Jeff's drinking; her father had been an alcoholic, and she certainly had no intention of getting involved with anyone else who had a drinking problem, but she was able to overlook her early concerns. "When I complained, Jeff drank less. Besides I was sure it was just a passing thing and that Jeff would settle down once he was out of school."

Susan and Jeff dropped out of college to marry at the end of their third year. Neither placed a high value on a college education as they both had good jobs waiting for them. Susan could work as often as she liked in her mother's gift shop, and Jeff had been offered a job as a sales representative for an electronics firm; they could see no reason to delay their marriage.

Alan, now ten, was born two years after their marriage, and Tad followed two years later. Susan reported that they were wonderful babies, happy and adorable. She enjoyed taking care of them and liked her part-time work in her mother's shop; Jeff was also doing well in his job. "It all seemed so perfect," Susan said, smiling.

At that moment, watching Susan smile, I could easily envision what must once have seemed a golden life. I knew it was hard for her to talk about Jeff's drinking and their problems; yet she was warm, engaging, and easy to like. She was also exceptionally attractive, with a bright smile and large brown eyes set perfectly against an olive complexion and long black hair. Hearing more of her history, I knew she was brave to face her problems, and I could not help but admire how well she had survived.

It was after Tad's birth, eight years before, that Susan had started to become seriously concerned about Jeff. At Tad's birth, Jeff left while Susan was in labor to go downstairs for a pack of cigarettes. He didn't return for hours, long after she had given birth, and then he was so drunk the nurses had to call a guard to get him out. A few weeks later Susan saw Jeff take a snort of cocaine at a party. "That did it for me; I was already worried about his drinking. And I also knew he had started to smoke marijuana again. He had stopped using pot when we were in college, but he was now using it several times a week. So when I saw him take that cocaine, I freaked out. I screamed at him all the way home, but he said he had used coke several times and that there was nothing to worry about."

"The next two years were terrible," Susan continued. Jeff was soon using cocaine several times a day, and then he started dealing. Susan reported that perfect strangers would come to their house, speak briefly with Jeff outside the door, and then leave. Occasionally she would overhear him making drug deals on the phone. Whenever she tried to express her fears about the cocaine and the dealing, Jeff would just ignore her or angrily tell her to mind her own business.

On several occasions, Susan reported, Jeff had been forced to stop using cocaine when his nose became too sore, and then he became so depressed that he couldn't get out of bed. "I pleaded with him to stop or to see a doctor, but he kept telling me he could handle it himself."

During this period, Susan said, Jeff's personality began to

change, and in addition to becoming more irritable he had abrupt and drastic mood swings; at one moment he would be on top of the world for no apparent reason, and the next moment so low he could barely speak or acknowledge her presence. The high periods often did not seem real to Susan and, even when he was high, she could sense an undercurrent of anger. "The least little thing would tick him off. He couldn't tolerate frustration of any kind."

She also noticed that Jeff was becoming very critical of other people. One of the things that Susan had always liked about Jeff was that he was a kind person. She had assumed that he was so secure about himself that he just never needed to put others down, but with the increased use of cocaine, marijuana, and alcohol, Jeff became increasingly arrogant in manner and disdainful of virtually everyone he encountered.

At the same time Susan spoke of how devoted Jeff was to his sons. Even though deeply involved with drugs, he managed to spend time with the boys on weekends and during the evenings when he was home. Susan said that he was also still devoted to her, buying her presents, taking her on vacations, and doing the kinds of things with her that he knew would make her happy. She said their problems were not constant at that time, and that it was fairly easy to pretend that things were okay.

At Susan's insistence, Jeff stopped dealing drugs when they moved into their new home. Susan thought he might have dealt elsewhere, but she was grateful no longer to be getting all those visits from strangers at her home. Still, she reported, his use of cocaine had often been a nightmare, and it was Tad who finally brought it to a stop.

"One day," Susan explained, "I was in the kitchen with Jeff when he was feeding Tad in his high chair. Tad must have been around two at the time, just beginning to talk in little sentences. Jeff was trying to get Tad to finish his meal when Tad put a straw into his nose and bent his head down and sniffed at his tray. Then he looked up and laughed and said he was just like Daddy."

Obviously, at some point, Tad had seen Jeff snort cocaine.

Susan said that Jeff burst into tears, sobbing because he was teaching his son how to be a junkie. "Anyway, that was it. Jeff never used cocaine or marijuana after that. I'm sure it was hard for him, but he stopped. Those kids meant the world to Jeff. I'm sure they still do, but you wouldn't know it. He's not willing to give up the alcohol for them or for me."

As she began to speak of Jeff's alcohol problems, Susan reported a marked increase in drinking once Jeff stopped using the other drugs, but said their life improved despite the drinking. During this period of apparent grace, Susan again became pregnant and gave birth to their third son, Scotty, now five. Susan was overjoyed to have another healthy baby, but said she also secretly hoped the baby would be as influential with Jeff's drinking as Tad had been with his drugs. "But having a new baby didn't work. Nothing worked," Susan complained.

I pointed out to Susan that it was very likely that Jeff could stop the cocaine and marijuana *because* he had another drug, alcohol, to fall back on—that otherwise he might not have been able to give them up.

"That's possible," Susan replied. "His drinking really picked up after he stopped the drugs. But I wasn't worried about the alcohol, except for the times when he got drunk. I was just so happy he stopped the drugs—alcohol seemed so much safer."

"Slower, perhaps," I said, "but not necessarily safer. Susan, you also need to know that if Jeff's addicted, it's not going to be enough that he just stops drinking. He's going to need treatment to take care of the personality deteriorations that occur in addiction."

"He's deteriorated, that's for sure. He doesn't even seem like the same person I married, but I don't know how you're going to get him to agree to treatment. He doesn't think he has a problem, and he's not going to listen or agree to anything."

"Don't worry, we'll get his attention; or more accurately, we'll help *you* do that. Susan, I know you've complained to Jeff about his drinking, but have you ever done that when he's sober?"

"Yes, repeatedly—early in the morning before he's had anything to drink. I've asked him to get help hundreds of times. I offered to take him to a doctor. I've even offered to take him to AA. It doesn't do any good. He doesn't listen. He says he doesn't need help."

"You've been going at a very big problem all by yourself with a bunch of home remedies. You are no longer alone, Susan; I will help you and so will others. Alcoholism treatment has finally emerged from the dark ages and there are many things that can be done today. You haven't told me anything about Jeff that leads me to believe he can't be helped."

"Oh, thank God! Do you really think there's hope? I feel like I'm about to give up. Are you sure there's hope? Maybe I haven't told you enough."

"There's hope, Susan, lots of hope. And I'm sure you haven't told me a tenth of what's been happening. How could you in just one session? But you've told me enough for me to know that Jeff is probably chemically dependent. He fits the addiction definition: *Addiction exists if a person's chemical use is interfering in any important area of his life—his physical health, family, social, or work life—and he continues to use chemicals in spite of that interference.* Jeff's drinking is certainly interfering with his ability to be a husband and a father and he's continuing to drink," I explained.

"But Jeff doesn't think his drinking is interfering in any way," Susan complained.

"Susan, is Jeff's drinking interfering with your family life?"

"Yes, of course it is—we don't even have a family life anymore."

"Then it really doesn't matter what Jeff thinks." When I next asked Susan if she planned to tell Jeff that she had come to me for help, she said, "Goodness, no! He'd freak out. I'd never hear the end of it."

"You are my client, Susan, not Jeff. I know you want to help Jeff and I'm going to help you do that, but first I need to help you. Jeff's drinking has been very traumatic for you. It's like you've been shot to pieces."

"Exactly!" she exclaimed, nodding her head as if in affirmation of feeling shattered.

"You can put those pieces back together so you feel whole."

"But the only reason I'm falling apart is because of Jeff's drinking," Susan interrupted. "Why can't we just help him? Then I'll be all right."

"I need you feeling stronger first, Susan. That's why I asked if you were going to tell Jeff about today's session. It might possibly be helpful. Telling him about this session might be an important message for him to hear—that his drinking is bothering you so much that you are seeking help—but telling him also might make your life easier. I appreciate the fact that he might freak out if he thought you were here in order to change him in any way, but how do you think he'd react if you told him you were here because you need help for yourself?"

"That's interesting. I think you're right. I think that is an important message. He won't like it, but somehow I don't think he'll fly off about it. Maybe he'll think it's a good idea; he's been telling me for years that I'm the one who needs help. Well, now I'm getting it!"

"He might be threatened and try to talk you out of coming back. How would you handle that?"

"Well, he can talk all he wants, but he can't stop me, can he?"

"I guess he can't, unless you let him. He also might respond by shaping up a little, by being less abusive. That's the reaction we see most frequently when spouses start getting help for themselves. We can't guarantee it, but it is a common response.

"If Jeff does shape up, you should realize it's only a manipulative tactic to get you to think there's no need for you to come here; then he has you fully under his control again and can return to his former behavior. But as long as you recognize that any shaping up on his part is a manipulation and only temporary, you might have a little less abuse in your life while we get some work done here. Why don't you play it by ear and tell Jeff if you think it might make your life easier," I advised.

"Okay."

"Do you feel up to some homework?" I asked. "I'd like to have you do some reading and I also want you to jot down as many specific incidents related to Jeff's chemical use as you can remember. Then we'll be able to make a more definite determination about Jeff's drinking and plan a course of action to meet his needs as well as yours.

"One last thing. Susan, you've said several times this morning that Jeff doesn't listen to reason. I believe you, but do you really believe yourself?"

"Well, yes. He doesn't listen at all."

"I think it would be safe to assume that he *can't* listen to reason. I'd like you *not* to attempt to reason with Jeff this week."

"I don't understand."

"Avoid trying to *convince* him," I explained. "What happens when you try to get Jeff to change or to believe you?"

"He starts arguing or yelling at me."

"Do you like that?"

"No, of course not."

"So don't invite it. Stop trying to reason with him. I'd like to see you have a little more peace in your life. We'll talk later about things you can do to help Jeff that are far more effective than trying to reason with him."

3

Compulsion

We all need oxygen. Without it, we will die within minutes. Yet, we rarely think of this basic need. Oxygen surrounds us abundantly; all we have to do is breathe, and we don't even have to think about doing that because breathing is an automatic reflex. It is only when we can't breathe or when oxygen isn't there for us that we truly feel this basic need of ours, and then we are overwhelmed with our urgency for air, we are able to think of nothing but getting oxygen back into our system, so that we can breathe easily once again.

Chemically dependent persons also need oxygen all the time. They feel they need a chemical as well, almost as much as they need oxygen, so that they, too, can breathe easily once again. Their urge to get the chemical back into their system is frequently as overwhelming and as primary as our urge for oxygen. When this urge is manifested, the chemically dependent person will most times be compelled to drink (or to use another chemical), and then he will go to any lengths to get the substance back into his system; nothing else will matter, not his wife, children, job, not anything; only the relief the chemical creates.

This compulsion develops very early in addiction, long before observable symptoms of physical addiction are manifested. The compulsion, the compelled urge for the relief obtained by using the chemical, strikes intermittently; it seems to have a life of its own and, while it will occur in reaction to external events, it seems to be far more dependent upon an internal direction and will come and go no matter what is happening in the dependent's life.

The compulsion is a subjective symptom of addiction, felt by the person, rather than an objective symptom such as tremors, observed by others. We belittle the power of this compulsion if we think of it as only a psychological craving, or something that can be overcome with willpower.

While we do not know how such a compulsion is formed, we do know its power is far beyond the cravings that nonaddicted persons experience from time to time in their lives. Perhaps with more knowledge of the brain's chemistry, we will better understand this compulsion. As of now we only know the *compelled urge*, perceived as a *demand*, exists. We would do well to remember that our inability to fully understand the compulsion does not in any way diminish its control over the chemically dependent person.

The compulsion is subtle in the beginning and, strangely, even as it increases in strength, it is not *thought* of as anything but a desire by chemically dependent persons. They do not recognize that they've crossed the line from *wanting* to *needing*; when they finally do recognize their *need* for the chemical, it's too late; they're trapped.

Interestingly, right from its onset, chemical dependency begins to dominate the person's life, even when the compulsive urge to use is not manifested, for not only does the dependent's behavior regarding chemicals change, so does his thinking. Once addicted, he develops a preoccupation with getting high, an obsessive thinking pattern characterized by un-

beckoned and progressively recurring thoughts about using alcohol and other drugs.

Thoughts of getting high will intrude upon him while he's
deeply engrossed in other matters. Or he'll have recurring
thoughts about future or past chemical use. He'll plot and
scheme about how to alter his life and that of others so he can
use without being chastised, discovered, or controlled. He'll
find that just thinking about chemical use will make his
whole day better.

As the compulsive urge and obsessive thinking increase in
both frequency and strength, his relationship with chemicals,
be it alcohol, other drugs, or any combinations thereof, will
become primary. Connecting with the chemical high will take
precedence over connecting with important people in his life
or with previously valued activities. His relationship with
chemicals will, in fact, become his most important relationship.

He will fall madly, passionately in love with getting high.
He will be able to think of little else. Unfortunately, his beloved object is a chemical, not a person. This compulsive, obsessive, primary relationship with getting high will most
likely go unnoticed in the beginning; nevertheless it becomes
his life's guiding force.

Several years ago three teenagers came to see me for an evaluation of their chemical use. While describing their alcohol
and drug histories, they spoke of a recent day when they had
wanted to attend a football game, but found themselves in a
conflict because they also wanted to smoke marijuana. After
some discussion they decided they might be able to do both at
the same time, if the wind were in the right direction. So they
checked the wind and sure enough, it was blowing from the
north and would carry their pot fumes out and away from the
crowd of spectators. All they had to do was sit on the top row
of the bleachers. They could have their cake and eat it, too!

They hooked up with their dealer, an unnamed neighboring
kid who dispensed all sorts of drugs from the rear window of
the basement of his home. They rolled their joints, climbed to
the top of the bleachers, and were all set to light up when the

principal of their school sat down next to them, ruining their best-laid plans. Two of the kids were ticked off, but stayed for the game even though unable to smoke pot. The third youth left. For her, smoking pot was far more important than watching the game, even though originally she had been the one who most wanted to see the game. With further probing, it became clear that using drugs had indeed become the primary guiding force of her life. While all three plotted and schemed to use, only one could not *not* use. Only one was consistently putting chemical use over and above the important people and activities in her life.

Usually it's only in their recovery, when no longer under its influence, that addicted persons can see the compulsive, obsessive, and primary force of their addiction in its entirety.

Recently, a young man named John, a college senior, came to me for an evaluation of his drinking, which showed addiction in its middle stages. John agreed to accept treatment at a residential facility and, upon his return, spoke of his former slavery to his addiction. "Every morning I'd wake up disgusted with myself for having gotten drunk the night before . . . and scared. I was on the dean's list, but I knew I wasn't going to be there much longer. Every morning I'd make all kinds of promises to myself that no matter what, I wouldn't drink that night. All day long, thoughts of drinking would creep in and I'd repeat my promises to myself. Then, after my last class, the moment of truth . . . the road to the left led to the liquor store; the road to the right to the dorm. Every goddamned afternoon, I'd force myself to go right—and I'd go left. Some days I actually made it to the dorm, but sooner or later, I'd be back at the liquor store. I scheduled evening classes, and I still was back at that store. I gave my money to my roommate to hold, then I'd scrounge the money off someone else and get the booze.

"I'd feel remorse for my drinking when I woke up. I'd think about drinking all day or about how not to drink. Then I'd drink all evening, pass out, wake up around three, study, fall asleep and the next morning . . . more disgust, more fear, more promises . . . all broken."

"John," I asked, "do you remember when you were here for

the evaluation of your drinking and I wondered if you were *preoccupied* with drinking—if you counted on it, waited for it, thought about it on and off throughout the day?"

"Yeah," he laughed, "but I don't remember what I told you."

"You said no. You told me you never gave it a thought, that you just drank at night because that's what everyone did. You couldn't see the *preoccupation*, how *obsessed* you had become with drinking, could you?"

John replied, "Not at all! My *whole* life evolved around my drinking, but I sure couldn't see that the day I was here; I'm glad you could."

The major mistake that families and virtually everyone else makes is to assume that John, Jeff, and others like them have control over their use—that they have a choice.

The hallmark of addiction is loss of control. Chemically dependent persons lose the ability to *consistently* predict what their chemical use will be like. They can often reduce the amount they consume, but can't keep it reduced. They can often stop using chemicals, but can't stay stopped. They can occasionally put their intentions about using into action, but not consistently. Eventually virtually *every* decision they make will be based upon how it will affect their chemical use. No amount of control will dominate their compulsion. No amount of reason will penetrate their obsessive thinking. Control is lost. Free will is lost. Drunk or sober, drugged or clean, addiction becomes the dominating force of the person's *whole* life.

Because the compulsion and obsession increase in frequency as well as strength, chemically dependent persons have to use more often as the addiction progresses. Initially they have rules regarding appropriate using times—never in the morning, only at parties, never at school or work, not before the sun goes over the yardarm, or whatever. In time they break some of their own rules and begin to drink or take drugs at inappropriate times. And of course they extend their regular appropriate using periods by starting earlier and stopping later.

Persons who become addicted to alcohol, tranquilizers, barbiturates, amphetamines, marijuana, or heroin also have to use an ever-larger amount to get the desired effect. Almost everyone who uses any of these chemicals will experience a tolerance increase to some degree, but persons who do not become addicted seem to hit a plateau so that they then continue to get the same effect from the same amount for years. There are people, for example, who take sleeping pills (barbiturates) who have not increased their dose in years, yet get the same effect. Nonaddicted marijuana users, once they reach their plateau, also deny any further tolerance increase. And we all know alcohol drinkers who've been drinking the same amount with the same effect for years. Persons who become addicted to any of these drugs do not know about plateaus. Their tolerance just keeps on increasing, at least until the late stages of addiction, when it begins to crumble.

Cocaine users, addicted or not, also develop a tolerance for the drug, but it is unlike the tolerance developed in response to almost all other drugs. No tolerance increase appears to develop toward the euphoric properties of the drug, even with chronic use. However, users do develop a tolerance for the drug's ability to ease anxiety, stress, and depression. And as cocaine addiction causes severe depression, cocaine addicts need ever-larger amounts of the drug to relieve their symptoms.

Another difference, described by the National Association of Drug Abuse, is that cocaine bears an *early* reverse tolerance effect. Even those who use it only occasionally find themselves becoming less tolerant. Thus, if they continue to use the same dose of cocaine, they increase their chances of accidental overdose, acute cocaine poisoning, and possible death from cardiac or pulmonary arrest, despite the fact they may have used cocaine for only a few months. Users of alcohol and all the other drugs will also experience a tolerance decrease or reversal, but usually not for years or until they are in the chronic, late stage of the illness. It is the reversed tolerance that causes alcoholics to switch to wine or beer or to drinking only periodically rather than daily. Very simply, their bodies can no longer handle alcohol as well as in the past.

Once the tolerance for the chemicals is developed beyond

the norm in addicted persons, but before the reduced tolerance develops, addicted persons have an increased tolerance for all chemicals of a similar nature. Thus alcoholics and addicts of the other sedative drugs require larger amounts of anesthesia during surgery, while narcotic addicts require larger than normal doses of painkillers following operations.

Some further differences: When persons addicted to alcohol and other sedative drugs stop using the chemical, their tolerance does not return to normal. If they resume drinking or using the drug, they may even find that they require more than ever to get the old effect. Heroin addicts find just the opposite. Abstinence from heroin will cause the tolerance to be decreased. Thus, heroin addicts can and often do reduce the cost of their addiction by staying off heroin for a week or two, finding that they require far smaller amounts to get the desired effect once they resume using.

Over the years many theories have been put forward concerning the cause of addiction: it has been considered to be the result of unfulfilled oral dependency needs, familial dysfunction, an impaired capacity for warm, human relationships, an unhealthy childhood environment, and so on. In other words, chemical dependency has been thought of as an illness secondary to something else. Yet, studies do not bear these theories out. In fact, one study of 456 persons conducted by George Vaillant and his colleagues showed no relationship between alcoholism and childhood emotional problems or growing up in a multiproblem family.[1] The theories of underlying pathology in the person or the family tend to raise more questions than they answer and cause more problems than they solve.

As often as not, chemically dependent persons are from intact, functional, nurturing families, and had healthy childhoods. More often than not, once treated, chemically dependent persons for the most part are without specific or significant psychopathology. If it is the cause, where did the underlying emotional illness go? As we do not get rid of a

1. George Vaillant and Eva Milofsky, "The Etiology of Alcoholism: A Prospective Viewpoint"; *American Psychologist* 37(5), 1982, pp. 494–503.

cause by treating a symptom, should not the emotional disorder remain once the alcoholism is treated? Chemical *abuse* may well be symptomatic of psychopathology or familial dysfunction, but chemical abuse and addiction are often not the same, and sometimes are not even related. Many abusers never become addicted. What makes them immune? At the same time, many persons use abusively *only after* becoming addicted. Why do moderate and even light users of chemicals become addicted when many immoderate and heavy abusers do not? The above theories have never answered such questions, nor do they provide satisfactory answers to questions related to addiction's underlying forces—the compulsion, preoccupation, and increasing tolerance. Also, such theories lead to the mistreatment of chemically dependent persons. When we believe alcoholism is secondary to something else, we tend to treat the something else, and the addiction progresses relentlessly onward.

One factor that must be addressed when considering cause is the mileage that a person gets out of the drug. The greater the euphoria, the greater the risk of addiction. We all react differently to the same chemicals. If a drug does inordinately good things for us, we are far more likely to return to that drug than we would if we did not like or only minimally liked its effect. Alcohol and the other chemicals are considered *reinforcing* drugs because they create a significant euphoria for many persons who use them and thus have an increased addiction potential for those persons. Of all the chemicals, cocaine and heroin are considered to be the most powerful drug *reinforcers* in existence, causing a significant euphoria in the greatest number of users, and causing a greater addiction incidence than exists in users of the other chemicals.

Today, through the tools of modern molecular science, barely a month goes by that we do not learn of another chemical, metabolic, or genetic finding pertaining to alcoholism.

From studies of biological sons of alcoholic fathers, we know that these sons are four times as likely to develop the disease as sons of nonalcoholics. *This is so even if the biolog-*

*ical sons of alcoholic fathers are adopted or raised by nonal-
coholic relatives.* It has been known for years that alcoholism
runs in families; now it appears to be *genetically* predisposed.
Children and perhaps grandchildren of alcoholics may inherit
factors that make them more vulnerable to the effects of alcohol. Alcoholism may be analagous to diabetes or hay fever,
where some people are born at risk.

We know that biological sons of alcoholic fathers show
higher blood levels of alcohol's first breakdown product, acetaldehyde, produced by enzymes in the liver. Acetaldehyde is
a stimulant, and its presence in high levels in the alcoholic's
system after drinking may account for why so many alcoholics
in their early drinking years report feeling less intoxicated and
less drowsy than others after drinking equal amounts of alcohol. *This ability to handle larger than normal amounts of alcohol is so common in persons who become alcoholic that it
has often been thought of as a precursor to alcoholism.*

Biological sons of alcoholics, after four or five drinks, gen-
erate 30 percent to 40 percent more alpha waves than social
drinkers without parental alcoholism. Alpha waves are corre-
lated with a sense of well-being. The marked increase in alpha
waves may account for why some people find alcohol far more
rewarding than others. *A profound euphoria from alcohol is so
frequently reported by people who later become alcoholic
that it, too, has long been considered a precursor to alcoholism.*

We often assume that dependents use chemicals to escape
from emotional pain, which is true *after* becoming addicted,
but that is often not the way it starts. Rather than *escaping
from* pain, many dependents report using alcohol or drugs
originally to *move into* great pleasure. In fact, their first experiences with the chemicals are often so profoundly pleasurable
that their memories are life-long. Social drinkers, on the other
hand, rarely remember the effects of alcohol from their early
drinking.

In laboratories, alcohol breakdown products have recently
been identified that are chemically related to the opiates. In

future studies, if these opiatelike breakdown products of alcohol are found in the brain as well as test tubes, we may one day have the explanation for the commonality of chemical dependency, which we can only subjectively measure today. Addicted persons can so easily substitute one drug for another that it *looks* as if the brain does not discriminate. It may be found that all the mood-altering drugs, in their breakdown products, have the addictive, reinforcing properties of the opiates; and thus ultimately *are* the same for the brain.

Studies are now underway to determine if alcoholics may be deficient in certain neurotransmitter receptors. People may become addicted when alcohol somehow corrects a deficiency. And it may be that alcoholics and social drinkers metabolize alcohol along entirely different pathways. Recently, a substance called 2,3-butanediol has been found to be present in the blood of alcoholics, though it is not present in the blood of social drinkers. Such intrinsic metabolic differences imply that genes may be influencing how alcohol is handled by the body.

While the recent findings indicate that persons who become chemically dependent may be responding to biological forces that are different or absent in others, the fact remains: we do not know what causes chemical dependency. But I do know one thing—in the fifteen years that I've been working with chemically dependent persons, I have *never met one who wanted to become dependent.*

4

Jim

I met with Jim and his wife, Virginia, very early one morning—early enough to not intrude upon Jim's work. He was concerned about his mother's drinking but was also determined to handle it in the most efficient manner possible. Jim, a tall, thin banker, neatly garbed in a dark, pin-striped suit, college tie, and black wing-tipped shoes, enumerated the problems his seventy-two-year-old mother was having with alcohol as if he were reviewing her net worth statement.

His mother, Margaret, widowed for thirty-seven years, lived alone in the same town as Jim, Virginia, and their two teenage daughters. While it was customary for her to drink cocktails before dinner, in recent years his mother had begun drinking during the day as well. This past year she had become increasingly isolated, dropping out of her bridge club, refusing luncheon and dinner invitations, and attending church only sporadically. On several occasions both Jim and Virginia had noticed alcohol on Margaret's breath early in the morning, but she angrily insisted that she had not been drinking and that they were deliberately trying to hurt her feelings. At least weekly during the past two years, his mother had called their home in the middle of the night, crying, slurring her words, and saying no one cared about her. Several of her friends told Virginia that they also had received many of Margaret's late-night intoxicated calls. When Jim and Virginia spoke to his mother about the calls, she could not remember having made them and viciously berated them when they told her the calls indicated that she needed help.

Margaret did not drink in front of Jim and his family at their regular Sunday dinners but was often intoxicated nevertheless. Jim assumed she carried a supply of alcohol in her purse, imbibing from it on her many trips to the lavatory. Virginia, who had recently assumed the responsibility of paying Margaret's monthly bills, found regular billings from three local liquor stores, each averaging close to $50 a month. During the past year, the several cleaning women hired by Jim to help his mother with her housework and shopping had abruptly quit within days, telling Jim that his mother was impossible to work for—arrogant, demanding, inexcusably rude, often blaming, never appreciative, and always drunk.

For quite some time Jim had known something had to be done about his mother, but he said he believed it was "probably hopeless." He was seeking assistance now because "the situation is very much out of hand."

The week before, his mother, described by Jim and Virginia as normally a kind, considerate, very proper lady, well respected by everyone who knew her, was so intoxicated that she had passed out in the beauty parlor. The police were called and his mother was taken to the emergency room of the local hospital. By the time Jim arrived she was somewhat sober and full of remorse, promising that it would not happen again, but refusing the hospitalization recommended by both Jim and her physician. Jim concluded by saying, "We've heard of the intervention process and wonder if it might be appropriate in this instance."

I was so taken with Jim's detached, almost mechanical, itemization of his mother's drinking that for a moment I didn't realize it was now my turn to speak. Good grief, I thought. He's talking about his *mother.* He must be torn apart inside. I was in awe of his enormous self-control.

I was also concerned about Virginia. Throughout, she had remained perched on the edge of her seat, mostly silent while her eyes darted anxiously back and forth from Jim to me.

"Let's see if the coffee's ready," I suggested, needing time to absorb the discrepancy between Jim's painful story and his painless reporting, as well as Virginia's apparent fear.

Jim's need for control was very obvious. Not only did he keep his emotions rigidly in check, he had also controlled the interview thus far. I wondered if he now would be able to let go of some of that control and I asked, "Jim, we probably will be able to help you help your mom, but I'm not sure the intervention process is our best route. I need more information in several areas. Will it be okay with you if I take the lead to seek that information?" Jim nodded his approval, stiffly.

Before continuing, I said, "Virginia, I've noticed you've been sitting on the edge of your seat, frequently searching Jim's face. You look a little scared; is that how you're feeling?"

"Oh, no, not at all," she replied. "I was just interested in his reaction. Well, yes, I am uncomfortable. This whole business with Jim's mother is most disturbing. I know it's bothering Jim a lot."

"I'm sure it is. How does Jim show you he's bothered?"

"Uh . . . what do you mean? Well, I guess he doesn't actually *show* that he's bothered, but I know he is."

"Do you think that might be contributing to your discomfort, knowing Jim's upset, but seeing him outwardly calm?"

"Yes, perhaps it is. That's certainly bothered me in the past."

"How do you feel about us talking about you like this, Jim?" I smiled.

"I find it interesting. I'm not sure what you'd rather have me do," he replied, sitting rigidly upright.

"Nothing. You're not here for me to change you. If I'm going to be of value it will be in helping you expand your options." I then suggested that we move on. While Jim retained his cool, controlled façade, Virginia was noticeably more relaxed, sitting back comfortably in her chair and speaking more freely.

Jim's father had died of alcoholism when Jim was thirteen, leaving him, his mother, and two younger sisters in such impoverished circumstances that they had to ask relatives for money to pay for his dad's funeral. Even before his dad's death, Jim had become the head of the household, taking over responsibilities not fulfilled by his disabled father. Throughout his junior and senior high school years, Jim held jobs before and after school, while his mother worked nights cleaning offices. Between them they cared for his younger sisters and managed to avoid going on welfare. Jim's grades were so high that he was able to secure full scholarships to Ivy League undergraduate and graduate schools, all the time working on the side to provide money for his mother and sisters. Upon graduation and a meteoric rise in his chosen profession, Jim put his younger sisters through college, purchased a home for his mother, married and purchased a home of his own, and set up a trust fund for his mother so that she, like his wife and children, could live comfortably, even luxuriously, free from financial worries.

"Jim, I also felt uncomfortable before. I found it hard to equate the painful things you were facing with your calm, cool, collected demeanor. Now it's much more understandable. If you had not taken enormous control over your life, you all might have gone right down the tubes."

"Yes", he replied. "I think that's correct. Someone had to shoulder the responsibility and there didn't seem to be anyone to do that but me."

"Jim, you've gone way beyond just shouldering the responsibility. You've achieved enormous success. I think you've done what few people could do."

"Perhaps," he replied, again showing no let-up in his controlled façade.

I then asked about their chemical use as well as that of their daughters. Neither Jim nor Virginia used alcohol or any other mood-altering substances. Jim said his father's alcoholism had taught him a lesson and that he had made a decision when a teenager to never drink, smoke cigarettes, or use any kind of drug. Virginia said she had never smoked and that alcohol had never been important to her so it was not difficult for her to comply with Jim's request that she not drink or smoke. To their knowledge, neither had any relatives who were addicted, other than Jim's parents.

Both expressed concern about the chemical use of their oldest daughter, Carla, a seventeen-year-old high-school senior. "She's the second person we wanted to talk to you about this morning. My mother's problems seem more critical at the moment, but actually we're just as worried about Carla."

For over a year Carla had been coming home intoxicated on weekends. A few months ago, Virginia had found rolling papers for marijuana cigarettes in a pair of Carla's jeans. Later she found a cellophane packet of marijuana on the floor under Carla's dresser. Both reported that Carla had become surly and rude, while all her life she had been sweet and considerate. Virginia said that Carla was often frightening to them, having abrupt and often violent mood swings for no apparent reason. She said also that Carla no longer seemed like a part of their family. "She's always a major source of worry and irritation, but she's rarely with us. She refuses to have dinner with us in the evening, and if we insist, she just sits there, slumped in her chair, refusing to eat or talk. She refuses to go out with us and is either off on her own or she stays in her room with the door locked."

Jim reported that Carla had dropped off the tennis team, of which she had been the captain and star player, and that they no longer saw Carla with the friends she'd had since grade school. "She's out every weekend, but we don't know where she goes or with whom." The school psychologist told them he had noticed Carla associating with a known "user-loser" group in the school. Jim said, "Nothing we do seems to have any effect. She quietly accepts her punishments for coming home late or for being intoxicated, but then she repeats the same behavior. We've told her that we do not want her to drink or use drugs, but she does as she wishes." He said he was particularly worried because he could see that she was destroying her future. Carla, always an honor student, in fact at the top of her class, no longer seemed interested in her education. Her grades had fallen the year before, and she did poorly on her SATs. "She could have had her pick of the very best schools. Now we'll consider ourselves fortunate if she gets accepted at a third-rate school."

Both Jim and Virginia agreed that it would be wise to have Carla's chemical use evaluated, and we set an appointment for me to see Carla the following week. They then went on to report that their youngest daughter, Lynn, a fifteen-year-old high-school sophomore, was "no problem." To their knowledge she neither drank nor used drugs. They said that Lynn often complained because so much of their attention was devoted to Carla's disruptive behavior, but that Lynn was a good student, a "happy" child with many friends, and that she was involved in several extracurricular activities at school.

"Do your daughters know of your dad's alcoholism, Jim?" I asked.

"No. Virginia of course knows, but it's nothing we've ever cared to discuss with the children. It's over, and nothing they need to be concerned about," Jim answered.

I said, "I wish that were true, Jim. The fact is that alcoholism has a strong genetic component, which means your dad's alcoholism increases their risk for addiction. I've never been impressed with the results of trying to scare people. On the other hand, it's in the interest of all of us to know about the predispositions we may have inherited for any illness—cardiac disease, diabetes, alcoholism, whatever. I'd be happy to talk to the girls later about their increased risk and what they might want to do to protect themselves, but in the meantime they do need to hear about their grandfather. Would you be willing to tell them about your dad?"

"Yes. They already know about my impoverished beginnings."

"So they're aware of the special significance of your considerable accomplishments?" I asked.

"Yes, I presume they are."

"Are *you* aware, Jim, that you've actually done what most people could not have done?" I asked.

"Well, I suppose I am," he answered, not very convincingly.

"You've carried a very heavy burden very well indeed. I think you deserve much more credit than you perhaps are giving yourself. Right now, your mom's alcoholism and your daughter's possible harmful involvement with chemicals, on top of everything you went through because of your dad's alcoholism, must be exceedingly painful."

When I next asked Jim to tell me more about what his mother is like when she is not drinking, his whole demeanor softened. He had always admired his mother. Through thick and thin, she never gave up. Even though she worked very hard at a demeaning job when he was a child, she remained cheerful and full of energy. She was always supportive and approving of Jim and his sisters. "I guess she was your typical Irish mother in that regard. None of us could ever do any wrong in her eyes."

Both Jim and Virginia said his mom was also always loving toward their daughters and in turn was well loved by both. Virginia said, "Jim's mother is such a lovely person—at least when she's sober. It's been very difficult for us to accept that she's alcoholic even though her doctor told us she was quite some time ago."

I asked, "Of the four of you, who do you think might have the closest relationship with your mom?"

"Neither Virginia nor I at the moment, I'm afraid," Jim replied. "She's angry with both of us because we've been trying to get her to do something about her drinking. But she's still close to both girls, especially Lynn. And even now, I think she feels more comfortable with Virginia than she does with me."

"Yes," Virginia agreed. "I think she's afraid of you, Jim. She thinks you disapprove of her."

"Yes. I expect she does think that," Jim responded.

"Do you disapprove of her?" I asked.

"Yes. Frankly, I do. I feel she should know better. Good heavens! She saw my father die right before her eyes from alcoholism."

"She lacks strength and resolve?"

"Yes, she does. That's what makes this so difficult for me to accept. My mother has always been enormously strong. She *never* faltered during our hard times. She's one of the strongest people I've ever met, and now she's not even trying. I can't understand it. It's not at all like my mother to give in like this."

"Are you Catholic?"

"Yes."

"Are you aware of the pledges given to alcoholics by the Church many years ago?"

"Yes . . . my father took those pledges."

"Did they work?"

"No—obviously, or he wouldn't have died."

"That's what the Church discovered also. That alcoholism seemed to be bigger than willpower—any amount of willpower. Do you know what the Church does today?"

"No."

"Last rites! It gives the Sacrament of the Sick. And that's much more on target, Jim. Alcoholics are sick. They have an illness. The Church accepts this, the World Health Organization and the American Medical Association have declared alcoholism an illness, but *you* are going to have trouble. Willpower has done everything for you that you've ever wanted. It's now going to be very hard for you to acknowledge that willpower cannot conquer your mom's drinking and your daughter's chemical use.

"You may be in serious trouble, Jim," I continued. "You love your mom and you love your daughter, but your tried and true method is not working with them. It's like asking someone with tuberculosis not to cough. If willpower is all you have at your disposal, Jim, you may lose them both."

Boom! Sometimes I hate my work.

Virginia looked at me with wide-open eyes. She started to

speak and then sat back, as if in shock. Jim remained silent. He looked at me. He looked down at his feet. He looked out the window, pulled his handkerchief out of his pocket, wiped his eyes, turned to me and asked, "What should I do?"

"Jim, you love your mom dearly. How do you feel when you see her drunk? Besides disgusted, how do you feel?" I asked.

"Hurt, I guess. Scared—afraid that she's going to die, like my dad," he replied softly, once again wiping his eyes.

"Can you tell her that?"

"Yes."

"Will you tell her that?"

"Yes, I will," he replied.

"Good. Do that for a starter. Leave your judgments and advice at home. Tell your mom how much you love her, how much she has always meant to you, how much she still means to you. And tell her how much her drinking hurts you. See if she might then be willing to see me or go to an AA meeting, and offer to take her; then I'll meet with you and Virginia again next week. Meanwhile I'll see Carla."

But first, I saw Lynn.

5

Lynn and Carla

Virginia phoned a few days after our meeting saying that Jim had met with each of the girls separately to talk about his dad's alcoholism. "It was a very difficult thing for him to do. He was tearful both times. Carla just seemed to laugh it off, but Lynn got very upset. She said she's been worried about her marijuana use. My God! We didn't even know she was using marijuana. What's happening to us? Everything seems to be falling apart. Lynn wants to talk to you. Can you see her?"

Lynn was stunning. A tall, thin, truly beautiful fifteen-year-old. But while she looked so good on the outside, she immediately spoke of not feeling well at all on the inside. The year before she had started using marijuana heavily, smoking three to four joints a day because she didn't care very much about anything in her life. Her chin quivered as she spoke. She looked sad, and so near tears. Her boyfriend dropped her when she refused to stop smoking, and her grades fell a little bit. Then she broke into tears as she told of stopping marijuana two months ago. "It didn't help. It didn't help to smoke pot and it hasn't helped to stop."

When I asked Lynn if she knew her source of pain, she immediately said, "Yes. Good is never good enough," and then sobbed so heavily that she could not go on. I held her in my arms. After several minutes, she said, "No matter what I do it's never good enough.

"I get five As and one B and they concentrate on the B. I'm the captain of the hockey team, we won the regional championship, and Dad wonders why I didn't go out for the cross-country team as well. I read Kerouac's *On the Road* and he tells me not to read such trash. I ask him if he's read it, and he says no, but he still knows it's trash. He hasn't even read it! I have! Why can't he see that I might have an opinion of my own? Religion's the same thing. How do I know there's a God—just because they tell me? I'm not saying there isn't, but can't I even ask questions? We can never discuss anything. It's either his way or it's wrong. Closed. No discussion. Mom's better—she's easier to talk to, but she's scared to open her mouth, too. Dad's so damned perfect. I mean he really is perfect.

"I just can't handle it the way Mom does. Mom says she sets a goal for herself and then when she makes it, she finds she's not really satisfied and sets a higher goal, and when she makes that, she's still not satisfied and sets an even higher goal. She says she expects to achieve contentment in heaven and is satisfied to go on striving until then. She doesn't expect happiness here on earth. I can't handle that! Can't I have some peace . . . some sense of accomplishment? Do I have to die to get that?

"You know what it is? I'm not perfect. Last year it became very clear to me that *I'm never, ever going to be perfect.* So why am I busting my ass—sorry, I didn't mean to swear—but that's when I started using pot."

And then she began to sob heavily once again, "I want him to love me. What can I do so he'll love me?"

Kids amaze me. So often they are able to put their finger right smack on the problem. Jim demanded perfection, in himself and others. *Anything* less was unacceptable. *Anyone* less was unacceptable. Everyone in Jim's life, Jim included, was paying a price for his father's alcoholism—the illness with the impact on future generations.

There are relatively few existing empirical and clinical studies that look at the effects of parental alcoholism on children. The problems of methodology are great; studies are usually based on small samples, self-report data, vague definitions of alcoholism, and all kinds of intangible variables. Still, the studies that do exist convincingly demonstrate that children of alcoholics are at high risk for a number of emotional and behavioral problems as well as difficulties with social adjustment.

Claudia Black, Sharon Wegscheider-Cruze, and others have described the roles children often acquire in response to family alcoholism that help them cope with the problem.[2] The oldest child, for instance, often becomes the "responsible one," the "family head," or "hero" who takes care of everyone else, may be a high achiever, and is concerned with always doing what is proper or right. Other roles are the acting out or "problem child"; the "forgotten child" who is a loner and lives in a fantasy world; and the "family pet" who gets attention through clowning and pretending to be carefree. While I find children of alcoholics who do not fit these roles or who only fit in part, many fit quite well and Jim filled the role of hero perfectly.

Now, there's a genuine good side to all these roles. Heroes, for example, are often remarkably competent and provide very real benefits and services to themselves, others, and society. I believe they should be given every credit due, not only for the many tangible good things they do, but because their method of functioning has been their means of surviving great emotional pain and life itself.

But there's a bad side, too. Each role exacts a price. Heroes

2. Claudia Black, *It Will Never Happen to Me* (Denver, Colorado: M.A.C. Printing and Publications Division, 1982). pp. 13–31, 53–67. Sharon Wegscheider, *Another Chance* (Palo Alto, California: Science and Behavior Books, Inc., 1981) pp. 89–149.

center upon abject failure. They watch their addicted parent fail and then they see themselves fail because nothing they do helps their parent. Even if the alcoholic should get well, the chances are it's not because of something the hero has done. In time, their sense of failure spreads to every area of their life so that nothing they do is ever quite good enough. No matter how much they achieve, they are haunted by the deep-seated, often unacknowledged, overwhelming belief they are failing or are about to fail. Their struggle to escape failure is unceasing and it is manifested outwardly by often extraordinary displays of control—control of self, others, and events; devotion to willpower as the only trustworthy means for success; and excessive demands for perfection from self and others.

Heroes in chemically dependent families often achieve worldly success, but rarely personal peace. They look good in the eyes of the world but not within their own hearts. They suffer, sometimes greatly; and often so do their families.

Lynn wanted help. She said she was willing to do anything in order to feel better and knew her answers did not lie in the direction of chemicals. Even though not herself the child of an alcoholic, Lynn shared the pain faced by so many second-generation children of alcoholics. She suffered a lowered self-esteem, feeling both inadequate and without personal power or influence. She said she couldn't get close to other people, had difficulty making decisions and completing projects, and was afraid of adults in authority, especially her parents and teachers. Like other second-generation children of alcoholics, she *hurt*; and while she could pinpoint the source of her pain, she could neither comprehend nor cope with it. I agreed to work with Lynn. She agreed to remain chemically free.

I am appalled by how many family members and chemically dependent persons are treated by mental health professionals who: (1) do not evaluate everyone's chemical use to see if chemical dependency may exist; and (2) treat families and chemically dependent persons without addressing their specific and primary conditions—co-dependency and chemical dependency. People can stay sick for years that way. People can get sick that way. People can die that way.

I don't have any set formula—my method of working with co-dependents and chemically dependents has evolved over the years with both experience and information—but always, I first evaluate chemical use, everyone's chemical use. Once it seems apparent that chemical dependency does not exist in the family members who first come to me, I begin to evaluate the chemical use in the person about whom they are concerned. Sometimes I see the chemical user in order to make the evaluation, but often I rely upon corroborated data from others.

When making evaluations, we don't have to come up with any final, end-all diagnoses. We need only determine the *probability* of addiction. That alone will steer us in the right direction, as the *probability* of addiction means the chemical use must be dealt with before anything else can be resolved.

Lynn probably was *not* addicted. While using marijuana came before her grades and her boyfriend for a while, it did not progress to the point that it took precedence in her life over the long haul. Nonaddicted chemical users, like Lynn, are *modifiable*. They can either see, or be easily made to see, that chemicals are not the panacea for their ills. Lynn did not seem to have suffered a loss of control over her use, nor did it appear progressive. She did not use alcohol or any other chemicals besides marijuana, which she stopped, rather than increased. She readily agreed to remain chemically free for the course of her counseling. Her sister presented a different picture entirely.

Carla, just as pretty as Lynn, if not more so, was ticked off— really furious that I had made her father tell her about her grandfather. "I mean that blew me away to see Dad cry. Jesus Christ! Why'd you open up that can of worms? Who needs that?"

"How did you feel when you heard your grandfather was an alcoholic?" I asked, not too sure what concerned her most, her dad's tears or her grandfather's alcoholism.

"Nothing. How'd you expect me to feel? I certainly wasn't shocked. I always knew *something* was wrong with him the way no one ever talked about him. Listen, I liked it the way it was in my family before you came along. And what's this business about me being at risk for alcoholism just because my grandfather was an alcoholic? You expect me to believe that? I listened to that crap in my health class at school and I wasn't convinced then by anything I read or heard and I assure you, you're not going to convince me now."

"What did you feel when you saw your dad cry?"

"Blown away," she answered. "I mean I couldn't stand it. That man's perfect and I'm not too sure I want to see him come undone."

"What's *undone*?"

"You have any idea how rigid he is? Jesus, he could blow apart. Do you know what you're doing?"

"Yeah, I saw the rigidity, too, but I guess that underneath I see a warm, caring person who's not at all about to fall apart. His shell might crumble a bit, Carla, but your father's much more than his shell. Your dad's not in any danger of falling apart."

"Well, that's a relief."

"Do you believe me?"

"Yeah, maybe you're right. At least I hope you're right. But I'm still pissed off. You want to talk about my drinking and drugging?"

"Okay."

"I drink! Big deal! Who doesn't? I smoke dope! Big deal! Who doesn't? I've used cocaine. I've gone on acid trips. So you want to call me a drug addict? Go ahead! Fuck it! This whole scene's ridiculous."

"Well, let's see if we can bring a little order to this," I said, and then asked her to trace the history of her chemical use from the time of first use of each chemical to today's use. I assured her that I would not reveal her specific chemical use to her parents, but that I would want to give them an evaluation, an opinion of what I thought her chemical use meant, and she agreed.

Carla reported that she first started drinking beer two or three times a month when she was in seventh grade, and started smoking marijuana five or six times a month when in eighth grade. By ninth grade, she drank alcohol nearly every weekend, and once or twice a week after school, and smoked pot several times a week. By tenth grade she had taken "every drug out there, including heroin, at least once," but claimed that the only things she really liked were alcohol and marijuana, which she preferred to use together. By eleventh grade, at sixteen, she had purchased a phony ID card and was drinking in bars every weekend. She also drank after school most days, "Someone's liquor from someone's house." On several occasions she cut school, forging her mother's signature, and spent the day stoned. By this time she was also smoking several joints of marijuana each day, before, during, and after school and in her room at home at night, "with the windows open of course." She felt there was nothing wrong with her use because almost everyone she knew used more. "They actually *drink* before coming to school."

This year, her senior year, she had dropped all her extracurricular activities because, "They were getting in the way. My parents know I dropped off the tennis team, but wait till they hear I didn't run for class president and dropped orchestra. I hocked the clarinet—needed the money, you know." Carla thought her alcohol and marijuana use was about the same that year as it had been the year before: "Maybe more but not much more." She said she frequently had *blackouts*, temporary periods of amnesia when she functioned, but couldn't recall what she had done. She also admitted that she had changed friends, hanging out with older men who bought her drinks. She denied that her friends dropped her, claiming she dropped them because she wanted more excitement in her life. She said her grades were lower this year and that she hadn't done as well on the SATs as she had expected. "So I'll go to a second-rate school, so what? Has all that great success brought my father any happiness? He never has any fun. Even when he plays, it's work. Who needs that?" She said she had never stopped using alcohol and marijuana, but did stop all the other drugs "because I didn't like them." When I asked if she had ever made any promises to herself about quitting or cutting down, she admitted she had, saying also that usually she broke her promises because "I'd decide the promise was a silly thing to have made in the first place."

Adolescents are often surprisingly open about their chemical use in evaluation interviews. Sometimes it seems as if they truly do believe their chemical use is normal. Perhaps they're open because they want help. Or maybe they get a charge out of flaunting their use and shocking staid adults. Who knows? It really doesn't matter. What matters is not their reasoning, but the chemical use itself.

In an evaluation, we look at three specific areas—the chemical use pattern; personality and behavioral changes; and consequences of use. And, of course, we look for loss of control and the importance of chemicals.

Carla was probably addicted. Her chemical use pattern was certainly progressive. She used an ever-increasing amount of chemicals and increased her variety. Even when she gave up everything but alcohol and marijuana, she continued to use those drugs more frequently and in greater amounts.

Most people remain true to themselves with respect to personality and behavior for life, even through the normally turbulent adolescent years. Chemically dependent persons do not remain true to themselves. Their personalities, and thus their behavior, become altered by the chemicals. Often their changes are so dramatic that others are apt to say, "He's just not the same person anymore."

Both Virginia and Jim talked about the changes Carla had shown, turning from a friendly, considerate person to a rude, surly, isolated person with abrupt, unexplainable, and often violent temper tantrums. An increase in hostility is always a part of addiction, and often the first change noticed by families. In addition Carla had switched friends to the older men in the bars, according to her, and to known "users and losers," according to the school psychologist. *All addicted persons find others whose chemical use is worse than theirs, so theirs will look normal.* Besides her former friends, Carla also had given up previously valued activities—class officer, tennis, and orchestra—in order to accommodate her chemical use, which may very well have become her primary relationship. Addicted persons, especially adolescents, will also eventually adopt an "I don't care" attitude, an attitude certainly very much in evidence with Carla.

Carla suffered several consequences as a result of her use of chemicals. No longer on the honor roll at school, she was also no longer eligible for a top college. While she claimed she chose to give up her friends and extracurricular activities, their loss was nevertheless a consequence of her chemical use. Additionally, she lost a certain friendship in her family. "Lynn says I'm a jerk and hardly speaks to me and Dad says I'm a 'bone of contention' for the whole family. Even my Gram's on my back. She's smashed herself, but she worries about me. How do you like that? She's ten times worse than me." Carla had also suffered at least one physical consequence, a loss of energy. "Everything's a drag. Christ! I can't even get through a set of tennis, much less a match." Carla also couldn't keep her promises about using, indicating a loss of control, one of the most frightening consequences of all.

"Carla, do you want help?" I asked.

"No, what the hell for?"

"All of this. It sounds like your life's become a real struggle. A downhill struggle."

"Yeah? So what?"

"*So what* is you can be helped. It doesn't have to be this way for you."

"Holy Christ! You think I'm addicted, don't you?"

"Don't you?"

"No."

"Carla, are you willing to give up alcohol and marijuana for a while? The best thing would be if you evaluated your own use, and the only way I know how to do that is not to use. You can only know how important chemicals are when you don't have them. Want to stop using and evaluate it yourself?"

"No."

"You're a tiger, Carla, or else you've got one by the tail," I said. "Listen, Carla, this is the way it is, as I see it. And this is what I'd like to tell your parents. You may very well be addicted. You have a progressive pattern of use, you've had several behavioral and personality changes that go along with chemical dependency, you've suffered significant consequences as a result of your chemical use, and you've indicated some loss of control by not being able to keep your promises about using. And that's the pits, Carla, when you can't even keep the promises you make to yourself. I'm not sure how extensively you're using the defense mechanisms of dependency, but it does seem that chemicals have become more important to you than your family, friends, education, future, and valued activities. I think you should be evaluated more thoroughly, either by entering an agreement of absolutely no chemical use and regular AA attendance so you can increase your knowledge about addiction and your relationship to it, or by entering a seven-to-ten-day residential chemical dependency evaluation unit."

"*That's* what you want to tell my parents?"

"Yes. It's all true, isn't it?"

"Jesus! I don't see it that way at all."

"I know. That's why it's so important for you to stop using, so you can see things more clearly. Is it okay with you that I give this evaluation and my suggestions to your parents?"

"Yeah, do I have any choice? What happens if I don't do any of those things?"

"I don't know. What do you think will happen?"

"I don't know. My parents are going to be upset, aren't they? They'll probably try to enforce some kind of action, but that's okay, I know how to handle them."

"I wondered why you weren't more upset about your parents' reaction. You've found a way to handle them. What is it, Carla?" I asked.

"Easy. I ignore them. I follow their rule about curfew most of the time so that I won't get grounded, but that's about all I do."

"What do you mean? Give me a specific. When they're in a tizzy about you, what do you do?" I persisted.

"That's the whole point. Nothing. Sometimes I smile. Sometimes I even agree with them; then I do my own thing. I just let it all blow over my head. I just hang in there, doing nothing, don't you see?"

"Yeah, I do see. That gives you a lot of power, doesn't it?"

"Right on. They do their thing, I do mine."

"That's how Gandhi brought down the whole British Empire—with all that passive aggression. It really does give you a lot of power, Carla. But it doesn't seem like you're using your power very well."

"What do you mean?"

"You complain about your dad's shell, Carla. But what about yours? You're talking tough, but what happens to you in the wee hours of the night? I bet you're crying your heart out. Your life's all messed up, Carla, and I think you know that and care about that a whole lot. Ever wish you were dead?"

"Yes."

"Want help?"

"No."

"Will you come back to see me next week?"

"I don't know. Maybe. When?"

"Thursday. Three o'clock."

"Okay."

"Carla, what you've got is treatable. I don't think you've wanted any of this to happen, and I think your parents will be upset *for* you, not *at* you. I think they're going to want to *help* you, not *hurt* you."

"Yeah, sure, but I'm not making any promises, okay?"

"Okay. See you next Thursday. Want a hug?"

"A HUG! Jesus! Yeah, why not?"

"Thanks. I need about five of those a day and I have a feeling maybe you do, too."

6

Coping and Defending

Addiction is an overpowering attack upon the person's sense of worth. To protect their self-esteem, chemically dependent persons unconsciously invoke psychological defenses that create and perpetuate increased dysfunction. The compulsion, obsession, and increased tolerance are bad; the defenses are worse.

Charles was a patient of mine when I worked in an alcoholism treatment center. He had been referred by a neurological institute in his home city many states removed. Charles couldn't walk very well; the nerves in his legs had been eroded by alcohol, and he was partially paralyzed. Charles couldn't think very well either; the cells in his brain had also been eroded by alcohol, and he scored at third-grade level on his intelligence tests.

Charles was forty-four years old. At one time he had been married, a senior partner in a prestigious law firm, active on several committees in his community, and while a student, he had been an Olympic skier and an editor of the law review. When I first met him he was a late-stage, chronic alcoholic who had lost his wife, his job, his health—virtually all his resources—yet Charles denied that he had a drinking problem. He was so massively damaged by alcohol I felt a need to tell him everything would be all right, when I really believed nothing would ever again be all right for Charles.

My director, Bob deVeer, confronted me with my dishonesty and pointed out that Charles could not afford my particular brand of kindness. "Who are you to consider him hopeless?" Bob asked and, in no uncertain terms, sent me out to confront Charles with the reality of his condition. "If he drinks again, Ruth, he dies or becomes a vegetable. What are you doing about his alcoholism?" Those were Bob's words. I don't know if they were easy for him to say; I do know they were not easy for me to act upon.

Charles and I met that afternoon in my office on the fifth floor. I felt anxious; Charles had already suffered enough; I couldn't stand the thought of adding to his pain. Yet, I did know that if he could *feel* his pain, he might *see* his illness. Charles, on the other hand, was perfectly comfortable, looking all around at my pictures and plants as if he hadn't a care in the world, totally out of touch with his illness. The buildup of the defenses he had used over the years to protect himself from his addiction was formidable. It was *his* illness, but *I* was uncomfortable; *he was not!*

I reviewed with Charles in detail where he had once been in his life, and I compared that to where he was now as a result of alcoholism. Nothing! No reaction! Charles smiled agreeably and wondered if I had anything else I wished to discuss.

Damn! Now I had to provide him with the results of his intelligence test, something I had hoped very much to avoid. I gave Charles the findings, blow by blow, and in conclusion, said, "Charles, what all this means is that you wouldn't make it through third grade today."

Nothing! Zilch! No reaction! Charles smiled sweetly and looked about my office. Now what was I supposed to do? Fifth floor or not, jumping out the window had a certain appeal.

Charles smiled, comfortable as a teddy bear. I fidgeted; he smiled. I fidgeted some more; he smiled some more. I don't know how long that silly charade went on, but it seemed endless. I truly did not know what else to do to break through his great defensive shield.

Then Charles spotted a copy of *Time* magazine on my desk. He humphed a bit, pulled himself up grandly in his chair, elevated his nose, and announced that *he* would never read such a magazine.

Oh God! Thank you! I *had* registered with Charles; at least there was a chink in that armor. He was responding defensively, and he gave me exactly what I needed.

"Charles," I said, "it's not a question of whether you *want* to read *Time*, it's a question of whether you *can* read *Time*." I underlined three consecutive sentences, handed him the magazine and asked him to read the underlined sentences and tell me in his own words what he had just read. He took the magazine and peered down his nose at the sentences. He put *Time* down, looked around, not nearly as comfortable as before, picked it up, read the sentences and put it down once again. I didn't say a word. I gave him all the space he needed to feel his pain, and he repeated his reading two or three more times. Finally, I asked, "You can't do it, can you, Charles?" He shook his head slowly, closed his eyes, forcing a big tear down each cheek, and softly replied, "No, I can't."

"That's alcoholism, Charles," I said, gently naming the illness he was finally feeling.

"If I don't drink will I get better?" he asked.

"There's a chance," I replied.

"I'll go for that chance," he announced.

With his agreement and in cooperation with his neurologist, we transferred Charles to a nursing home in his home city and made arrangements for local AA members to take him out to a meeting daily.

Charles is once again a senior partner in his old law firm. He has remarried and is today a father. His peripheral nerves remyelinized; he is no longer paralyzed and is skiing again. He read *Time* magazine hour after hour for months, until he could finally, once again, concentrate, absorb, and abstract. Since brain cells aren't supposed to regenerate, he must have tapped into an excess supply, for he is no longer intellectually impaired.

Charles went for the chance and got well. Certainly his message is one of hope—chemical dependency is a profoundly serious illness; recovery from chemical dependency can be equally profound.

But Charles went for the chance to get well *only after he finally perceived his illness,* which brings us to one of the greatest hurdles in chemical dependency. Addicted persons cannot see their illness. In time, you can see it, I can see it, the whole world can see it, but the dependent cannot.

To understand the conflict that the alcoholic like Charles faces, it's helpful to recognize the distinctions between the inner and outer worlds we all inhabit. Each of us has a private inner world, a psychic world, separate from our intellect. This inner world is where our instincts and conscience reside; what goes on in our inner world is in large measure governed by interactions between our instincts, conscience, and the outer world, which contains important people, our own behavior, and physical reality. Conflicts between our instincts and conscience or our inner world and the outer world often result in an erosion of our self-esteem, which is our blueprint and guide to our ideas, feelings, and actions.

To be healthy, we all need to regard ourselves and be regarded by others as worthy. In fact the need for self-worth may very well be one of the most fundamental human needs. When we are in psychic conflict—for example, when our behavior violates our own values or is rejected by persons important to us—our self-esteem is cast in doubt, and we must find some means for resolving this doubt. We seem to have two basic ways of safeguarding our self-esteem; we can either *cope* or *defend* ourselves.

Coping means that we acknowledge the conflict, confront

it, and modify our behavior to be more in accord with the values and prohibitions of our conscience or of society. As Daniel Anderson describes in his pamphlet "Psychopathology of Denial," coping does not base self-worth upon a childlike idealistic image of the perfect self, but values the self despite its imperfections.[3] Consequently, coping seeks to bolster self-esteem through realistic accomplishment.

If we do not cope, we must defend ourselves by unconsciously invoking a psychological mechanism. Rather than facing up to the conflict and attempting to overcome it directly, we evade the threat to our self-esteem. Our sense of self-worth is thus preserved through self-deception.

Using psychological defense mechanisms is not a conscious avoidance of problems, nor does it have to do with willpower, perseverence, or turning to others for help. Instead, defenses are subtle, automatic, and largely unconscious psychological processes that, in turn, are reflected in our behavior and affect, which is our emotionality: its color, tone, and heat.

As our intellectual and physical maturation seems to have a natural continuum, so does our use of defenses and our resulting emotional development. Anna Freud, in her book *The Ego and the Mechanisms of Defense*, points out that children use defenses that are different from those used by adults. George Vaillant, in examining healthy people as they move through life, has categorized defenses in a hierarchy.[4] Defenses of childhood evolve into defenses of adolescence and then into defenses of adulthood: they go from primitive to immature to neurotic to mature. In the normal course of things most of us are able to move through life with different defenses for different years—using as adults mature defenses for everyday crises and neurotic defenses for severe life crises.

Generally speaking, the better we feel about ourselves, the less defended we need be. Nevertheless, defenses are necessary.

3. Daniel Anderson, "The Psychopathology of Denial," *Professional Education* pamphlet (Center City, Minnesota: Hazelden Educational Services, 1981).
4. Anna Freud, *The Ego and the Mechanisms of Defense* (International Universities Press,) London, England, 1937. p. 58–100. George Vaillant, *Adaptation to Life* (Boston: Little, Brown and Company, 1972). pp. 73–91.

Being without them in a mild crisis would be like being in an April shower without an umbrella, and in a severe crisis, like being in a blizzard without a parka. Defenses can oil the machinery of everyday life, as when we *displace* anger by kicking a chair instead of our boss. Defenses can give us the time out we need in order to heal, as when we face the death of a loved one and go through the various stages of grief.

Defenses can, indeed, be very helpful. If we use defenses appropriate to our age, if we use them on occasion, and if we use them flexibly, they can pave the way to increased emotional strength. In fact, when used in this manner, defenses can help us cope.

Still, defenses are risky. Coping increases emotional strength, which increases our ability to tolerate stress and decreases our need for defenses. Coping makes us, defenses can help make us, but if rigidly overused, they break us. Then they reduce our ability to tolerate stress, increase our need for defenses, and become part of the creation of emotional illness.

Chemically dependent persons are in trouble right at the outset. Their addiction compels them to behave in ways that conflict with their conscience, which in turn causes an erosion of their self-esteem and results in a great number of negative feelings. Dependents can face their conflicts on occasion, but they cannot effectively resolve them and thus preserve their self-esteem by coping for the very simple reason that they are compelled to use chemicals and, thus, ever to repeat behavior that is in conflict with their inner world.

The power of their addiction is beyond coping. Chemically dependent persons can only defend. Because the onslaughts upon their self-esteem are perpetual and the cause of an ever increasing store of negative feelings, they must defend repeatedly and rigidly. Such unhealthful use of defenses in turn causes a decrease in emotional health and an ever increasing need for defenses. As the addiction progresses, the accustomed mature defenses—even rigidly overused—no longer are enough; chemically dependent persons have to retreat to less mature defenses, until finally they reach the bottom of the defense barrel, at which point they qualify for chemical insanity to one degree or another. Then, they are like John, the college senior, saying he gave drinking little thought when, in fact, he thought of little else; or Jeff, insisting he had a wife problem; or Carla, going downhill with chemicals while thinking she was ahead of the game; or Margaret, Jim's mother, arrogant and angry at those who offered help.

All the crazy, irrational, insane thoughts, behavior, and attitudes displayed by chemically dependent persons are reflections of the underlying forces of their addiction and their desperate use of defenses to reduce the stresses associated with their reduced sense of worthiness. In time, they suffer such a marked loss of self-esteem that they come to believe, on some level, that they are less than human. Along the way, they suffer drastically increased levels of hostility, until at last they become volcanoes, festering with resentments, steaming at the least slight, dripping with cynicism and sarcasm, and set to blow at any moment. Eventually, they become so depressed that death seems attractive; then they scream out in defiance of God, while they pray for help, feeling hopeless, helpless, and totally alone in the midst of their families. The fact that the dependent uses chemicals more heavily in the face of all this is not at all surprising. The fact that so many recover is a miracle.

7

The Tyrant

One of our greatest needs if we are involved with a chemically dependent person is to understand his defensive behavior. Much of the trauma we experience is needless and occurs only because we take his defenses personally or at face value. Then we feel victimized and powerless.

Recall Charles for a moment. After I presented him with specific data on the destruction he suffered as a result of his alcoholism, he pompously belittled *Time* magazine. My data was an enormous attack on his distorted view of himself, his *false* self-esteem. True to form, Charles went to bat to protect himself from the assault, and the message of his defensive response was loud and clear, "I, Charles, am superior to *Time*, *your* magazine, Ruth; therefore I am superior to you, and anything you have to say is not worth listening to." Isn't that terrific? By *defending*, he eliminated a whole set of concrete, specific facts regarding his very real destruction.

But I then had a choice—to play his game or not. I could recognize his behavior as being defensive and without face

value and avoid buying into it, or I could be blind to his defensiveness, assume it had relevance and take it personally; perhaps by entering a discussion with him on the relative merits
of *Time*, hoping he'd then elevate his opinion of me. If the
latter had been my choice, who wins? Charles, of course. Except by winning the game, he loses his life.

Dependents go on the *offense* every time they employ defense mechanisms. They carry the ball. If we join their game,
we automatically go on the *defense*; we can try to keep them
from scoring too many points, but we can't score ourselves.
It's their game, not ours. They've got the ball, not us.

The only way we can be truly protective of ourselves and
helpful to the chemically dependent person is to learn enough
about his defensive behavior so that *we do not play his game.*
Without us, he has no game. When I told Susan that it does
not matter what Jeff thinks about his drinking and suggested
that she not attempt to reason with him, I was beginning
the process of showing her how *not to buy into his defenses,*
how not to play his game; how, in effect, to render his defenses
powerless.

There is a multitude of behaviors that can be labeled defenses; joking can be a defense, or clamming up, or changing
the subject. Rather than including the multitude, I will limit
myself to the defense mechanisms described in Freudian no-
menclature. It will not matter one iota if you forget the names
or definitions of the defenses; my intent is to enlarge your
awareness of *defensiveness.* Then, we will move on to seeing
why this defensive behavior is so powerful.

In early addiction, the chemically dependent person unconsciously invokes defenses common to most adults, the neurotic and mature defense mechanisms. Like most of us, the
dependent will *repress*, forget the unbearable; *minimize*, play
down the seriousness or significance of an event; *rationalize*,
use a plausible but inaccurate explanation for his behavior;
and he will *intellectualize*, speak in generalities or theoreti-
cal terms in an impersonal manner, thereby removing himself from his feelings about specific events. But, unlike most

adults, the chemically dependent person in time will use these defenses rigidly and repeatedly. Then, to make matters worse, much worse, he will invoke two additional defenses that are not routinely used by healthy adults: *projection* and *denial*.

It is the chemically dependent person's use of these latter two mechanisms that causes the most problems for others. They become the main components of his defensive personality. Thus, of all his unconscious protective measures, they are the ones most deserving of our attention.

As I mentioned, in emotional maturation, we move from the use of the primitive defenses of early childhood (those used to age five) to the immature defenses of early adolescence (those used to age fifteen) on to the neurotic and mature defenses used by most adults from time to time. Consequently, in emotional maturation or progression, we move up the hierarchy of defenses.

Emotional illness may be thought of in terms of a regression back down the hierarchy. The mature defenses of health give way to the overuse of the neurotic defenses, which results in neurotic disorders. Further regression down the hierarchy to the overuse of immature defenses results in the more serious forms of emotional illness, personality or character disorders. Further regression into the use of primitive defenses, and perhaps a genetic predisposition, result in the most severe forms of emotional illness, the psychotic disorders.

Chemically dependent persons like to think of themselves as unique, and they are—uniquely ill. *Projection* falls into the immature bracket in the defense hierarchy while *denial* falls into the primitive bracket. Chemical dependency represents a severe regression on the defense hierarchy; yet *chemical dependency does not fall neatly into either character disorders or psychoses. It's somewhere in between, but far more severe than the most common forms of emotional illness, the neuroses.*

The purpose of *projection* is to quiet the inner unacknowledged chaos of painful feelings about oneself by attributing them to someone else.

At its simplest, projection allows dependents to dump their own painful but unacknowledged feelings onto others. Feeling unworthy, for example, they call others "garbage," "stupid," "insignificant," "mere animals," etc. In transactional analysis lingo, this form of projection states, "I'm OK; you're not OK."

Or, suffering unacknowledged guilt, dependents blame. Like young teenagers the world over, rather than their being wrong, others are the "wrongdoers." The cause of the problem is "out there" someplace, and not within them. Unlike healthy teenagers, addicts are not able to modify this stance—the blame is *always* elsewhere. Healthy teenagers eventually come around to facing the fact that the dog really didn't eat their homework; in fact, they didn't *do* their homework. Dependents, on the other hand, insist that dogs eat homework; and, if you don't want to believe that, it's *your* problem.

A more complicated form of projection, also commonly invoked by chemically dependent persons, is the assumption that others feel about them what they unconsciously feel about themselves. In other words, feeling unworthy, but unable to acknowledge that feeling, they project it, assuming others view them as unlovable, unworthy, or no good. Or they feel that "no one loves me, or "you hate me," and so on.

It is this form of projection that causes dependents to become paranoid or suspicious of others. Some develop unwarranted suspicions of everyday social interactions, wondering, for example, "Why is he being so friendly when I know what he's really thinking about me." Others become injustice collectors, racking up lists of persons who are "out to get me," "trying to do me in," "making me fail," etc. Believing they deserve the worst, they assume others believe the same and are acting in ways to make sure they get what they deserve.

Another form of projection that I see time and time again with dependents was reported by Susan at her first meeting when she mentioned that Jeff "rambled on for hours about the wars in Central America." Dependents focus on the wars of the world almost as if they could resolve their inner wars by resolving outer wars.

Whatever its form, projection is an externalization of inner chaos, and as a result, is a highly manipulative defense. It gets others to change for one's own gain and, therefore, helps chemically dependent persons become excellent con artists. But projection is also spooky because it invades the boundaries of others.

In my first session with Susan, she spoke of the time Jeff got so drunk he was thrown out of the hospital when she was giving birth to Tad. She reported that when he visited the next day, he said the only reason he drank was because she moaned too loudly with her contractions and took too long. He ended his blaming (projecting) tirade by asking Susan why she couldn't have fast labors like other women. In turn, Susan started to believe there really was something wrong with her and that it probably was her fault that Jeff got drunk. Jeff transferred his unacknowledged guilt onto Susan, as if he went right through her skin. He invaded her boundaries, giving her his feelings. That's Caspar-the-Ghost stuff, though not nearly as friendly.

Healthy toddlers occasionally employ the defense of *denial* of external reality. If a two-year-old doesn't like the looks of something, he simply announces, "That's not so," and toddles off, and we think, "How cute!" When my son was two and presented with twin sisters, initially he handled the whole situation by firmly shaking his head and telling us there was "only one baby, not two," though two were clearly right before him.

After the age of four, denial is rarely used rigidly by healthy people. While we may *minimize* and even temporarily *deny* from time to time, when faced with concrete evidence, unlike chemically dependent persons, we will accept reality whether or not we like it. In adults, a rigid, nonmodifiable, and repeated use of denial is a defense that is usually associated only with psychotic disorders and addiction.

When dependents deny, it often looks as if they are lying, and they often are. But frequently, what looks like lying is the strange defense of denial, wherein the chemically dependent person grossly alters his world.

With denial, the dependent can drink around the clock, yet claim he drinks no more often than anyone else, and *believe* his claim. Or like Carla, be presented with the results of her chemical dependency evaluation and say she doesn't see things that way, and believe her view. Or like Jim's mother, she can look you straight in the eye, claiming she's had absolutely nothing to drink, and believe her claim.

The chemically dependent person can get into all kinds of trouble—inadvertently overdose, lose his job, fail courses in school, pass out in a snow bank, fall downstairs, lose friends and family, be sapped of energy, suffer profound depression, get coke holes in his nose, clog his veins, develop liver damage— yet insist that his chemical use is not the culprit.

For many chemically dependent persons denial also includes fantasies, many of which take the form of dreams of a better life elsewhere. AA members sometimes refer to these former fantasies as their "geographical escapes." Unfortunately, the fantasies can seem so real that some have actually attempted to make them real. One former patient of mine, an Eastern Establishment Ivy League internist, left his family, his practice, and his faculty position to move to the hills of Kentucky, believing he would find the glory of a Nobel prize as he brought peace, health, and wealth to the Hatfields and Mc-Coys. With his pin-striped suits and "lockjaw" accent, he must have seemed like an extraterrestrial to the mountain folks of Kentucky. He couldn't even find their stills, much less a Nobel prize.

Families, needless to say, go absolutely bananas with the defense of denial. On the one hand, such behavior qualifies the chemically dependent person for immediate admission to the nearest "cuckoo nest"; on the other hand, he looks so normal when, as Susan says, "He goes off to work, smiling, neat as a pin, as if nothing were wrong." Families *think* their view of things is accurate, but dependents are absolutely *sure* of their view; so sure that, in time, family members begin to question their own sanity—"Maybe he is right and I am wrong." Once again, their boundaries have been invaded. Denial may be cute in toddlers, but it's maddening in chemically dependent adults.

Unfortunately, not only do chemically dependent persons repeatedly and rigidly use primitive and immature defenses, they also exhibit associated narcissistic or self-centered attitude and behavior traits that are most commonly seen in young children; such as sustained feelings of unwarranted or deluded superiority, a sense of entitlement ("the world owes me"), supersensitivity (to oneself, not others), arrogance, grandiosity, and omnipotence. Members of Alcoholics Anonymous hit the nail right on the head when they refer to their former selves as "his majesty the baby."

We see these traits operating each time the chemically dependent person pompously acts as if he has the right and power to get whatever he wants whenever he wants. We certainly saw them in Jeff when he expected Susan to cook a three-course gourmet dinner late each evening, without regard to her needs or wants, and without regard to the fact that most evenings he was too drunk to eat.

We saw them more subtly in Carla, but she, too, really believed she could do whatever she wished whenever she wished. It was not without considerable arrogance and superiority that she described her all-powerful means of handling her family.

These childlike traits are reflected in the chemically dependent person's disdainful manner; in the fact that he needs to be handled with kid gloves and is so easily slighted; in all his grandiose statements that if it were not for him "the company would go under" or that he is the "only one who can do anything right"; and in his treatment of others as if they were objects to be used as he wishes.

Such traits put the dependent on a lofty perch where he can look down critically upon others, yet miss the messy nitty-gritty of his own life; a perch that allows him to demand perfection in others, while remaining blind to his own increasing number of imperfections.

They cause the chemically dependent person to present an image to the world that does not match the realities of his world; an image that says "look at how important I am"; an image that the dependent will protect at all costs. Often the image-protecting is very much in evidence when the chemically dependent person is first admitted to treatment; when the movie star marches in snapping her fingers for round-the-clock nurses and the surgeon enters clutching his black bag, despite the fact that neither has made a film or a house call in years. Or when the school dropout enters my office quoting Nietzsche, when an author brings along his latest book, and the executive asks for the nearest phone. In each instance the chemically dependent person is announcing his importance while hiding his illness. At other times the image-protecting is more subtle, only becoming apparent when things don't go the way the dependent wishes; then, as Susan says, "Anything and everything happens."

In time, these childlike traits have a belittling impact. Repeated exposure to his often angry, impervious, self-centered demands begins to cause others to feel diminished, as if he had greater importance; in turn, they tend to give in and cater to "his majesty the baby." Receiving his negative feelings through *projection* is never pleasant, to say the least, but it is far more traumatic for family members to adapt themselves to his self-centered demeanor, where he's the master and they're his slaves.

Another defense mechanism employed by some chemically dependent persons is *passive aggression*, an immature defense seen most commonly in young teenagers which reflects serious pathology when employed repeatedly and rigidly by adults. One hoped Carla had not become locked into this defense, for it does have considerable power. Adult chemically dependent persons who use passive aggression as one of their major defenses can tie everyone's hands. Coming on as goody two-shoes, they smile sweetly, promise all kinds of good things, and then do whatever they wish, giving nothing to others to work with—no anger, no energy, no nothing.

Let's take another look at defensive behavior. The purpose of the neurotic defenses used by adults in times of severe life crises or in neuroses, is primarily to protect oneself from inner-world conflicts—conflicts between instinct and conscience; thus they are *intrapsychic* in nature. *Observers* of these defenses may consider them quirky or neurotic hangups, even moderately annoying, but rarely are they seen as grossly disturbing. *Users* of the neurotic defenses often consciously suffer discomfort, are apt to be highly motivated for change, and tend to respond dramatically to reason, interpretation, and conventional psychotherapy.

The primitive and immature defenses of chemical dependency are altogether different. The purpose of these defenses is to provide protection from conflicts between the inner world and the outer world; thus they are *interpersonal* in nature. *Observers* of these defenses consider them grossly inconvenient, inexcusably objectionable, and socially undesirable. *Users* of these defenses *do not* consciously suffer discomfort, *are not* motivated for change, and *do not* respond to reason, interpretation, or conventional psychotherapy.

Most of us employ mature and neurotic defenses; consequently we tend to view the chemically dependent person from the perspective of our own defenses and to assume he's like us. He isn't.

The chemically dependent person's defenses are particularly troublesome because they invade the autonomy of others—dependents merge boundaries just like infants merge boundaries with their mothers. Both passive aggression and projection will make others feel what the dependent feels but does not acknowledge. Denial will make others question their own sanity. The associated childlike narcissism will render others into subservience, tending to the dependent's needs while unmindful of their own. These defensive mechanisms induce a breakdown of clear knowledge of what is mine and thine. Relationships with the chemically dependent person become entangled; individual boundaries become fuzzy; outsiders looking in will have trouble determining where one starts and the other leaves off.

Parents of rebellious teenagers are often made painfully aware of the murkiness of boundary invasion. Being rational parents, we reason, and our child continues to rebel. Pretty soon we're not so rational, and then he really lets us know what rebelling is all about. Before long we lose our cool altogether, and he calmly points out how crazy we are. We've been invaded! Suddenly we're crazy and he's sane! My three children are now in their late teens, and they take great glee in recalling my freak-outs of past years. I no longer bother reminding them of their former crazy behavior; all they can remember is mine.

Any one of us suffering from *intrapsychic* conflicts, if placed on a desert island, will continue to suffer. Our defenses will continue to operate; they do not need a sounding board. We can stay quirky all by ourselves.

In comparison, the chemically dependent person suffers *interpersonal* conflicts, and if he is placed on a desert island, his defenses *will not operate*; he needs a sounding board. *The dependent cannot stay crazy all by himself; he needs people to react to his defenses. If we don't react, his defenses will not work*; then he will have to give them up and do something else instead. When it comes to the defenses of chemical dependency, virtually *any* change is an improvement.

Unfortunately the dependent's defensive behavior is so profoundly inconvenient and disturbing that unthinkingly we take it personally or at face value. We buy into it and play his game; as a result, we give him the one thing he needs for his defenses to work—our reactions.

We find his defensive behavior so glaringly provocative that we feel compelled to make him change, and with each attempt at change, we are drawn ever closer to his craziness. The closer we get, the more urgent our need for him to reform. Thus, it is no wonder chemically dependent persons and their families become inextricably entwined. While outsiders may find the entanglement mysterious and express amazement at the family members for putting up with him for so long, the reality is that we all react unthinkingly to the dependent.

Also, few of us are aware of how much families react to dependents out of fear. Alcohol- and drug-dependent persons tend to be on their best behavior with outsiders, but not with their families.

Sometimes, as an outsider, I am exposed to an impervious smirk or a subtle but hurtful put-down. I *know* I was reaching an addicted person who recently came to see me for an evaluation of his drinking. Several times, as I went through his chemical dependency history and the inventory of chemical dependency symptoms, he reacted as if stunned. Yet in closing he smiled ever so coldly and through gritted teeth gave me the name of an office supply company so that we could improve upon the quality of our stationery. His anger was barely contained, and the message was very clear: "Nothing important happened here today!"

For families, the expressions of anger are far less subtle and far more hurtful. I have been working in the field of chemical dependency since the early seventies, and I have yet to meet a spouse, parent, or child who was not afraid of the dependent. They are repeatedly, if not daily, exposed to his great well of pent-up hostility.

All chemically dependent persons are angry. Angry at themselves because nothing works; no matter how hard they try, they keep blowing it. Angry at others for refusing to understand them, for not leaving them alone, for assuming they can't take care of themselves, and for making unreasonable demands upon them. As with his other emotions, the dependent's anger is stored away; as it mounts, it becomes diffused into a hostile aura and lingering resentments. The defenses of chemical dependency permit some venting; but rather than ridding him of his vast store of anger, the venting serves only to pave the way for future outbursts. Even the periodic eruptions, when anger spurts forth in destructive rages, do not effectively release the dependent from his anger.

Recently, while I was working with the wife and two teenage sons of a dependent, they asked, "Why are we so afraid of him? Why do we feel such an impending threat of violence?" Never had their dependent husband/father actually been physically violent. They even described him as rather bland, a no-action type of person. On the surface their fears seemed to them to be irrational. They had underestimated the impact of their continued exposure to his angry, grandiose put-downs, when he referred to them as "worthless eunuchs." And they had underestimated the impact of their nightly exposure to his angry, drunken gloom and doom ravings about the impending nuclear "wipeout." Later, when I finally met him, he looked at me, a woman, straight in the eye, and made a scathing attack on the "castrating" females holding public office in the federal government, whom he felt should be "yanked back to their caves by their hair." I confess my immediate reaction was to wonder how to hasten the close of interview.

One wife, a competent, forceful university president, denied being afraid of her dependent husband. Their grown children tended to feel the same, unafraid of his anger. Yet when it came time to decide who should ask him to come to see me, all were immobilized with fear. Their dependent husband/father, in the late stage of dependency, was unemployed and quietly stoned most of each day and night. Their fear of him could be dormant only as long as he remained dormant.

One client, a father, routinely made trips in to one of the most dangerous sections of New York City to secure heroin for his fifteen-year-old daughter. When I questioned his assumption of this responsibility, he replied, "If I don't get her the heroin, she'll kill us!" He was an officer of an international corporation, responsible for thousands of employees; yet putty in the hands of his angry, addicted teenage daughter.

Look at the demagogues of history. All were angry, paranoid, and felt omnipotent. While misperceiving reality, they performed outrageous, impulsive, often violent actions. All imposed their will upon others and dominated through fear. So it is with chemical dependency. In every household, we find a demagogue, a tyrant, whether it be a two-hundred-pound fifty-year-old or a ninety-pound teenager.

Only rarely do we find people deliberately entering such a tyranny. Instead, we find Susan, the wife who watches her warm, loving, cheerful husband turn into a tyrannical, angry, abusive stranger. We find Jim, who watches his loving, sensitive, and considerate child and parent become tyrannical, frightful strangers. Most family members with whom I've worked can recall vividly the person they once knew, and most describe moments in the active addiction when they can still see the person of old.

When we see the demagogue of active addiction, the kind, loving, considerate person is still there—just hidden behind his defensive shield. The tyrants of history may have been truly evil. The tyrants of addiction are not evil; they are only attempting to survive overwhelming internal forces not of their own choosing. Their addictive forces are like a bacterial invasion; their defenses are the increased white blood cells, pus, and inflammation required to combat the invasion. The tyrannical defensive behavior we see is the chemically dependent person's desperate attempt to heal himself. At the same time, his defenses are the building blocks of a solid barrier that deforms his personality. In his deformity, he sees others, not himself, out of step. In his deformity, he causes illness in others.

8

Stoics, Saints, and the Like

My way or no way! Like tyrants the world over, the chemically dependent person presents either/or terms to her family. She must use a chemical; it has become as important to her as oxygen, necessary for her survival, or so it seems. Therefore, she must impose her will upon others. So it's her way or no way. Only rarely does she state her terms aloud, but she shows them daily in her actions.

As her addictive forces contain inordinate power, so do her defenses. As her compulsion, obsession, and increasing tolerance manipulate her, her defenses manipulate others. As she is governed, she governs—totally. Families have no choice; they must react; they can get out, adapt to her terms, or get help, but they must do something.

One common reaction to chemical dependency is to get out; my descriptions are of defensive adaptations seen in those who've chosen to stay with the addicted person. While these responses are the ones I've seen most commonly, they are by no means the only possible responses for family members who attempt to adapt to the chemically dependent person. Dependents all eventually use the same major defenses to one degree or another. But co-dependents, while governed by the addiction, exhibit a range of adaptations.

In the early stages of addiction, most family members will play down or *minimize* the dependent's behavior; and they will excuse or *rationalize* her chemical use. Often they will project their feelings onto others by *blaming*, but unlike dependents, most do not seem to regress to all the manifestations of the defense of *projection*. Instead as the dependency progresses, they will add other defenses that, in time, will become their main defenses. Then, like chemically dependent persons, the co-dependents will assume rigid attitudinal postures and behavior, but, rather than becoming tyrants, they become stoics, or escape artists, or the obsessed, or saints. If they stay trapped in the addiction, many will regress further into illness and become martyrs.

Jim might have put up with his mother's alcoholism and his daughter's deteriorating personality for quite some time if it had not been for his mother's episode of public intoxication. Until then, Jim had seemed content to bite the bullet and overlook the turmoil surrounding him.

At the beginning of our first meeting, Jim seemed inscrutable; he kept so much inside that it was difficult for me to sense his affective response. His body was stiff, I could almost see him clamping down on the bullet, and he frequently looked at his watch as if to see how much longer he would have to endure my probing.

But endure he did—my probing and his family's chemical problems. Jim regularly worked sixty-hour weeks but admitted that while he liked his work, he used it as a means of putting off facing problems at home. Frequently over the past year, knowing he'd have to face one of Carla's "rotten" moods or Virginia's "nagging" concerns about both Carla and his mother, he had chosen to stay late at the office, eating in a restaurant before returning home late in the evening. "By then I knew Carla would be holed up in her room, and I hoped that Virginia would be calmed down." On Saturdays, Jim often worked mornings in his den on material brought home from the office and spent afternoons playing tennis at the club. Sundays were devoted to church, the "traditional family brunch, which we all dreaded," and more office work in his den in the afternoon. Consequently, Jim avoided as much as possible the turmoil in his family and quietly "rode out the storms" of their periodic angry outbursts, saying he churned inside, but no one ever saw him angry.

Are you familiar with Grant Wood's 1930 painting of a farmer and his wife standing rigidly side by side in front of their house with the Gothic window, pitchfork in hand, bespectacled and unsmiling? Two stoics—not meek, but rigid, solid, upright endurers. Looking at that painting, don't you get the feeling that a mammoth dust storm could sweep down upon them from the prairie, and they'd still stand there, enduring? That's Jim, and to a large extent, Virginia.

Jim was well aware of the problems in his family, and he was also well aware of his pain, but "inclined to overlook both." The defense of *suppression* allowed him to hold his tongue and "not let things get to me." While Jim filled his hours, and either avoided or endured, he admitted he was lonely, sad, and worried. Suppression, one of our mature defenses, allowed Jim to see his mother's and his daughter's deterioration, but it also allowed him to put those problems and his associated pain aside when he "kept a stiff upper lip." His defense got him through the rough spots, but his life hurt, and he knew it.

In actuality, many of Jim's feelings were quite close to the surface, not deeply buried at all. With only minimal probing on my part, Jim was able to express a wide range of feelings for and about his mother and Carla—love, admiration, anger, and fear. When speaking of his loneliness, he looked at Virginia and said with much warmth, "I miss you." Later when telling his children about his dad, he shared his pain with tears. Stoics feel—they feel a lot—they just do not readily show those feelings to others.

Generally, if the mature defenses are overused, as suppression certainly was by Jim, a regression to a lower level of defenses will occur. But this did not seem to be the case with Jim or many of the other co-dependent stoics I've seen who've used suppression as their main defense. It's as if their use of suppression is so effective that they have little need for other defenses.

The use of suppression is often partially conscious, and of all the defenses, it is the one most commonly used by most adults. From time to time, we all suppress a conflicted event; we know about the conflict and we feel distress, but we, semiconsciously or otherwise, put off dealing with it. It is only the stoics among us, however, who use suppression repeatedly and rigidly against the neverending crises of chemical dependency.

Virginia, also a stoic, found that her controlled façade was giving way. Suppression was no longer working very well for her, and she was becoming markedly anxious, "Feeling very frazzled indeed." Nevertheless, she tended to put conflicts aside, like Jim, and seemed able to postpone gratification forever. Recall Lynn's story of her mother's expectation of achieving happiness in heaven, not here and now on earth—a story confirmed by Virginia.

The adult co-dependent stoics with whom I've worked are frequently devoted to willpower as their primary, if not only, means for achieving success and dealing with life's problems. Consequently, control of self and others is a dominant issue in their lives. Many have actually made contracts about their behavior with themselves while in their youth—contracts to which they've remained committed for life; contracts that they've kept by the application of rather heavy doses of willpower and outward manifestations of self-control.

Jim told us that he had made a decision while young never to use alcohol, drugs, and tobacco. Both Virginia and Jim decided, separately in their youth, never to swear or show violent emotions of any kind; in other words, to be proper and calm through thick and thin. Like so many stoics, both Jim and Virginia appeared to have consciously chosen to keep their emotions suppressed. What's so remarkable is that they succeeded for so long. The price they paid for their success, however, was the delay in the gratification of pleasure as well as pain.

Because suppression integrates conflicts between one's inner world and outer reality, it helps create a tenuous sense of peace. Thus co-dependents who use this defense are not apt to seek assistance until driven to it. Though their lives hurt, their defense permits some comfort, and it is usually at someone else's urging that we see these family members. Nevertheless, they respond well; suppression does not bury pain, and stoics, not being martyrs, are often quite willing to give up their pain, especially if encouraged to do so within the framework of what they consider proper or acceptable. Stoics may accept "lives of quiet desperation," but given a choice or a push, even though skeptical and fearful, they are apt to select a life with increased pleasure.

Next come the escape artists. Their energy seems boundless and it can be exhausting just listening to their various escapades. Ostensibly they come for help but often concentrate on their escapades and not their problems. Their two main defenses, *repression* and *dissociation*, both neurotic level, tend to alter their inner world and, as a result, keep them from facing their difficulties.

Repression is characterized by a curious forgetfulness, which often looks too deliberate to be unconscious; nevertheless it is. With repression the co-dependent forgets that which he cannot bear. He puts the memory of the problem aside, down, or under—anywhere but in his conscious realm. But, while he forgets what happened, he remains vaguely distressed. Repression splits the conflict; the event is forgotten, but the feeling remains, albeit in a rather amorphous state. People who repress, and most of us do from time to time, are apt to say, "I really don't feel very well, but I can't for the life of me think why."

With dissociation co-dependents are aware of their conflict, but they drastically alter both their perception of the problem and their associated distress. One young lady, enormously disturbed by her husband's alcoholism, was referred to me by her supervisor when I worked in the employee assistance field. She was about to be discharged because each day she took several twenty-minute periods away from her work in order to meditate. Sitting in the lotus position alongside her desk, she was totally oblivious to her conflicts, assignments, and the consternation of her fellow employees. But, rather than repressing knowledge of her husband's alcoholic behavior, through meditation she temporarily disassociated herself completely from both her knowledge and her associated distress.

More common forms of disassociation among co-dependents are the use of tranquilizers and/or innumerable extramarital affairs. But there are many other ways to obliterate one's inner world. One young actress claimed that more than anything she wanted to stay home to care for her infant son. But whenever her husband went on a cocaine binge, she ran out to audition for another play, hoping to lose herself in the make-believe theatrical world.

Edgar, a successful film editor, used several different forms of escape. At our first session, I could barely keep up with him; in between pacing, he plopped from one place to another, lying flat out on my sofa at one moment and sitting on top of my desk at another. He told me he had just returned from a three-week trip to the Bahamas: "The first week I popped pills and slept; the second week I drank and gambled; the third week I nearly drowned taking scuba lessons." When I asked him if he had been accompanied by his wife, I quickly discovered how stupid some of my questions could be, for he indignantly replied, "Of course not, why the hell do you think I went? I had to get away from her for Christ's sake!"

When Patti, his wife, began to be "stoned around the clock," Edgar increased his escapes. He slept throughout much of every weekend, talked his doctor into admitting him to a hospital for a week so he could read and sleep undisturbed, and started seeing a psychic to explore states of trance. About the only thing he didn't do was hook himself up to a biofeedback machine. Each of his escapes followed crises associated with

Patti's chemical use, as did his visit to me. Interestingly enough, he tempered our session by announcing that he had scheduled an appointment that same day with a lawyer in order to "divorce my beloved, besotted wife." Then he burst into tears saying he could not possibly divorce Patti.

Though disturbed by Patti's use of barbiturates, alcohol, and marijuana, Edgar initially had considerable difficulty providing specific data. He knew her chemical-related behavior was "terrible," "too much," and "gross," but when I asked him to describe her behavior of the evening before, he seemed to go blank, and finally said, "I can't remember, but you can be sure she was bombed." He was unable to describe specifically what she was like when she was, in fact, "bombed." Repression is indeed a curious forgetting.

Co-dependents who use heavy doses of repression and dissociation as a means of defending themselves against chemical dependency often have dramatic personalities, measuring rather high on the scale of exhibitionism. They are able to express their emotions fully and appear marvelously spontaneous. Sometimes they have a naive, Pollyannaish quality; perceiving silver linings where only the darkest of storm clouds exist.

Like Edgar, they can seem like bunny rabbits—hopping from one escape to another; never staying long enough in any one place to see the details of their lives, never *wanting* to see those details lest they interfere with their contrived inner comfort. When they seek help, they are frequently seeking another means of escape, another way to *extract* themselves from their predicament, and many will hop to divorce rather than face their conflicts. Perhaps because divorce was the one means of escape that was not acceptable to Edgar, he stopped hopping and allowed us to help him face his conflicts, feel his pain, and see his defenses. As he gained in emotional strength, he was able to get Patti to seek treatment for her chemical dependency.

If Edgar, the Escape Artist, couldn't see the trees of his life, Orville, the Obsessed, missed the forest, but could describe exactly the bark, leaves, and branches of each tree. While paying attention to details made Edgar anxious, ignoring details was upsetting to Orville. While dramatic personality types like Edgar's seem to lend themselves best to the use of repression and dissociation, obsessive-compulsive personality types like Orville's lend themselves best to *intellectualization* and *displacement.*

Edgar needed to stop to *think,* so he could more appropriately *feel.* Orville needed to stop to *feel,* so he could more appropriately *think.* Edgar presented the extremes of one position, Orville the extremes of the opposite. Co-dependents will commonly use defenses in one or the other of these directions, but often not to such extremes.

Users of the defenses of intellectualization and displacement often appear uptight and exhibit traits of excessive orderliness. Leaning toward stubbornness and overscrupulousness, they are rigid in their attention to details that others consider insignificant. They have difficulty expressing their feelings but are quite adept at verbalizing their ideas.

Orville came to his first appointment with several typed sheets of paper outlining in detail the history, progression, and present state of his wife's drinking, beginning with her acne at age thirteen and ending with their many recent visits to several different dermatologists for her current "reddened blotches" at age fifty-two. Orville read off to me exactly how much Marianne drank every day and how he marked her bottles and measured her consumption. He listed the hours of the day when he could call from work and find her sober and the hours when he could find her drunk. He described exactly how he helped her to bed each night and the various means by which he "almost" had her weekend drinking "under control." He reported warning their two daughters in advance of their visits from college about how to talk to their mother so as not to upset her. And he cautioned me on what to say to Marianne if the occasion arose that she would agree to see me.

So many words, but not one mention of his distress! Before Orville completed his pages with all his details, I asked him to stop for a moment and tell me how he *felt* in response to Marianne's alcoholism. Rather than telling about his feelings, Orville immediately went into a convoluted and one-sided discussion about the various definitions of alcoholism. While he thought one or two definitions fit in some ways, none fit in all ways. Before he could proceed to his description of all the ways the various definitions did not fit, I asked, "Orville, how do you *feel* when she's drunk?" But he again didn't "hear" me and I knew it would be a while before he could. For Orville, feeling meant thinking, and he proceeded to discuss the various meanings of the word "drunk."

Years ago, in Italy, I encountered by accident a friend from college, and we agreed to see Michelangelo's *David* together. Within minutes, I knew I'd have to return alone. I didn't want to see each chisel mark, and that's all my friend cared about. I wanted to be hit by the full force of that magnificent sculpture. Before dissecting, I wanted to experience it fully. By being obsessed with each "chisel mark" of Marianne's drinking, Orville was able to avoid being hit by the full force of her alcoholism. By dissecting, he did not have to experience her illness fully.

And that's the way it is with some co-dependents. The defense of intellectualization allows them to put aside their feelings. They split conflicts just like persons who repress, but rather than burying the idea of the conflict as in the curious forgetting of repression, intellectualizers bury the associated feeling and remember the event. Then, by compulsively paying strict attention to the many details of these events, intellectualizers can adjust their inner, unfelt chaos to their outer orderliness.

By adding the defense of displacement, they can further insure their inner comfort. Rather than burying feelings, displacement channels feelings attached to highly charged problems to those lesser charged. By displacing his feelings about his wife's alcoholism onto "reddened blotches" and by taking her from one dermatologist to another, Orville made his life seem more manageable; he had very effectively turned the mountain into a molehill.

Intellectualization and displacement are neurotic defenses and when overused can cause considerable dysfunction. Nevertheless, overusers of these defenses often respond dramatically to therapy. With but a few sessions, Orville could hear the word *feel* and, while he still considered abstract thought a "logical means" of handling feelings, he became able to face and share some of his feelings. Also, it became possible for him to extrude from his mind some of his many ideas about the various facets of Marianne's drinking, and he began to see the larger picture. Once he could face the mountain of her alcoholism, he recognized his many molehills, one of which turned out to be his compulsive overworking. While it took Orville considerable time to learn how to relax and play, within weeks he was able to effectively address Marianne's chemical dependency.

By her second meeting with me, Susan no longer had any doubts about Jeff's chemical dependency. She had worked hard preparing her list of specific incidents related to his chemical use and said that each incident she remembered reminded her of ones she had forgotten. Upon finishing she was shocked to see how far Jeff had progressed into addiction.

While he apparently did not drink before work, his hands frequently shook at breakfast and often he felt too sick to eat. Jeff also had been encountering problems at work. Arnie, a friend of theirs who worked in the same company, had spoken to Susan several times about his concern over Jeff's drinking, saying Jeff was often intoxicated at afternoon meetings and that the president had warned Jeff not to drink so heavily at lunch.

Their social life had also become virtually nonexistent. Susan had so frequently been embarrassed by Jeff's drinking when they were with friends that she no longer made social engagements. She also attended all the kids' school functions without Jeff, again not wanting others to see him in a drunken state.

Susan had spoken to her mother about Jeff's drinking, but

only at her mother's insistence. "She's been concerned about
Jeff's drinking for years. I just assumed she was exaggerating
because of my Dad's drinking, but I didn't want to talk to anyone, not even Arnie. It bothered me to talk about it; it always
made me feel like I was doing something wrong. I know it's
stupid, but I kept thinking Jeff would get over it somehow."

Susan reported several occasions during the preceding two
years when Jeff had attempted either to cut down or to stop
drinking altogether. "He never stayed cut down for long, and I
don't think he ever made more than a week without alcohol.
He always says that he can stop any time he wants, but I can
see now that he can't stay stopped."

Both Arnie and Susan had become increasingly worried
about Jeff's blackouts, which had recently seemed to be much
more frequent. On several occasions, Jeff had called Arnie at
home at night but the next day would not remember the calls
he had made. And Susan was shocked when Jeff could not recall their arguments or fights of the evening before. "He just
didn't remember anything about them."

When I asked to meet with her children, Susan at first was
reluctant to have them involved, saying, "They've already suffered enough. I'm not going to put them through any more."
When she then admitted that she now was "feeling relieved
and hopeful for the first time in years," she agreed that it might
be as helpful for her sons to talk about the problem as it was
for her.

At the beginning of the session with Susan and the boys,
they were all very much locked into defensive behavior. Susan
played down the problems in their family and Alan agreed
with her. In fact, he didn't think they even had any problems.
Tad was angry because he was missing a softball game, and
Scotty didn't want to talk about anything. My experience with
children of alcoholics is that sooner or later one of them will
break the ice, and then often it's as if a whole dam has spilled
over. And so it was with Susan's children.

Scotty, the five-year-old, asked me if I was helping his
mommy so she wouldn't have to cry, and then he started to cry

as he talked about how scared he was; "I get scared when Mommy cries . . . and my daddy falls down. He drinks alcohol and he falls down." Alan then became exceedingly restless and asked to leave, but when Tad began to talk about his dad's drinking, Alan, too, began to share his concerns. Then it was a matter of getting them to speak one at a time. Tad said he shouted at his dad when he was drunk. Alan said he threw the alcohol away or "sometimes I hide it in my closet." They all talked about being afraid, especially of their parents' arguments, and finished by talking about how much they loved their dad when he didn't drink so much. "Then he's lots of fun." And they said they were glad their mom was getting help, adding, "You're never any fun, Mom. You're always so worried, and you're always making us do everything."

Susan said she had no idea that the boys were so concerned about Jeff's drinking. She truly thought she had kept his problem hidden from them. At first she was angry when the boys complained that she was too serious and not fun to be around, but she also admitted that her life had become a very burdened and serious matter. They all said that talking made them feel better, and when the boys asked to come back, Susan agreed to bring them.

Jeff's chemical dependency had become very clear, but so had Susan's adaptive response. Throughout each of our meetings, even though Susan often appeared "scattered" and said she felt helpless, she was, in fact, very much in control and incredibly competent. Rather than either telling or showing her feelings about the trauma in her life, she reported events. While saying she couldn't do anything right, she held down a job and managed a busy household all by herself and claimed "it was nothing." Over the years, as Jeff had become increasingly irresponsible, Susan had become superresponsible. As Jeff had become increasingly cavalier in his attitude toward problems, Susan had become superserious. And supersweet. She was heavily involved in the neurotic defense of *reaction formation*, the creator of saints.

The main defenses used in chemical dependency seem almost made to order. Certainly denial of external reality is a perfect response for chemically dependent persons as they are faced with dreadful, uncontrollable happenings and tremendous loss of self-esteem. For co-dependents facing constant crises and the dependent's increasing irresponsibility, reaction formation is also the perfect response. For both chemically dependent persons and co-dependents, the consequences of such defenses are exceedingly maladaptive; nevertheless they are perfect in that each is invoked to resolve unconscious distress diametrically opposite to the defensive behavior itself.

In the early stages of Jeff's addiction, the either/or conditions he imposed upon Susan were, for the most part, limited to his ability to use chemicals as and when he wished (needed). Thus, initially the tyranny of his addiction did not affect many areas of Susan's life. As the addiction progressed and consumed more time and facets of Jeff's life, it began to intrude significantly in many areas of Susan's life as well, and in time it consumed her life. Then virtually all her decisions and actions were based on what his drinking and his anger would be like, and she became totally preoccupied with Jeff. She did her work and cared for their children, but her concerns, thoughts, and actions centered upon her addicted husband.

In the process of the growing tyranny, two additional things happened to Susan. First, she was repeatedly used and abused by Jeff's defensive behavior; being fearful of Jeff and not knowing how to confront such behavior effectively, she was forced to give in. None of us can repeatedly and then continuously subjugate our will to that of another without experiencing great anger. Susan learned early and quickly that Jeff's anger would beat hers any day of the week. He countered any expression of her anger with increased anger of his own, and without even being aware of it, Susan knew her rage was not safe; it only resulted in Jeff's unspeakable wrath and had to be submerged.

Secondly, as the addiction progressed, no one met Susan's emotional needs; not Jeff, not even herself. We all have ways in which we must care for ourselves and ways in which we need others to care for us; thus, we all have dependency needs. Emotionally, alcoholics are among the world's neediest people. They cannot meet their own needs, much less those of others. While alcoholics will mask their dependency needs with great claims of independence, underneath they are totally without emotional self-sufficiency, and Susan learned painfully that Jeff simply was not there for her when she needed his emotional support. Nor was he able to give emotional support to their children. Nor, in time, was he able to meet the many physical needs of his family. While he worked and provided them with their main source of income, that was about all Jeff provided. As the illness progressed, both the emotional and physical needs of everyone in the family became so great that Susan's needs could no longer be counted. Her unmet dependency needs, like her rage, became "unacceptable," unsafe, and had to be submerged.

Even though unconscious of her anger and unmet dependency needs, Susan was governed by them. The conflicts resulting from these unsafe, unconscious feelings were great and required a strong defense. For Susan and many co-dependents, *reaction formation* fills the bill; it is such a strong defense that it can take on the conflicts resulting from these two powerful but unacknowledged feelings at the same time.

Reaction formation may not be fun for anyone, but it serves a very important purpose: it preserves the marriage and the family. By behaving exactly the opposite of what she was feeling unconsciously in her inner world, Susan created the safety they all required for their preservation. While she was used, abused, and dominated, reaction formation allowed Susan to feel love for rather than anger at Jeff; thus they all could be "safe." While her needs were ignored and neglected, reaction formation allowed her to feel supercompetent, independent, and in need of no one; thus again they all could be "safe."

Because the affect and behavior are in direct opposition to the unacknowledged feelings, reaction formation is an inflexible defense—a very serious matter. It leaves no options open, which is another reason why it is such a perfect defensive response to chemical dependency. The co-dependent's no-option response fits perfectly with the dependent's no-option imposed conditions.

When the dependent does not do the things that need to be done, someone has to do them, or so it seems to the co-dependent, so she does them. That certainly is compensating behavior, but by itself, such behavior is not a psychological defense mechanism. Compensating behavior, if *not* reflective of a defense mechanism, will reflect affect appropriate to the situation. Sooner or later, if we have to keep picking up the pieces after somebody, it would be natural for us to feel some annoyance or anger. It's when we don't feel anger when it would be appropriate to feel anger, that we can tell something strange is happening, and that strange "something" is very likely to be a defense mechanism. And, so it is with reaction formation as employed by co-dependents. Outsiders shake their heads; to others her behavior is no longer plausible. They know they would be furious in the same situation, and they can't understand how she puts up so sweetly with it all. They know also that they wouldn't be able to exist in that kind of situation, and they wonder where she gets her strength.

Because reaction formation allowed Susan to keep in consciousness an idea and affect quite opposite to those in her unconscious world, she could sweetly say and believe, "It's my duty to love Jeff no matter what he does." Or, as she often said in our early sessions, "If I don't do everything, no one will, but I'm strong, and I really don't mind." On several occasions, while she and Jeff were still socially active, Jeff had been so verbally abusive toward Susan that either their friends complained to Jeff, or they left the party, yet Susan said, "It wasn't so bad, I know Jeff didn't mean the things he said."

Susan did all the parenting in their family. She took care of *everything* in regard to the children: she supervised their homework, attended PTA meetings, taught them how to play softball, had their braces fitted, tended broken arms, bought and laundered their clothes, chauffeured them about, cooked their meals, resolved their fights, attended their soccer and baseball games, located lost skateboards, fed and walked the dog, kept the kids out of Jeff's way, and all the rest, yet, "Jeff's a wonderful father. He works hard to provide for them. He loves them very much, I know he does."

Susan worked from four to six hours every day in her mother's store; she cleaned their house, marketed, laundered, did *all* those "kid things," and at nine or ten each evening, she cooked a three-course gourmet dinner for Jeff, who never thanked or complimented her and, more often than not, left the meal uneaten; yet upon my further questioning, Susan said, "I like to cook; I guess I've spoiled him."

Reaction formation led to a marked loss of pleasure, and it decreased Susan's ability to relate closely to others, but it did have its payoffs. Besides *appearing* to preserve the fabric of all their lives, it made Susan feel *important* and *well.* While she frequently complained about Jeff's irresponsibility, she also was proud that she was the one who got everything done. And she said and believed, "He's sick, not me." After all, she was moving ahead at high gear, or so it seemed, while Jeff was shifting into reverse.

At one of our early sessions, when I suggested to Susan that it would be helpful for her to start attending Al-Anon meetings, she was very resistant. At first, she said she could not possibly go to Al-Anon because then, "Everyone would know about Jeff's alcoholism." Susan didn't seem very impressed when I reviewed Al-Anon's concept of anonymity and told her she wouldn't have to tell anyone her name. Nor was she impressed when I suggested that she could go to Al-Anon in a neighboring community if that would make her feel safer. Finally, she said that she didn't want to go to Al-Anon because she resented my implying that she was in need of help. "Why do I have to do all these things? Jeff's the one who's sick. Why don't you get Jeff well; then I wouldn't have any problems."

In describing Susan's defensive behavior, I have not done

justice to her as a person. She was an absolute delight to work with. Her defense of reaction formation would strongly tell her to do one thing, and I would just as strongly suggest that she do the opposite. Susan would at first argue and look at me with disgust, then she would shake her head, mumble a bit, and do as I suggested. She went to Al-Anon, didn't like it too much at first, but soon reaped its rewards.

Susan was very big on cleaning; because of her defense, she took *everything* very seriously, and so when I, at another point, suggested that she let her house get dirty and take Saturdays off to play with the boys, she looked at me as if I were out of my mind. She was even more flabbergasted when the boys said they'd help her clean in the evening if she'd play with them on Saturdays. Having those kids running around with vacuum cleaners, mops, and dustcloths must have seemed like a fate worse than death, but Susan turned Saturdays into their play day. They went to movies, played ball, hiked, rode bikes, ate at McDonalds, and Susan forced herself to smile, and then she laughed at how serious she had become. Susan was willing to take the risk of doing the very things that her defense told her were wrong. In my book that's courage of the highest order.

Within a very short time Susan was able to perceive that she was crucifying herself with her reaction formation—*that it was the very reversal of her needs and that it stood in her way of rescue.* She said she had desperately wanted help for years but had shunned offers. She could see that their offers of help called into question her whole mode of operation, her whole supercompetent "act." She also said she wanted to be normal, like other people, but could see that her saintliness made her "inhuman." "My mother once called me Joan of Arc. I guess being a saint rankles."

Reaction formation also frequently exacts another price. Because it is such a demanding defense, it can easily lead co-dependents into functioning beyond their strengths, and thus sets them up for serious physical illness. Susan was lucky; she had avoided the ulcers, bad backs, hypertension, and migraines—the ailments common to other co-dependents, especially those who use reaction formation as their main defense.

But she had not avoided the bitterest pill of all. Her defensive behavior had begun to turn her children against her. Because she felt compelled to see to everything, she had become controlling and manipulative. The boys felt she was always on their backs, and they began to identify with Jeff, believing if she would leave him alone, as they wanted to be left alone, that he then wouldn't drink so much. Also because Jeff was anesthetized much of the time, he let the boys get away with a lot, while Susan let them get away with nothing. Sometimes Dad was fun, but Mom was never fun. Mom had become the ogre, not carefree Dad. More than anything, whether or not Jeff got well, the boys and Susan needed their day of play.

When co-dependents stay trapped in the addiction without assistance, sooner or later it is highly likely that the defenses they have used to adapt will no longer be sufficient, and new ones will be called forth. Sometimes the users of intellectualization and displacement, the Obsessed, may enter the paradoxical world of reaction formation, where the passions that rage the strongest are the passions that are held under the tightest rein. Persons whose main defense has been reaction formation may begin to use tranquilizers, sleeping pills, and antidepressants, and thus obliterate their inner world through dissociation.

The whole point of a defense is to insulate one against the pain of conflicts, but the reality is that the world of chemical dependency is too disordered. None of the main defenses I've described, even when used in combination, will work forever against the onslaughts of the loved one's addiction. So, too, though the main defenses may have created a sense of comfort for the short term, in the long run, defenses provide protection from emotional pain only at great sacrifice to the co-dependents' sense of self-worth, and as the conflicts mount, their tolerance for stress decreases. Consequently, many co-dependents regress to the immature defenses of *passive aggression* or *hypochondria—the two defenses that reflect an extraordinary acquiescence in the humiliating tyranny of chemical dependency.* While both of these defenses modulate distress arising from the co-dependent's unacknowledged rage, they are enormously provocative to others. Either defense creates a martyr out of the user.

With passive aggression the co-dependent's rage is close to the surface, felt by everyone *but* the co-dependent. Now, while she outwardly disavows her anger, she drives everyone crazy through petty, self-defeating actions. After years of domination, she finally gets even, but she does not fight back openly; instead she uses indirect expressions of anger and sneaks her attacks. Though not consciously aware that she is provoking others, she's now late for everything, "forgets" to do what she has promised, "puts off" anything important to others, and frequently becomes a compulsive overspender on nonessentials. Albeit unwittingly, she starts arguments among her family and then withdraws; in turn, they become infuriated when she does not fight back or finish what she's started, while she literally gloats in their discomfort. The supreme passive aggressive act is suicide—the ultimate revenge—and the enraged martyr, with a great sigh and forlorn look, often alludes to the fact that she might as well be dead. While she may not speak openly about suicide, it is nevertheless an implied threat. The martyred co-dependent makes life miserable for everyone; there is no way others can combat the rage they correctly perceive but which she denies.

The defense of hypochondriasis transforms covert rage into physical complaints, which soon become exaggerated and take on a life of their own. While the physical complaints are rarely accompanied by physiological symptoms, they become the co-dependent's chief concern and they, of course, reflect her attempts to obtain much-needed care and to contain her hostility. Unfortunately, she is incapable of being consoled. While she goes out of her way to let one and all know of the excruciating details of her physical agony, her agony is not the issue; it is in lieu of openly complaining of how she has been neglected and mistreated. She uses her imagined pains to covertly accuse and punish others, and she is not going to give them up easily, so no matter what others do, nothing will work. If they attempt to comfort, reason with, confront, or ignore her, she expounds on her agonies in even greater detail.

Susan was perilously close to moving into the defense of hypochondriasis. She already exhibited its first sign—self-reproach. Repeatedly, in virtually all our early sessions, Susan spoke of how she couldn't do anything right. She always apologized profusely; at one point when I asked her to *not* say "I'm sorry," she replied, "I'm sorry." I am very happy Susan got help when she did. Hypochondriasis is a very debilitating defense and difficult to leave once established.

The defenses of passive aggression and hypochondriasis are similar to the chemically dependent's main defenses in that they are profoundly irritating to others and merge personal boundaries. As with flypaper, families can't get unstuck from these defenses. They are so irritating that families, as well as friends, become (or remain) oblivious to the co-dependent's covert rage and believe it to be their own; thus, they assume responsibility for her anger for her. Their boundaries have been invaded by these defenses: they will feel the rage; she will not.

Not surprisingly, children of chemically dependent families tend to clear out as soon as possible, and then the dependent, if he survives, and the co-dependent, if she survives, are left alone together. Neither will care very much about anyone or anything. They will have become wasted by their defenses, not preserved. The predominant affect as they approach the end of the line of addiction will be pity—pity for themselves and pity for each other. Their great store of unconscious hostility will remain amorphous, but it will not contain the energy of earlier years. They will have burnt themselves out, and now about the most they can do with their unacknowledged rage is fantasize each other's death.

Children leave the chemically dependent home *without having learned how to say good-bye.* They take the illness with them: never having had well-demarcated boundaries, their future relationships run the risk of being as entangled and murky as the ones they've left; never having been able to trust, they are apt to remain emotionally isolated while their *love* for others will often be confused with *need;* never having been emotionally nurtured, their initiative is frequently marked by pessimism and passivity. Children of chemically dependent families are at risk for serious emotional illness as adults; while they may be able to work, few will be able to fully love and play.

The most important childhood learning tasks have not to do with the three Rs, but with trust, autonomy, and initiative. In chemically dependent families, trust is destroyed, autonomy is invaded, and initiative is lost. Unless treated, chemically dependent persons go right down the tubes, but they do not go alone; they take their families with them. It starts subtly and slowly, but in time the illness of each person in the family is apt to become profound.

9

The Enabling Equation

Lest we cast stones at ourselves or others, we would do well to remember that chemical dependency, stigmatized and poorly understood by our society, requires the co-dependent family member to combat by herself, in secrecy, and without specific knowledge, two, not just one, but two forces beyond her power—his *compelled chemical use* and his *unreasonable defensive behavior.* Either would defeat the strongest among us.

Control and reason are the missing ingredients. Everyone, and I mean everyone, automatically assumes the solution lies in the realm of supplying these missing ingredients. *Every co-dependent attempts to control the uncontrollable and reason with the unreasonable; in turn every co-dependent is destined to fail. Lack of control and reason are definitely the problem, but neither control nor reason is the solution.*

Also, lest we cast stones, we would do well to know that our selection of defenses is *preordained* and *out of our conscious control.* To ward off the onslaught of attacks against their decreasing sense of worthiness, co-dependents must invoke defenses repeatedly and rigidly. Our selection of defenses is unconscious; if they work, we cannot take credit; if they don't work, we cannot take blame. Our use of defenses is dependent upon our biological readiness, the genes we've inherited, the role models with whom we've identified, and other forces as yet unknown.

As you were reading about Jim the Stoic, Edgar the Escape Artist, Orville the Obsessed, and Susan the Saint, you may have thought that one response seemed worse or better than the others, or that you would do something altogether different, and you might. Then again, you might invoke the defenses you liked the least. We do what we can do. Defenses can't be willed, nor can they be faked. Defensive adaptations are given to us, for better or for worse.

With chemical dependency, it really doesn't matter which defensive adaptation is invoked. None of them is effective; and no one adaptive style is any better or worse than any other. Each is maladaptive. Each leads the co-dependent into ever more desperate applications of control and reason; in turn, each contributes to the progression of illness—her illness and his illness.

One of the most outstanding characteristics found in virtually all of the maladaptive responses to chemical dependency is that the co-dependent's focus is on the dependent, not on herself. Before she can help either herself or the dependent, she must shift her focus from him to herself. Before discussing this shift, let's consider how the misplaced focus comes about and why it is so traumatic for both.

As we've seen, the chemically dependent person's defensive behavior is so provocative that the co-dependent feels compelled to react; thus the dependent's main defenses—*projection and denial*—work. Because these defense mechanisms are both belittling and invasive in nature, they work to make the co-dependent feel shattered, without boundaries, as well as unworthy, guilty, inadequate, and subservient.

When his uncontrolled chemical use is coupled with these

belittling, invasive defenses, the co-dependent not only loses her autonomy so that she is unable to differentiate herself clearly from others, she also loses every shred of trust in the dependent, learning that she can depend upon only the worst from him. Add to that her repeated failure at attempting to supply the missing ingredients of control and reason, and the co-dependent loses every shred of trust in herself, learning that she can expect only her further failure. Without trust in herself, she can have little trust in anyone else. Additionally, with her repeated failure, she loses initiative; not only is she riddled with indecisiveness, pessimism, and doubt, she eventually feels utterly hopeless and helpless.

Having lost her autonomy, trust, and initiative, the co-dependent cannot focus upon herself—she has lost her identity and feels there's nothing there to focus upon. She no longer feels like a separate, complete, and worthy person; instead she feels herself to be an extension of the dependent; he is after all the dominating force of her life. Thus, she can only focus outward upon him—as if he were her host and she his parasite—which sets her up for a whole chain of negative behaviors, beliefs, and feelings.

Without identity as a complete, separate, worthy person, she needs the dependent (and others) to be strong. If others crumble, she will crumble, or so she believes. So the co-dependent becomes a *fixer*. If others are sad, she feels compelled to make them unsad. If others share fears, she is compelled to pooh-pooh those fears, or avoid persons she considers weak. But most especially, feeling attached to the dependent, she suffers an all-encompassing need for him to get well. She does not believe she can feel well until he feels well.

Without identity, she fears being disconnected, abandoned, so she becomes an *appeaser*. Her fear of rejection is so great that she will do anything, anything at all, to remain connected. She'll permit the chemically dependent person to slap her around, to rape her, beat up their kids, and to treat them all with utter disdain. Anything goes as long as she can remain connected.

Without identity, she must be dishonest in her relationships—compelled to say what others want to hear and afraid
to say what she is really thinking or what others need to hear.
Her need for approval is so great that she becomes a *people
pleaser*, willing to be whatever others want her to be.

Without identity, she feels powerless; in turn she has a great
need to control, to be on top of everything, so she becomes a
manipulator, incurring the displeasure of others.

Without identity, she is unable to accept responsibility for
what is wrong with her life; she puts that responsibility onto
the dependent instead. Thus, he and others are the cause of
her problems, and she becomes the *victim*.

Without identity, she knows how to be passive and how to
be aggressive, but she does not know how to be assertive. She
knows how to cater to the dependent's whims and how to
throw frying pans at him, but she does not know how to express her needs and wants openly.

Without identity, she does not believe she has any rights,
much less needs or wants. He has rights, she does not. His
needs and wants matter, hers do not. He can be decisive, she
cannot. He leads, she follows. He has worth, she does not. She
has become so shattered that she believes, feels, and acts like
his appendage—as powerless, as worthless, and as amorphous
as his shadow.

It is a beautiful and exciting thing when the co-dependent
family member comes to grips with these manifestations of
her loss of autonomy, trust, and initiative. For the most part,
co-dependents do not regress as far down the defense hierarchy
as chemically dependent persons; thus they tend to be conscious of their discomfort, motivated for change, and able to
respond to reason. The place to start back up the hierarchy
into health is with the shift of her focus from him back to
herself. She cannot regain her autonomy, trust, and initiative—the necessary ingredients for being able to fully love,
work, and play—and she cannot help the chemically dependent person until she becomes self-focused. While being other
focused is symptomatic of her loss of integrity, treating that

symptom results in her reintegration, and the renewal of that integrity.

Shifting focus is not easy, nor is it accomplished overnight. Susan tried to avoid it altogether. In one of our early sessions, while no longer perched on the edge of her seat, Susan continued to be bogged down with her crammed datebook, cigarettes, lighter, and pocketbook, which now spewed forth innumerable newspaper clippings and several dogeared books. Once she appeared more or less settled, I asked, "How are you feeling, Susan?"

"I can't stand it," she replied. "You know what Jeff did this morning? He gave me a list of things he wants me to get done before he gets home from work. I can't stand his lists. He was passed out . . . drunk all evening, and *he* gives *me* lists. He's falling apart and *he* tells *me* what to do. I can't stand his lists."

"We'll get to the lists in a moment, Susan, but I asked about you, not Jeff, and I really do care about how you're feeling."

"Well, I'm fine, but he's not! He's just getting worse," Susan complained.

"You're *still* talking about Jeff. I care about you, Susan. What are you feeling right now?" But Susan kept on talking about Jeff and, finally, at my insistence, she picked a feeling out of a list I named, saying she felt mad as opposed to sad and glad. Then she looked at me as if wondering why I attached importance to such an insignificant thing as her feelings and returned once again to talking about Jeff, describing how impossible he had been since our last session. During a lull I asked, "Do you know that you're a lot like Jeff?"

"*I'm* like Jeff? How can you possibly say that?" she asked, obviously not pleased with the comparison.

"Do you think there's something harmful about Jeff's preoccupation with alcohol?"

"Of course," she replied, "it's his whole life . . . his drinking is more important than anything else. That's what I'm trying to tell you."

I said, "*You* are acting as if Jeff is your whole life, as if *he's* more important than anything else. That's why I said you and

Jeff are alike. He's totally preoccupied with drinking, and you're totally preoccupied with him. Your preoccupation with Jeff is just as harmful as his preoccupation with drinking. That's why we need to talk about you, and your feelings are *part* of you, an *important* part of you. Talking about you may not interest you too much, Susan, but it is what we need to do."

"I know what you're saying," she replied, "and I've read everything you've given me, but I guess I still don't understand; why can't we just help Jeff? None of these problems would exist if he didn't drink."

"Then you'd have different problems and you'd still be in the same boat. Right now both you and Jeff are placing all the responsibility for your problems outside yourselves. Jeff blames the world and everyone in it, and you blame Jeff. Problems get replaced with problems. They'd be a whole lot different, and no doubt easier, without Jeff's drinking, but as long as you both blame outside factors, you'll continue having trouble.

"Susan," I continued, "I know you want me to help Jeff, and I agree with you that he needs help, but I don't have a magic wand. I don't have any influence with Jeff. My only way to help Jeff is to help you increase your influence. Then we can get him to do what he needs to do in order to survive his illness. But it doesn't seem as if you have much influence with Jeff right now. I'd like to help you feel stronger, and that means concentrating on you, not Jeff."

I then said, "Under the circumstances, I think I'd feel mad, too, Susan, if I were given a list of things to do from someone who's not doing his own things very well. It's like Jeff can't manage his own life, but he's managing yours."

"That's it exactly," she said, "and I can't stand it. I hate his lists."

"Do you?" I asked.

She replied, "Yes, I really hate them."

"Do you do the things on the lists?" I asked.

"Yes, but I can't stand doing them," she responded.

"But it looks as if you do stand them," I pointed out. "Listen to what you've just said. You can't stand the lists, but then you follow them and do stand them."

"That's crazy, isn't it?" she asked.

"That's not the point. What does tolerating the intolerable do to *you*? And it's not just lists we're talking about. You've been tolerating a lot of intolerable things for years, month in, month out, week in, week out, day in, day out. *What has that done to you, Susan?*"

Susan answered—with tears, not words. For the first time, she was able to reach beneath the scattered, helpless, yet all-competent image that she presented to the world; she was able to share her great pain, and she sobbed bitterly for several minutes. And then she spoke of how much her life hurt; how she cried herself to sleep at night, how each morning she felt as if she wouldn't be able to make it through the day, how she often wanted to die, saying, "I've thought of suicide a lot, but I just can't leave the boys."

"You're not going to have to suffer that kind of pain any longer, Susan. You've taken an enormous step this morning. You're really seeing what hurts—what doesn't work—aren't you?"

"Yes, and I don't know why, but I feel better already." She smiled as she wiped away her tears.

"You've reached your turnaround point. Now you can start on your voyage out of pain, Susan, and I'm so very happy for you," I said as I returned her smile and embrace.

The universal response to the chemically dependent person is first to reject and then to tolerate his objectionable behavior, which results in enabling his illness, furthering its progression. Even though the co-dependents' maladaptive responses to chemical dependency can vary widely, they each result in the devastating and life-threatening enabling equation: *rejection + tolerance = enabling.*

The enabling equation has profound negative ramifications, but when articulated, it's really quite simple. "I can't stand what you are doing, and I'm going to make some accommodations because I want to continue our relationship, which means I'll help you get away with your objectionable behavior." First, the co-dependent rejects the behavior, then she tolerates it; in turn, she enables and thereby promotes the progression of addiction.

When the co-dependent gives an inch, the dependent takes a foot; then she has to give a foot, and he takes a yard. The more she tolerates, the more she has to tolerate.

Chemically dependent persons do not listen to words— words do not penetrate their defensive barrier—they listen only to action. Each time the co-dependent tolerates the intolerable, her actions tell the dependent "Hey, you're not so bad after all." While her words tell him repeatedly that he's sick, in need of help, and all those kinds of very accurate pronouncements, her *actions* tell him the opposite, that he's okay. If she puts up with it, how bad can it be?

Co-dependents do not intend to promote illness; everything they do, in fact, is an attempt to make things better. Yet, despite their different defensive responses and despite their good intentions, the end result, a worsening of the illness through enabling, is the same for all spouses who attempt to adapt to their partner's chemical dependency. Jim, Virginia, Orville, Edgar, and Susan were all very different in their defensive responses to the dependent person, yet all *rejected and tolerated* the dependent's behavior; thus all invoked the *enabling equation*.

All co-dependents find the dependent's chemical use and defensive behavior gross, irresponsible, embarrassing, frightening, terribly inconvenient, inexcusable, painful, worrisome, and unacceptable. In their own unique ways, they each *reject* such behavior. They rant and rave; withdraw in tears or unspoken rage; beg, plead, pout, and reason; denounce; threaten; and extract promises of reform—each response a very clear statement *rejecting* the dependent's objectionable behavior.

Then, co-dependents add the second part of the equation and *tolerate* the very behavior they *reject*. Their defensive responses, though different, are their means of accommodating and tolerating the intolerable.

Every time Jim bit his tongue and studiously put Margaret's

and Carla's unacceptable drinking and defensive behavior aside, he tolerated such behavior. Edgar matched his wife's chemical use with escapes of his own; in turn, he was able to tolerate her dependency. Susan became superresponsible and thus able to tolerate Jeff's increasingly irresponsible behavior. By obsessing over unimportant problems, Orville was able to tolerate his wife's drinking. Though intentions are good, one plus one makes two; *rejection plus tolerance makes enabling.*

Initially the co-dependent's enabling often takes the form of ignoring or belittling the objectionable behavior, or of excusing it by saying such behavior is due to acne, pressures at work or school, too much idle time, too little idle time, other people, places, and things. Eventually, though their defenses may differ, all co-dependents will attempt to control the dependent—they will try to get him to stop taking drugs and to drink less.

Jim thought that if he set rules and gave advice, Carla and his mother would drink less. Orville thought things would get better with his wife if he measured her consumption and everyone's reaction to her. Edgar, between escapes, threw his wife's pills away and set up her drinking rules—one cocktail before dinner, two glasses of wine at dinner, one ounce of brandy following. Susan overspent so Jeff would have less money for drugs; she threw his alcohol away and assumed his responsibilities for him, believing that if she made his life easier, he would have less reason to drink.

Each co-dependent also repeatedly tries to make the chemically dependent person *see* reason. Jim quietly, politely, and frequently spoke to both his mother and his daughter, explaining why their behavior was unacceptable and advising them about what they should do instead. Margaret either wept with remorse, making promises of reform, or she viciously berated Jim. Carla smiled sweetly, saying, "You're absolutely right, Dad," and went upon her merry way, drinking and doing drugs. The calmer and more reasonable Jim became, the more bizarre were their reactions.

In addition to all their attempts at rational discussion, both Edgar and Susan took innumerable pictures of their intoxicated partners, assuming Patti and Jeff would then be able to see the error of their ways. Instead, like bulls, Patti and Jeff saw red, and charged forth in rages. But Edgar and Susan didn't give up easily; they continued their endless, futile attempts at rational talk and snapped even more pictures.

Orville, not willing to confide in his secretary, but compelled to get everything down in neat detail, stayed at the office after closing in order to type lengthy descriptions of Marianne's drinking, which he then read to her. She, in turn, ripped up his beautifully prepared descriptions, threw them in his face, and marched grandly out of the room. The next day, Orville added *this* behavior onto his new description.

Additionally, co-dependents repeatedly rescue the dependents from the consequences associated with their chemical use. Susan occasionally called Jeff's office to say he had the flu when in fact, he was hung over. Edgar bailed his wife out of jail when she was arrested for impaired driving, saying, "Jail's no place for a woman." When his mother fell down the stairs with a load of laundry while drunk, Jim hired a housekeeper to do the heavy work, and he obtained tutors so Carla could raise her grades. Orville kept his daughters away so they would not see their mother's intoxicted states. They each accommodated the intolerable, and they all unwittingly contributed to the disease's progression.

Rejection plus tolerance equals enabling is not an unusual equation. We enable sloppiness if we pick up after our litterbug teenager. We enable tardiness when we wait for a friend who's habitually late. We enable irresponsibility when we do for anyone what that person should do for himself. If our enabling—which always has as its base our acceptance of unacceptable behavior—is a one-shot affair, the resulting damage may not *seem* extensive. But, by enabling, not only do we blow an opportunity to be helpful, we do not show respect for ourselves or the other person. We knock ourselves down a peg on the ladder of self-esteem, and we negate the worth of the other person. Enabling is *easy*, but it is *never helpful*; it is usually far more destructive than it seems.

Leo Buscaglia, in his book *Living, Loving & Learning*, relates an incident in his life when he sought enabling, but received something altogether different.[5] When young, he had gone to Paris against his mother's wishes. She felt he was too young, but that if he chose to go, he was declaring himself an adult, and she would expect him to be self-reliant. When after several months he wired home for money saying he was starving, his mother responded not with money, but a succinctly worded telegram inviting him to starve.

My heart goes out to that woman. How many of us could have done that? Buscaglia reports that his mother later said it was the most difficult thing she had ever done. I'm sure it was. How many of us perceive, as Buscaglia does, that it was also the most helpful thing she could have done?

Detach yourself for a moment. Any kid who's got the spunk to go to Paris by himself *is not going to starve.* That's the reality. He may not eat well, but he'll eat. The spunk that got him to Paris will get him to food, and it will get him to adulthood *if it is respected,* as it clearly was in Buscaglia's case.

Enabling diminishes! What if Mama sends money? What's her message? "You silly little boy, I knew you couldn't make it on your own"? "I told you you weren't old enough"? "You're a stupid kid who needs rescuing"? Even if she says, "I'll rescue you this time, but no more," what is she really saying? Don't play this down now. Incidents such as this have the power to make us or break us. If Mama sends money, what's her statement about his adequacy?

Sure he'll be grateful when he gets the money, but how will he feel about himself for having asked for it when both he and she clearly knew that was not part of their original agreement? Inside someplace, he's not going to feel very good about himself, is he? And he's not going to feel so good about his mother either, is he?

Enabling belittles everyone. The dependent, beneath his defenses, feels increasingly disgusted with himself and with the

5. Leo Buscaglia, *Living, Loving & Learning* (New York: Ballantine, 1983). pp. 230–231.

co-dependent for going along with his horrible behavior. The worse he feels about his own behavior, the worse he feels toward her for accepting such behavior.

He'll focus, of course, on her behavior, not his own. As his illness progresses, her accommodating behavior will seem increasingly bizarre to him. He won't be able to fathom, for example, why she can't get the message to leave him alone. And in many ways, he has good reason for his views. If he nearly tears the house apart after seeing pictures of himself intoxicated, one might question the wisdom of taking more pictures. If he beats her up when she throws his alcohol away, one might think she would stop throwing it away. If he wins *every single argument* resulting from her attempts to get him to see reason, which he invariably sees as nagging, one would think she'd learn not to bother trying to reason with him. But she has become as locked into her defensive behavior as he is in his. So, he can say and truly believe, "With a wife like you, anyone would drink," or "If anyone's crazy around here, it's you, not me," or the very common and perhaps most hurtful comment of all, "You want to know why I get stoned? Look in the mirror!"

While the chemically dependent person needs the crazy enabling behavior in order to continue using alcohol and drugs, he nevertheless does not respect it, and he turns it around to mean only one thing: he's normal, she's crazy.

The co-dependent puts the enabling equation into action because she feels she has no other choice, because she wants to help, and because she feels too weak to do otherwise, and that's the thanks she gets—his scorn, his ridicule, and his loss of respect.

The other side of the enabling picture, as we have seen, is that by accommodating herself to his intolerable behavior, the co-dependent allows herself to be used and abused; ultimately she sacrifices her integrity as a human being. *She knows no other way; without guidance and support, there is no other way.*

10

Reversals

When you're barreling down hill in your car and see off in the distance that the bridge has collapsed and troopers are waving everyone back, what do you do? You slow down, stop, and reverse your direction. If you are living with a chemically dependent person, you should do the same thing. Slow down, stop, and go in the reverse direction.

Is your way working? Have you helped yourself over the long haul? Are you feeling better now than you were a year ago? Has anything you've done for the dependent helped over the long haul? Is he better now than she was a year ago?

If your answers are "no," your bridge has collapsed. You just can't go any further on that road unless you want total destruction. Can you see that? If so, your solution is simple, not easy, but simple. *Stop doing whatever you're doing. Start doing just the opposite.*

In any interaction, or contemplated interaction, with the chemically dependent person, slow down. Ask yourself how you've handled this kind of situation in the past. Then do something different, something as close as possible to the opposite of your former response. Actually, anything different will be helpful, but the more opposite the better.

Your actions in the opposite direction are called *reversals*. Reversals will take you on the voyage away from illness into wellness.

Because each of you is unique, many of your reversals will differ. Susan readily acquiesced to Jeff's demands, so some of her reversals were in the direction of standing firm. Jim stood firm before his mother and Carla, passing out admonitions and advice all over the place, so his reversals were quite different from Susan's.

On the other hand, each of you shares some similarities. The specific nature of chemical dependency is such that it has forced each of you to: attempt to control his alcohol and drug use; get him to see reason; take her defenses at face value; and focus on him rather than yourself. Consequently, each of you, assuming you now see that these behaviors have collapsed your bridge, will share many similar reversals.

You'll do the opposite. You'll stop controlling the chemical use, knowing you can't make him do what he can't do; you'll stop advising, warning, and explaining, knowing he's beyond logic; you'll ignore his ideas, opinions, explanations, and attitudes, knowing that virtually everything he says and shows is defensive and, therefore, irrelevant; and you'll start thinking of yourself, looking at and meeting your own needs and wants, not his, knowing that if you don't, no one else will.

Keep it simple. Ask yourself how you handled it in the past, then do the opposite. Reversals! They'll save your lives.

Susan arrived at our fifth session *uncluttered*. Finally, she was free of all her various forms of evidence regarding Jeff's alcoholism—pictures, tape recordings, newspaper clippings, dog-eared books—evidence proclaiming his uncontrolled drinking; evidence proclaiming his inability to listen to reason; evidence she wanted known but had not fully accepted herself. While Susan was now virtually bubbling with energy, she also

seemed more at peace, as if she no longer had to prove anything either to herself or to me. She had been *heard* in our last
session when she shared her innermost feelings; most impor-
tantly she had *heard* herself. As you'll recall, I never once
doubted Susan's claims regarding either Jeff's uncontrolled
drinking or his irrational behavior; all along, in fact, my efforts
were to allow Susan to feel and believe her own claims.

Susan had reached that marvelous moment when she could
fully *see* what hurt and what didn't work; in turn, she could
enlarge her insight, *accepting*, not just saying, but *accepting*,
that Jeff's *drinking* and *thinking* were unmanageable, as much
out of her control as his. Susan was then, for the first time, in
a position to stop enabling and to start reversals—her voyage
out of illness.

As we had parted at the session before, Susan spoke of her
intentions of letting Jeff *drink* and *think* as he wished, two
major reversals, to be repeated daily, hourly, if necessary. And I
asked Susan to consider another reversal as well, to make a list
of the things she most resented so we could begin to concentrate on what she wanted instead, thereby starting the process
of shifting her focus from Jeff to herself.

She began our next session by saying, "Something's really
happened to me. I just couldn't take cooking those late dinners
any longer, so I told Jeff that if he wanted me to make his dinner, he'd have to be home by seven to eat with me and the boys.
He stayed out late twice and came home so drunk that he
passed out on the sofa in the den, but you know what? Last
night he was home early and had dinner with the rest of us.
Jeff joked around and acted like the whole thing was his idea,
and I almost straightened his thinking out for him, but then I
remembered not to buy into his defensive behavior and . . ."

"Wow, Susan, stop a moment. I saw you just a few days ago
and you were still very much the meek little kitten around Jeff.
Now you're a tiger. What happened?" I asked, truly amazed.

"There's no reason for him not to be home by seven. He
finishes at the office by five or six at the latest. He can easily
get home by seven," she explained.

"I know that, Susan, but . . ."

"Oh, I've been going to Al-Anon," she interrupted, "and almost everyone there has gone through these same things, and they told me how they've changed. I have a wonderful sponsor now, and she helped me. She did the same thing with her husband."

"That's terrific, Susan, but this is a major change that you're making. Less than a month ago you had trouble asking Jeff when he *wanted* to eat; now you're telling him when he *can* eat. If that isn't a reversal, I don't know what is. Are you scared?"

"Yes," she answered.

"But you're doing it anyway," I said softly, still amazed.

"I'm doing it anyway," she replied softly, equally amazed.

Susan then reported how members of Al-Anon had listened to her fears and shared their experiences. While she was afraid, she knew her sponsor was never farther away than a phone call. Not only did the Al-Anon members inspire Susan, they showed her how to change and then stood behind her every step of the way. "It's so helpful to know that I'm not the only one that this has happened to. I feel if they can change, so can I. When I first told Jeff about the new dinner arrangements, I was so scared that my knees were trembling. But when he started screaming at me and telling me that I would do as he said or else, I was able to get up and walk out of the room. He followed me into the kitchen, yelling and swearing at me, and I told him he could either stop shouting or I would call the police. He didn't believe me at first, but when I picked the phone up and started dialing, he left the room and banged all the doors on his way out to work."

"Would you really have called the police?" I asked.

"Yes, absolutely," she replied.

"What if he had ripped the phone out of your hand or hit you?" I asked.

"I was prepared to scream my lungs out and I knew I could get away from him long enough to run out the door to the neighbors," she explained.

"You really would have done that?"

"Yes, I rehearsed the whole thing with my sponsor and with the boys. Since they've been seeing you, they're eager for changes. We all knew exactly what to do if Jeff became violent. We don't care as much anymore about what the neighbors might think. Before, we would have been too embarrassed, but now we don't care."

"That's another reversal, Susan. Now you're not making empty threats. You're announcing definite actions instead. I don't know how exactly, but addicted persons can *always* tell the difference. They ignore threats but listen when they know their families really mean what they say. I would guess that you're presenting yourself to Jeff in an entirely different manner."

"I think I really am," Susan replied. "I know I feel stronger—scared, but somehow much more sure of myself."

"Susan," I said, "you're using Al-Anon very profitably now, and I will continue seeing the boys. If you continue to stick close to your sponsor and to Al-Anon, you're going to be able to go on making changes while you keep your focus on yourself, which means, if you feel ready, you and I can work on some more reversals that will certainly help you and that might get Jeff to seek the treatment he needs."

Over the next few weeks, Susan continued her major reversals of letting Jeff think and drink as he wished while she focused on and assumed responsibility for meeting her own needs and wants. Throughout, each time she interacted with Jeff in any way, she first asked herself what she would have done in the past, and then, to the best of her ability, she did the opposite.

One morning Jeff awoke with a severe hangover and for two hours scuttled back and forth from his bed to the toilet, unable to stop his dry heaves. When he asked Susan to call his office saying he had the flu, Susan refused. She told him she would no longer lie for him, but that she would call a doctor of AA, if he wished. Jeff complained, feebly, but refused her offers of help.

When Jeff objected because she and the boys were away too

long on Saturdays, Susan told him they were having their play day and said that if he was willing to get help for his drinking, they'd love to have him join them. When Jeff passed scorn on her day of play, Susan walked out of the room. When he announced that from now on he'd take the boys out on Saturday, they all said that would be great, but they wanted him to get help for his drinking first. He ranted and raved, but they did not give an inch.

For Tad's birthday, Susan and the boys decided upon an early evening bowling party with Tad's friends, but without Jeff. Together, they all told Jeff they loved him but didn't want him at the party because he had ruined too many parties in the past by getting drunk. When, after much abusive language, Jeff promised not to drink, they reminded him of the times he had made and broken that same promise in the past and again did not give in.

Jeff arrived home by taxi late one night, so drunk that once again he passed out on the sofa. The next morning he vaguely remembered having gone from one bar to another the night before but could not remember where he'd left his car. When he asked Susan to drive him around to find his car, she refused, saying she was no longer willing to help him with any of the problems caused by his drinking. Then she drove off in her car, leaving Jeff responsible for resolving his own crisis.

While Susan had told Jeff that she and the boys were seeing me, she had kept Al-Anon a secret, attending only day meetings. Because she felt stronger each time she met her needs and was finding that Jeff's bark was greater than his bite, she soon felt able to tell him about Al-Anon and that she would be attending evening meetings as well. When he said she had no right to attend Al-Anon and tell the whole world everything about him, she told him that every time he drank, he told the world all there was to know, and once again she insisted upon her right to get help for herself. Then Jeff threatened to kick the baby-sitter out of the house, and Susan told him he could do whatever he wanted, saying she'd alert the police and the baby-sitter in advance so everyone would be prepared for his violence. Next, he said if she got a sitter, he wouldn't come home, and Susan said she thought that might be best.

Susan and the boys often told me how afraid they were, and Susan and Alan in particular also spoke of feeling guilty; yet all of them said they also knew they were doing what they had to do, and they spoke of how much better they felt. Whenever Jeff threatened in any way, and whenever they stated their views or intended actions, Susan was careful to make sure no room was left open for discussion, thereby avoiding the trap of buying into any of his defensive behavior. Susan now really knew that Jeff could not listen to reason, and she was able, most times, not to play his game.

Reversals are the opposite of enabling; rather than abetting, they interrupt the disease process and, thus, are a form of intervention, which has its own equation: acceptance + confrontation = intervention. When articulated, this equation states, "I truly do accept the fact that your behavior, which includes your reasoning, is intolerable, and I will take no part in it, which means you'll have to change or handle your crises and emotional pain yourself."

When co-dependents follow the enabling equation of rejecting then accepting the unacceptable, they flee from reality and, in a very real sense, are in a state of denial. Following the intervention equation brings them home, back on target, in touch with reality. As we saw with Susan, accepting reality makes the co-dependent feel at peace, while the second half of the intervention equation, confronting the reality of intolerable behavior, increases the co-dependent's emotional strength.

In essence, intervention confronts the dependent on two levels—his outer world and his inner world. When the co-dependent no longer accommodates herself to his intolerable behavior, he is forced to face his behavior. When the co-dependent no longer reacts to, or buys into, his defenses, they are rendered powerless, and he is forced to face increased emotional pain. Then, the dependent is up the proverbial creek, faced with his own aberrant behavior but without the means to squelch the emotional pain associated with that behavior. Then, and only then, can he "hit bottom," "see the light," perceive his illness.

Even though Jim and Virginia had spent a good part of their lives keeping their feelings well checked, their bond was strong. When I told them I thought both daughters were in need of treatment—Lynn because she was depressed, feeling powerless, and unable to cope with what she perceived as "never being good enough," and Carla because of the probability of chemical dependency—Jim and Virginia reached out to hold hands, immediately offering each other support. I was relieved. Their mutual support would make all our tasks easier in the days to come.

Though they were initially shocked to hear of the extent of their daughters' problems, both also said they had known underneath that something was very wrong with each of the girls. Our first order of business then seemed to be one of strategy—how best to meet everyone's needs. We decided that I would continue seeing Lynn in individual counseling and perhaps in group counseling later. I also suggested that I see Carla a few more times to increase her insight into her chemical involvement, hoping she'd then become motivated for treatment. Jim and Virginia agreed to meet with me together once a week in double-length session to address their problems related to both Jim's mother and their daughters.

I suggested that Lynn be included in their plans for helping both Margaret and Carla, and Lynn said it felt good to "be wanted." They all agreed to attend a series of lectures on chemical dependency given at our office as well as several AA meetings open to the public. Jim planned to speak to Margaret's doctor to seek further information on her condition and to enlist his support.

Jim, in the meantime, had met with his mother to share his feelings as we had planned at our first session. He reported that their meeting "did not go off very well." But in fact it had.

Jim's mother cried when he told her how much he loved her. *They held each other for the first time since Jim was a child.* He said it felt "good" to hug his mother, and I bet it felt good to her as well. But then Margaret pulled herself together and "scolded" Jim for getting upset, adding that she was surprised that he "wasn't able to handle himself better." A typical defensive response! Jim was worried about her drinking; she reacted as if there were something wrong with him! Nevertheless, something very important had happened. Jim validated his mother's worth by sharing his love for her, and she was moved, even though she quickly covered herself in her defensive cloak. Now, Jim was in a far better position to separate her drinking from her personhood—he could love *her* while hating her *drinking.* And even though Margaret refused to get help, she now knew, at least on some level, that she was, in fact, valued and loved, *despite* her drinking. While the meeting had been painful for Jim, he could see that it was "well worth the effort." Jim, Virginia, and Lynn decided to visit Margaret, individually and together, repeatedly over the next couple of weeks to tell her how much they loved her, how her specific drinking incidents hurt them, and of their desire for her to seek help. Lynn called it the "shotgun" approach—"We'll go at her from all sides."

The problems associated with helping elderly chemically dependent persons are great. They often live alone; families do not have the emotional leverage they would have if they were living with them. While co-dependents can schedule meetings with the dependent for their reversals, the impact cannot be as great simply because the reversals cannot be constant—repeated several times daily. Also, by the time elderly persons are identified as chemically dependent, many are in the late stages of their illness, and thus are harder to reach. Often elderly chemically dependent persons no longer feel closely connected to either their children or anyone else, and it is difficult to break through their great psychic isolation. So, too, being elderly is a ready reason for the dependent to lose hope for life, to have little motivation for change other than death itself.

Before moving on to last-ditch efforts, it seemed most appropriate to see if Margaret could be reached by her family's "shotgun" approach. Margaret was well defended against moral pronouncements and advice, but I thought her family's repeated reversals of expressions of love and offers of help might very well sneak through her defensive shield.

I was wrong. Margaret stood firm, denying her drinking and refusing all offers of help. We then decided to move ahead with a planned intervention. Virginia agreed to call Margaret's friends and three other children. Jim made plans to meet with the priest of their church as well as with Margaret's doctor— all would be asked to join the intervention team to help Margaret.

But Lynn made all that unnecessary. She called just prior to one of our scheduled appointments to say she was bringing her grandmother with her. "She wants you to tell her how to 'enroll' in AA!" Lynn had dropped by to see her grandmother and found herself getting angry at her continued refusals to seek help. "I did just what you said to do. I asked myself how I had handled this in the past and then did just the opposite. Instead of remaining silent, I told her I was angry with her . . . that we were all worried about Carla and that she should be helping us. I said we needed her, but that she was botching things instead of helping us with Carla."

That did it! Margaret was indignant that no one had told her about Carla, saying she would have stopped "this foolish business about drinking long ago if she had known Carla needed her." She announced grandly that she would go to AA to "get their minds off me," but in fact she agreed to even more.

Withdrawal from alcohol can be a risky business for persons of any age who are physically addicted—causing tremors, hallucinations, convulsions, and even death—but it is especially dangerous for the elderly. Therefore, prior to her enrollment in AA, I insisted that Margaret be detoxified in the local hospital under her physician's supervision, and she agreed, haughtily and reluctantly. But she agreed and that's all we wanted—her compliance.

Five days later, alcohol- and drug-free, she joined AA "to keep my family happy." Not only did she not return to drinking, she became an active AAer, helping herself and others.

Keep up the reversals. Over time, repeated, caring, but honest reversals have a softening effect on the dependent's defensive wall. Keep them up. You can never tell when one will work, or which one will work. Like Lynn, feel free to express your feelings as well as reality as you perceive it; and use good judgment when doing so. Keep your cool; otherwise the dependent will zero in on *your* "craziness," not hers. Describe reality factually and specifically, so she can better perceive it. Guard yourself to ensure that you are not being deliberately provocative; otherwise she might want to fight back. Speak to the dependent when she is chemically free, or at least on the down side of intoxication; otherwise the chemical will screen out your words.

Usually I make it a policy to work with the co-dependents first, then the dependent, for the very simple reason that the dependent will either refuse to see me or refuse to cooperate. So, rather than trying to get the horse to drink the water, I help the family make the horse thirsty, very thirsty.

It seemed wise to alter this policy for Carla. She had given some hints in our first session of being at least a little thirsty—of hurting, of perhaps wanting help. She did not deny "crying her heart out"; she admitted to thoughts of death; she agreed to come back even though I was giving her parents an evaluation of her condition that she saw differently; and she had even accepted and returned my hug. It seemed as if there might be a chance that I could help her enlarge her insight into her chemical involvement. Also, I knew that if I concentrated on Carla, the rest of the family would have a better chance of regrouping to support each other and address Margaret's more immediately critical needs.

In advance, I met with Carla, Virginia, Jim, and Lynn to help set some ground rules, which included some reversals on all their parts. Carla wanted Lynn to stay out of her room and her parents to stop telling her what to do. Lynn agreed to stay out of her room and Virginia and Jim agreed to refrain from advice, warnings, criticism, and comparisons. Lynn wanted Carla to stay out of her room and Jim and Virginia wanted Carla to attend school without cutting classes, keep her curfews, eat dinner with the rest of the family, and not swear at or in front of them. Carla agreed to stay out of Lynn's room, attend school regularly, keep the curfews, not swear, and be *at* dinner, but not necessarily *eat* dinner. They each wanted a whole lot more, of course, but no one was ready to agree to anything further at this point. Frankly, I was aiming at reducing some of the chaos in the household as well as achieving some emotional distance between Carla and the others. They all needed some peace to heal their enormous anger-hurt wounds, and they needed space for self-reflection. I was quite satisfied with the simple ground rules they agreed upon, thinking they were followable and capable of providing the needed peace and space.

My *only* goal at this point in my work with Carla was to help her increase her insight into the extent of her harmful chemical involvement, so that she could become motivated for change. Chemically dependent persons as well as those with a chemical involvement harmful enough to qualify for probability of addiction *have to take care of their chemical problem first*. They are not amenable to conventional psychotherapy as long as they continue to use chemicals for the very simple reason that the chemical use itself, in any amount, will keep them locked into the lower-level primitive and immature defenses.

Remember what we know about these lower-level defenses and one of the ways they differ from the neurotic and mature defenses—*they do not respond to reason or conventional psychotherapy.* Additionally, neither reason nor conventional psychotherapy has shown success in getting persons with either addiction or probability of addiction to modify their use. *The only approach that works is confronting the chemical use and the defensive behavior.* So I, of course, had no intention of getting sidetracked by any red herrings about *why* Carla used the way she used or *why* she behaved the way she behaved. *Fortunes* and *lives* are lost because of those red herrings.

Carla completed the first two assignments I had given her very well. I had asked her to complete a chemical history form, listing every chemical she had ever used, starting from first use to her present use, much the same as I had asked her to *tell* in our first session. Now she had to write it, *so she could see it.* Next I had given her a blank pie-chart and asked her to fill in how she spent her time in a twenty-four hour period, including her using and stoned time. Carla barely had room on the form for all her chemicals, and she had only four hours out of twenty-four that were chemically free, and those were sleep hours. At no time when she was awake was she without chemicals in her system. Yet, Carla continued to insist that she was no different from anyone else—"Everyone uses like that."

"Maybe you don't use any differently from those you hang around with, Carla, but I've got news for you, most people do not use chemicals this way at all."

Reality was presented, denied, and then more reality was presented. Then she balked. She didn't like the third assignment at all—to write out four specific incidents of how her chemical use had interfered with her ability to function in each of four areas of her life, as a student, daughter, sister, and friend; but she did it. It took three sessions, but Carla eventually looked at the fact that chemicals had indeed had a significantly negative impact on her life. Fortunately, Carla's hidden emotional pain was always accessible enough for her to be able to share at least some of her feelings, which allowed her to feel nurtured; then she was willing to work on increasingly difficult assignments.

At the end of our first month together, Carla asked in a round-about fashion if she could join one of our groups, "like Lynn is in." And I said, "Sure, but you're not going to like the criteria for group membership."

"Like what?" she asked.

"Like no alcohol or drug use and active involvement in a self-help group," I replied.

"None of these guys use?" Carla's appointments with me preceded "group time," so on each occasion she was exposed to a large number of clients, many her own age, arriving for their various groups—cheerful, smiling, hugging people. Carla asked more questions about what kinds of groups they were in and what I meant by self-help groups. Then she decided she didn't want anything to do with either type of group. But the horse was now sniffing the water, and we kept on with assignments enlarging her view of her harmful chemical involvement.

Then she arrived one evening announcing that she had gone to AA over the weekend. "It was okay. I went with a kid I used to know, but I'm not giving up pot. Maybe I'll stop drinking, but I'm not going to stop smoking dope. No way!"

"Maybe you should try NA as well," I said.

"What's that?"

"Narcotics Anonymous."

"Jesus, you don't give an inch, do you?"

"Yeah, there's always that," I agreed. "But actually I'm concerned about something else, Carla. That was a real neat move you made to go to AA. You deserve some strokes for that. I'm sure it wasn't easy, but my concern is whether it's going to be possible for you to do it that way without being detoxed first. Your alcohol and drug use has been enormous for a long time, Carla. I'd hate to see you try to do something, like going to AA or NA or both and trying to give up pot and alcohol, which might be too much for you to do without help. What do you think, Carla? Do you think it might be best to check into a detoxification unit for a few days to get some help to get off alcohol and pot?"

"Jesus! I don't need detox! You must think I'm as bad as Gram, for crissake! You know, you've always had this problem about thinking my drinking and smoking is worse than it really is."

"Okay. It's there for you if you want it," I replied, and we proceeded with more assignments dealing with her chemical involvement. Note that we're now talking about giving up both alcohol and marijuana. And that's the way it went with Carla. She'd throw something out, like going to AA and stopping alcohol "maybe," as if inviting me to take it further, which I'd do, which she would then partially accept as if it were a decision she'd already made. It was pretty clear to me that this was Carla's way of saving face, of doing what she knew she had to do without actually taking it all the way herself or coming up with any verbalized admissions of need.

By the end of three months she was chemically free, without hospitalization for detoxification, active in AA as well as one of our young people's chemically dependent support groups, and at last making very constructive changes in her life.

It's usually safe and often wise to give chemically dependent persons space and time to come to grips with their illness, as long as they are in some form of program that will assist them in this specific task, and especially if, like Carla, they indicate a willingness to cooperate.

Unfortunately, most chemically dependent persons are not like Carla. Most absolutely refuse to have anything to do with any counseling or group that insists they come to grips with their chemical involvement. There seem to be more Jeffs than Carlas in the world.

Susan's life was "a whole lot better," but she now wanted to do something more. Despite all her reversals and her greatly increased emotional strength, Jeff continued to drink and refuse all offers of help. "Tell me about the planned intervention process," she asked, so I told her about the worst intervention I'd ever been involved with.

This particular intervention was the worst for several reasons; first, the family members were among the most fearful and downtrodden that I've ever known. Their chemically dependent husband/father, Peter, dominated them in the cruelest of ways. He weighed well over two hundred pounds, was six feet tall, and was both verbally and physically abusive, once strangling his wife to the point of unconsciousness. While wealthy by anyone's standards, he kept his family in poverty as they lived among the affluent. He forced his wife and three daughters to assume almost the total responsibility for the maintenance of the house and grounds of their rather sizable estate. They had to cut their own hair and sew most of their own clothes. He did not permit them to take jobs and gave them no money for socializing. Not only did they feel they could not afford friends, they felt unworthy of friendship. Each evening, even though intoxicated, Peter selected their dinner conversation topics and, if he did not like their responses, he shouted, swore at them, threw furniture, or assaulted them, on one occasion breaking his daughter's arm and on many occasions locking the girls in various closets. While he was the most tyrannical of alcoholics, they had become the most meek and terrified of families.

It was also the worst intervention because only the wife and her teenage daughters took part; no friends or other relatives were involved. If any family ever needed outside support, this one surely did, yet their isolation was so great that they had no one they could call upon to be part of the intervention team. And it was the worst intervention because Peter had just been promoted to the presidency of his company, hardly the ideal time for him to perceive his powerlessness over alcohol. Finally, it was the worst intervention because the family's greatest fear was fulfilled—Peter refused to accept treatment.

Under the circumstances, you might ask why we decided to proceed with the intervention in the first place. We proceeded because the family knew they could no longer live as they had in the past. The strangling incident was the final straw. Two of the children had just left home for college and all were afraid for the wife and youngest daughter to remain home alone with Peter. But mostly we proceeded with the intervention because the family had gained sufficient knowledge and strength to be able to break out of their tyranny. They were prepared for the intervention, which always means being prepared for the worst.

On the day of the intervention, Peter accompanied his wife

to my office to talk about his drinking; he did not know his three children would be there waiting for him and was not even aware that the two oldest girls were home from college. When he walked in and seated himself, he looked at his children as if they were stones, and then with ice in his voice he peered down his nose at his wife and said, "I can't *believe* you've gone behind my back like this."

For a moment she looked like she was going to sink behind the pillows on the sofa where she was seated. I started to say something to Peter, but he turned his back to me as if I did not exist. I then tapped his arm to get his attention and asked, "Tell me, Peter, would you have come here today if you had been told your daughters were going to be present?"

"Of course not," he growled.

"That's why you weren't told," I announced, and then Peter agreed to listen and the family proceeded with the intervention. They were fantastic. They didn't attack him in any way, they simply spoke of how his drinking had hurt them. They described specific drinking-related incidents and shared their feelings—their fear, shame, hurt, and anger. And they told Peter how much they still cared for him and that they wanted him to seek treatment. They let their defenses down and revealed their vulnerability. Throughout the intervention, at one time or another, all were in tears; all but Peter. He remained rigidly silent, staring coldly at each of them in turn. At the end, when his youngest daughter asked him if he would get help for his drinking, he looked around at each and then asked, as haughty as ever, "Have you finished?" They nodded their heads. Peter then clapped his hands and snarled, "What a marvelous performance!" He then got up and marched out of the room.

That's cruelty for sure, but that cruelty was also a measure of Peter's sickness. At first, his family was speechless and in a state of shock. They now had to go home and live with this very angry and disturbed person, but they had made great changes in the preceding weeks, and we discussed those changes. They felt they were going to be okay and were pretty sure they would be able to avoid buying into his defenses once they got home. As they left, they were all determined to work together to continue at home the intervention process that they had begun that morning, by carrying on with the same kinds of reversals as they'd made prior to the planned intervention.

Soon after they arrived home, Peter went out to the garage where his oldest daughter was gathering some things to take back to school the following day. Peter told her he was shocked to see her, his oldest child, take part in a scene such as that morning's intervention. He said he thought she had more sense than that, and then he proceeded to tell her that he was reconsidering paying her college tuition.

"Dad," she said, "the intervention didn't work for you and I'm sorry about that, but it worked for me and I'm glad we did it. Now I know that I really love you. For years I've only felt hate for you. It's been horrible hating my own father and I feel so much better knowing that I love you. So, Dad, I'm sorry the intervention didn't work for you, but I'm so grateful it worked for me."

Wow! Talk about not taking defenses at face value. Her reversal was a classic example of the intervention equation. She acknowledged what had happened, she confronted his perception of reality by lovingly and respectfully stating her own, and she kept the intervention process going. As you can see, when reversals are presented in as receivable a manner as possible, they do not invite retaliation.

Peter left the garage without a further word, his head bowed, and went out to buy his wife a plant, the first present he had bought her in years. When he handed it to her, she shook her head, did not take the gift, and said, "It was not a gift I asked for, it was your health."

Three weeks before, this wife had not believed she had *any* rights. Now she was able to make a request and stick to it. She, too, continued the intervention process. Chemically dependent persons are incapable of listening to reason, but they do heed confrontations, especially if they are presented firmly and lovingly.

Later in the day, Peter told his wife that he had spent a lot of money on his gift and was disappointed that she had not yet unwrapped it. She again told him she wanted his health, not a gift.

In the middle of the night, she awoke and heard Peter sobbing in the nearby bathroom. She later told me she had to literally hang onto the mattress, for she felt the strongest urge to go to him to say that everything was all right and that she was sorry she had upset him, which would have been a classic enabling act and which would have surely invited retaliation. By apologizing as if she had done something wrong, she would have become the culprit, the cause of Peter's misery, and consequently she would have invited his abuse.

Instead, she remained in bed and Peter was left alone with his pain. When he returned to their room, he asked her if she really believed he was sick enough to warrant treatment. Again, his wife desperately wanted to take the easier enabling route of saying no; instead she said, "Yes, Peter, you are very sick and you need treatment." And he went off to a treatment center the following day.

His family did not return to their former defensive, enabling posture of tolerating intolerable behavior. They knew they had a need and a right to intervene in Peter's illness; consequently, they, rather than Peter, were on the offense. By consistently invoking the intervention equation, wherein they confronted intolerable behavior, they rendered his defenses powerless.

With guidance and support the co-dependent can turn her whole life around—almost overnight. And she can make it possible for the dependent to turn his life around—almost overnight. By focusing upon herself and by replacing the enabling equation in its many forms with the intervention equation in its many forms, the co-dependent has only one thing to lose—illness; and one thing to gain—wellness. Hers for sure; his most likely.

11

Susan's Planned Intervention

Planned interventions are a sudden, dramatic, and highly successful method of motivating chemically dependent persons for treatment. They are especially appropriate for chemically dependent persons who've resisted the co-dependent's reversals and attempts at getting them to seek help or who are facing life-threatening crises. Planned interventions, in my opinion, are not appropriate if the co-dependents are still locked into enabling behavior, as under those conditions the dependents have hardly been given a chance to seek help. Planned interventions are also not appropriate if the co-dependents have not previously asked the dependent to seek help.

Planned interventions, in addition to motivating dependents for treatment, also help strengthen the emotional security of the co-dependents. This is especially true if they have been involved with Al-Anon and/or counseling specific to their condition and have become able to focus upon themselves as well as others.

Susan wanted to do the planned intervention for Jeff, who seemed to be resisting all her changes and reversals as much as ever. Concerned about Susan's problems with shifting her focus off Jeff, I asked, "Do you think you're going to be able to reach out to Jeff now without once again putting all your eggs in his basket?"

"I don't really see any difference. If I can keep my focus on myself with all these reversals, why can't I do the same with the planned intervention?" she asked.

"You can," I answered, "but there is a difference. All the reversals were designed to help you meet your needs as well as Jeff's. The planned intervention is primarily to help you meet Jeff's needs. You've gained a lot of emotional strength, Susan, and you've started the process of rebuilding your own boundaries. I'd sure hate to see those crumble and have you become totally focused on Jeff again. Do you think you're ready to focus on both yourself and Jeff?"

"Yes, I think I can do both now," she answered.

"I think you can, too. Okay, let's at least get prepared for the intervention, and you can decide later if you want to go ahead with it. As you know, we like to have as many people on the intervention team as possible, people who know about Jeff's drinking problem and who care enough about him to want to help. Have you thought of people you'd like to have on your team?"

True to form, Susan was several steps ahead of me. She whipped a sheet of paper out of that bottomless purse of hers and said, reading from her list, "My mother will help. She's wanted me to do something for a long time. As you know, the boys will help. Steven, Jeff's older brother who lives in Chicago, says he'll do anything to help. He would leave his job and come here tomorrow if we wanted, and he says he thinks Chris, his wife, should be part of the team also. Chris likes Jeff, and apparently she talked to him about his drinking over Christmas vacation last year. Arnie, of course, will help. He works with Jeff and has been trying to get him to do something about his drinking all along. That makes eight so far, including me. What do you think about Roberta and Bill? They're friends of ours from college and they live near us, but we don't see them anymore. I think they've given up on Jeff."

"Maybe they haven't," I said. "Maybe they've just not known what to do. Why don't you meet with them, explain what you're planning and ask if they would be willing to help. Are there any other relatives, brothers, sisters, parents, nieces, or nephews?"

"No, Jeff's parents are no longer living, and we don't have any other relatives."

"How about clergy? Are you or Jeff at all connected with a church?"

"Ha! Jeff stopped going to church years ago," she said.

"What about you?" I asked.

"I've spoken to our minister several times, and he's been very kind. I think he might be willing to help, but he doesn't really know anything about Jeff's drinking except what I tell him."

"His knowledge of how Jeff's drinking has hurt you and the boys might be very valuable at the intervention. It's also often very comforting for the whole team to have a member of the clergy present. Would you like to ask him? The worst that could happen is that he'll say no."

"Yes, I'll ask him. Now let's see how many we have. With Bill and Roberta, it's ten and with Reverend Barnes, it's eleven. Is that enough?"

"That's enough and it sounds like a great team, but I don't want to leave anyone out who might be significant to Jeff. Are there any other friends or people from his job you think should be involved?"

"Well, the head of Jeff's company must know something. Arnie's told me that Jeff's been warned about his drinking, but I frankly don't know where the warnings have come from."

"Why don't you ask Arnie if he thinks anyone else from the office should be involved. I'm never comfortable involving people from work, unless I'm sure they already know about the problem and are committed to trying to help, rather than punish. We certainly don't want to get Jeff into any more trouble at work than he's already in. Let's see what Arnie says. How about friends? Anyone else besides Roberta and Bill?"

"We've become so isolated. Everyone dropped by the wayside years ago when Jeff was on drugs, so I really don't know of anyone else," she explained.

"You have an excellent team with the eleven people you've listed."

"What should I do about Al-Anon?" Susan suddenly asked. "Some of the members don't approve of intervention. They think it will get me back into a negative attachment to Jeff. They say that intervention is another form of manipulation, another way of trying to fix Jeff instead of myself."

"I know that's how some members feel," I explained. "It's my experience that co-dependents can become secure enough to help both themselves and the dependent. And I think you've reached that point. Al-Anoners are concerned about manipulation because it was such a large part of their lives at one time and served only to make matters worse. But, have you felt you were manipulating with all your reversals?" I asked.

"No, I haven't really thought much about it, but no, I don't think they were manipulative," Susan answered.

"I don't either. You were confronting reality and offering Jeff a clear choice of either changing or accepting the consequences for not changing. You *let go* of the results of your reversals. You let Jeff make his choice, and whatever his choice, you went about your business of meeting your own needs. When people are able to *let go*, they tend not to manipulate. You'll see as we move into the planned intervention that it's very similar to the reversals. You'll offer a choice and then *let go* of Jeff's response. What does your sponsor say about intervention?"

"Oh, she's all for it," Susan replied. "My sponsor did one for her husband. It was the reaction from some of the other members that I found confusing."

"Stick with your sponsor, Susan, but I also want you to stay close to the Al-Anon program because that will help you keep your focus on yourself while you do the intervention. The purpose of Al-Anon is to help the family members, not the alcoholic, as you know. Do you think you'll be able to separate this out and work with Al-Anon to help yourself while you work with me on the intervention?"

"Yes, I think so. My sponsor will help, and I think the other members will too. What do you think about having the boys involved? My mother's worried. She thinks the boys are too young to handle the intervention."

"They're too young to handle active addiction, but they're sure not too young to handle an intervention. Look at how much they've already changed. They're far more open now, which means they're feeling more secure. They talk freely about their fears and Jeff's drinking, and they've been very much allied with you on all your reversals. Intervention tends to be strengthening, so it should help the boys as much as all the reversals you've been doing together. But I can understand your mom's concerns. Let's have the boys involved in the preparation, then we can all decide if it's going to be helpful to them to be part of the actual intervention."

There are various methods of preparing families and friends for a planned intervention. While there is probably no one best way, the point is that the team should be *well* prepared. A planned intervention creates a *sudden* change in the equilibrium of the team members' interactions with the chemically dependent person. In advance of that change, all should be well informed and comfortable with the nature of that change as well as with the intervention process.

In our practice, we ask that all the members of the intervention team who live within the area, before committing themselves to an intervention, attend a series of evening classes to learn more about the illness, its impact on others, the various ramifications associated with change, as well as the intervention techniques themselves. During the classes, the team members have a chance to express their concerns about several issues, not the least of which is the subversive or sneaky nature of preparing for a planned intervention behind the dependent's back, so to speak. Many members of the team feel guilt as they review their past enabling behavior, and most are fearful of their future relationships with the dependent. While our counselors impart much information during the classes, considerable time and attention is paid to helping each member of the team with these very real and valid concerns. Tape recordings of the classes are often made and sent to the long-distance team members, and at the end of the last class, the team decides whether the planned intervention is right for them. Almost without exception, they agree that it is.

Next, the family and their counselor decide which form of treatment is best suited to the chemically dependent person's needs—sometimes Alcoholics Anonymous or Narcotics Anonymous seems appropriate, especially if the chemically dependent person is not physically addicted and has only minimal denial. Often detoxification, out-patient or residential treatment is required in advance of the self-help groups; in that case, admission and travel arrangements are made. Next, the entire team assembles at our office with their counselor to rehearse the intervention, and by this time all participants will have completed lists of concrete, factual, specific incidents related to the dependent's chemical use with which they've been involved. Included on their lists will be their description of how they felt as a result of the incident. In addition to rehearsing the presentation of their data and feelings, they will select the order and seating arrangement. Finally, they are left with two items of unfinished business. What if the dependent, like Peter, refuses to accept treatment? And how do they get him to the counselor's office for the intervention?

Each year over 80 percent of the interventions we do result in the chemically dependent person seeking the treatment of the family's choice. In our six years of doing interventions, less than a handful of families were unable to get the dependent to attend the intervention session. Nevertheless, prior to the classes and the rehearsal, many families choose the losing odds, even though the winning odds are heavily weighted in their favor. They are sure the intervention will not work, that there is absolutely no way they will ever be able to get the dependent to the intervention. They feel powerless.

At the end of the intervention preparation, they feel empowered. They have become emotionally strengthened, and their changes are reflected in their entire demeanor. They walk taller, speak more firmly, laugh more frequently, and openly nurture and support one another. Thus, by the end of the rehearsal, they easily decide upon how they will get the dependent to the counselor's office, while sober, to discuss his chemical use. By then, they are also pretty sure he'll agree to seek help but are prepared for his refusal. The once overwhelming questions of how to get the dependent to the intervention and what happens if he refuses to get help are problems only when the family feels powerless.

Susan never wavered in her decision to do the intervention and, at the end of their rehearsal, her team—which included everyone on her original list as well as her minister, Richard, and Roberta and Bill, their former friends—felt pretty sure that Jeff would seek treatment. In the past, Jeff had talked to several of the team members about how sick he felt. He once admitted to Arnie that he feared his drinking problem was too big for him to handle alone, and he once told his mother-in-law that he thought he needed some kind of treatment. They all also felt that their collective data and love as a team would have a powerful effect upon Jeff, but they were each also prepared for Jeff's refusal.

Susan and the boys knew that if Jeff refused to seek help, then they were going to continue treatment for themselves. They had begun to feel well and had no intention of backsliding to their former painful existence. Consequently, if Jeff refused treatment, he was then going to have to face living daily with a family united in their support of one another and actively involved in their own recovery; which, of course, would also mean that they would be actively involved in the continuation of the intervention process at home through their reversals.

Each of the other members was prepared to tell Jeff what his refusal would mean to him or her personally. Katharine, his mother-in-law, no longer wished to see him. Arnie was not going to cover for him anymore at work. Steven and Chris decided to continue seeing Jeff, but planned to be more confrontive. Roberta and Bill said they'd see Susan and the boys, but not Jeff, and Richard expressed a desire to continue supporting Susan and the boys.

Jeff was very strongly trapped in a whole system of denial. While he had occasionally expressed his pain, most of the time he denied any chemical problem and did not seem at all motivated for help. Also, Jeff was showing signs of physical addiction. Susan noticed frequently that he had the shakes, especially early in the morning, and we were all concerned about both Jeff's safety and his ability to withdraw from alcohol without medical assistance. Thus, because of his inordinate denial and his physical addiction, residential treatment seemed the most appropriate choice for Jeff. After having checked his insurance coverage, Susan made reservations at a well-known facility in another city. She had the airplane ticket purchased and Jeff's suitcase packed and in the trunk of her car. Now they had to complete their plans for getting Jeff to my office the following morning for the intervention.

The week before Susan had told Jeff that she had made an appointment for him to see me, using the date scheduled for the intervention. When he refused, she said I had asked for the appointment. When he still refused, she told him that she wasn't asking him to *continue* seeing me, she was only asking him to attend one one-hour appointment. When he continued to refuse, she said, "We have big problems in this family. You think I'm a problem and I think your drinking is a problem. We need to talk, Jeff, and I need you to be with me, at least once. I really can't go further without you." And then he agreed, tentatively.

At the end of the rehearsal, Susan felt sure Jeff would keep

the appointment the following morning as long as he thought
it was for just the two of them and not the boys. She now wondered if she should tell him that the boys would also be present. Her team discussed several options and finally Susan decided she would tell Jeff the session included the boys. If he
refused to attend, his older brother, Steve, would then stop at
their home early in the morning to say that he was also involved and to use his considerable influence to get Jeff's cooperation.

One of the most wonderful things about planned interventions is that the co-dependent is no longer alone; others are
now available to help her with both decisions and actions. As
it turned out, Jeff agreed to attend with the boys at Susan's
request. She, in fact, thinks Jeff *wanted* to see me, so that he
could give me what he thought of as a more accurate picture
of their problems. Jeff, of course, was not aware that all the
other members of the team would be present.

When Jeff, Susan and the boys arrived, I introduced myself
to Jeff and led them into my office, where the others were
seated in their pre-arranged places. Jeff, like so many chemically dependent persons, played it cool. He acted as if he were
only mildly surprised, as if he were happy to see everyone. He
kissed the women and shook hands with the men. Then he sat
down and smiled politely while I explained that his family and
friends were very concerned about his drinking and wanted to
talk to him about their concerns. When I asked him if he
would agree to hear them out, he said that they really didn't
have to be concerned as he had already decided to stop drinking. I then said, "Jeff, they are scared and they really need to
talk to you, will you listen?" He nodded his agreement.

Steve started. The team had earlier decided that he carried
the most influence with Jeff and should be the first to present
his data, and he said, "Jeff, you're my baby brother, my only
brother, and I love you a lot. Last year at Christmas you were
so drunk that you fell off your chair while we were having dinner with the whole family. I was ashamed. Three summers ago,
when we took Alan and Tad fishing in Canada, you drank a

lot. Most mornings you were so hung over that you couldn't get out of your bunk. I felt sad—sad for you and sad for your sons. When I saw you blowing coke a few years ago, I was angry, and scared. But I'm even more scared now about your drinking. When we took the boys down to Florida last year for the spring baseball training, you were hardly around, Jeff. The boys and I would be on the bleachers, and you'd be in the bar. Twice you were so drunk Alan and I had to practically carry you out to the car. Once I found Alan sitting by himself in the motel lobby. He was crying, Jeff, crying because of your drinking. I was so angry at you for hurting your sons, my nephews. Mom and Dad never had much money. You know that, Jeff, but you know they really loved us. Two years ago, when Dad was dying, he gave me five hundred dollars in cash. He had so little left after Mom's illness, but he saved that money, Jeff, and he gave it to me so I could get help for your drinking. Oh! God!" Steven sobbed, unable to go on for a few minutes. Finally, he said through his tears, as he handed an envelope to Jeff, "Here's the money, Jeff. He loved you so much, and he was so worried about you. Please use it to get help for yourself."

As planned, Bill then said, "Jeff, we've been friends since our first year of college. You're the best friend I've ever had, and I really care about you. When you were using cocaine, you used to brag about it and try to get the rest of us to use. That made me mad, and I felt scared for you. I was visiting Susan when Tad was born and you were so drunk the guards had to drag you out of the hospital. Susan cried her heart out—we both cried, Jeff. Two years ago, when you were at our house, you had so much to drink that Roberta didn't want to give you any more. Then you pushed her into a wall. Jeff, I almost hit you, but you were too drunk to hit—you were already keeling over. I decided right then to cut you out of my life. No one, but no one, is going to push my wife around. But, Jesus, I miss you, Jeff. I love you," he continued as he blew his nose. "Your drinking is destroying the best friendship I've ever had. I hope you get help, Jeff; I'd like you back."

"Jeff, you're my son-in-law," Katharine said as she started

her list of data related to his drinking, "and I love you as much as I would if you were my own son. But I'm so afraid for all of you. Last year at Scotty's birthday party, you didn't show up until it was nearly over. Scotty kept looking for you. All his friends were there, but he only wanted his father. Then, when you arrived and he finally got what he wanted, you were so drunk you fell over an end table. Scotty went into his room in tears. I felt so sad, Jeff—sad for Scotty and sad for you. Several months ago when I spoke to you about your drinking, you promised to stop. But you didn't stop, Jeff, and that scares me. Three Saturdays ago you came charging into my store, drunk, demanding that I tell you where Susan was. When I said I didn't know, you started swearing at me. I had customers in the store, Jeff. I was embarrassed. Several months ago, Tad didn't want to go home after spending a weekend at my house. He said he was afraid to go home—afraid of your drinking." Starting to cry, Katharine said, "You are much more to me than just a son-in-law, Jeff, and these boys are my grandchildren. Susan is my daughter, you are my only children. Your drinking is destroying you. It's destroying all of us. I want you to get help."

Arnie said, "I'm here because I care about you, Jeff. Last month at the luncheon meeting of the regional managers, I picked you up off the floor of the men's room after you passed out, and I put you on the train instead of letting you go back to the office in that condition. I was so disgusted with you. You had promised me you wouldn't drink at that meeting. But you blew it. A lot of people at work are concerned about your drinking, Jeff, and I know you've received some warnings. Your job will be protected, Jeff, if you agree to seek help, but I'll tell you right now, your days are numbered if you don't get help. I've covered for you a lot, Jeff. Last year I rescued you when you got drunk in Hartford by taking over your meeting for you. Twice this year I've sent you home from the office before others could see how drunk you were. Two months ago, you ran out into the hall screaming for people to call the maintenance men. You thought water was coming out of the sprinklers. There was no water. You were having some kind of drunken hallucination, Jeff. My God! I was scared for you. I'm still scared. Please, get help while you can still be helped."

Alan said, "I love you, Dad. When you drove me home from scouts last week, you were so drunk we almost went into a ditch. I was scared, Daddy. I don't want to be killed, and I don't want you to be killed. Last fall, you and Mommy were fighting in the kitchen and I came downstairs. You were drunk, Daddy, and I saw you hit Mommy. When I tried to stop you, you hit me. Daddy, your drinking is hurting us." Alan then learned over, his head on his knees, and sobbed deeply. Jeff, also in tears, reached over, hugged Alan, and kept him enveloped in his arms throughout the remainder of the intervention. Alan continued, wiping his tears with his fists, "When I won the trophy for tennis, you were so drunk you threw it across the room. I feel like you don't love me. I want you to get help for your drinking."

Roberta said, "Jeff, we've been friends for years and I love you. At our clambake three years ago, you drank so much you nearly fell into the pit. I was scared. One night two years ago you came over to our house and you were drunk. You ranted and raved. When we tried to stop you from leaving, so you wouldn't drive in that condition, you pushed me into the wall. I was scared. You are such a nice person when you are sober, but you're mean when you're drunk, Jeff. Four years ago, Susan asked me to speak to you about your drinking. You told me to mind my own business. That hurt, Jeff. You're my friend. You *are* my business. Last winter, Tad came to my house, and when it got dark and I tried to get him to go home, he wouldn't go. He cried and said he was afraid of you when you drink. He said he thought something terrible was going to happen. Oh, Jeff, he hurts. We all hurt. I miss you as a friend, Jeff. Please get help so we can all be together again."

Scotty, the next to present, sat in his seat next to Jeff, in tears and unable to speak. He looked at Jeff and then crawled into his lap, saying, "I'm scared when you fall down, Daddy. You drink, Daddy, and then you fall down, and I'm scared when you fight with Mommy. Please don't drink any more, Daddy."

"I won't, Scotty, I promise you," Jeff said through his own tears, and he then looked up at the others and said, "I've got the message. I appreciate all the trouble you've gone to and I promise each and every one of you that I'll stop drinking."

"Jeff," I said, "they haven't finished, and you've agreed to listen. I know it's hard for you, but they need to talk; then you'll have plenty of time to say whatever you wish." Jeff then nodded his agreement to listen to the others who had not yet spoken.

"Jeff, you're my brother-in-law and I love you like a brother," Chris said. "Last Christmas, after you fell off your chair, you and I went for a long walk. You said that you knew your drinking was getting out of hand, and you promised me you'd get help. You broke that promise, Jeff, and I feel scared for you. Several months ago you were in Chicago on business and we all met for dinner. You got drunk, and you started attacking me in the restaurant. You called me all kinds of names, Jeff. I love you and that hurt," she said as she wiped her eyes. "I was with your dad when he died. He was such a loving, kind man. His last words were of his concern for you, Jeff. I felt sad, so sorry he had to die worrying about your drinking. It seemed unfair. Last year when we came to New York, you had cut way down on your drinking, and I felt like I had my old brother-in-law back. You were kind and full of all your old charm. It was fun to be with you then, and I felt so sad when I heard you had started drinking heavily again. You're such a good person when you don't drink, Jeff. I want you to get help."

"Jeff, I'm here out of my concern for your wife and your sons and out of my concern for you," said Richard, the minister. "I, too, think you're a valuable person. You stopped attending church services several years ago, but it was only this year that I knew what was happening to you and your family. Before one of the Young People's meetings, I overheard another boy tell Tad that his father was a drunken bum. Tad cried out that you weren't, and he started to beat on the other boy. Later he cried like his heart was broken, and he told me the other boy was right, that you are often drunk. Alan has never wanted to talk to me, especially about your drinking, and I've noticed that he's become very withdrawn. He just doesn't seem to have the friends he used to have. He doesn't seem to be able to have fun any longer. Tad came to me again about six months ago to see if I could help. I felt helpless. I didn't know what to do, but I told him I would speak to his mother. Susan seemed offended at first. She didn't want to talk about your drinking, but then she told me that sometimes she hurts so much that she's thought of suicide. Your family is very loyal to you, Jeff, and they love you very much, but they need you to get well. Your drinking is destroying all of you. I hope you will get help."

"Jeff, I love you very much," Susan began. "But it's true, there have been many times in the past few years when I've wondered how I could go on, when I've wished I were dead," she sobbed. "A few months ago, you hit me when I said something you didn't like, and then you threw Alan across the room. You hurt us, Jeff. Alan and I held each other and cried. I was scared. Last year you disappeared for three days. No one knew where you were. I thought you had been killed. You were on a drunken binge and couldn't even remember where you'd been. I was more scared than I've ever been. Last Thanksgiving, you were drunk, but you insisted upon driving home from Mom's. You were weaving all over the road, Jeff, and the boys were screaming, they were so scared. Then you turned around and smacked them. I'm scared that you will kill yourself, Jeff, and I'm afraid to drive with you. I'm scared that you will kill us all. You came into the store several months ago when I was working. You had been drinking and you fell flat on your face. I was embarrassed. Two of the customers tried to help me get you up, and you flung your arms out and hit one of them. They've never been back. Your drinking is hurting my business and my Mom's business, and that makes me mad, Jeff. When I gave birth to Tad, you got drunk and then blamed me because I took too long in labor. I felt guilty, Jeff. I felt so inadequate. When I went into labor with Scotty, you were so drunk I had to go to the hospital in a taxi—all alone. Oh God! Jeff, I was scared," she sobbed, "so alone and so scared. I love you Jeff, with all my heart. I want you to get help."

Tad said, "I love you, Daddy, but I hate your drinking," and then he burst into tears, sobbing, "Why'd you throw Alan's trophy? Why do you drink? You like alcohol better than us; I know you do. My friends call you a drunken bum all the time, Daddy. You spanked me 'cause I got in fights at school, but I have to fight when my friends call you a drunken bum. Don't I?" Crying too hard to continue, Tad leaned back and buried his head in his uncle's shoulder. After a few moments, he said, "I don't want you to drink, Daddy. Will you get help?"

Jeff looked around the room, tears flowing freely down his face, and he saw everyone else in tears. He seemed unable to speak, and Tad asked him again if he would get help. Jeff then looked at Tad across the room, in his uncle's arms. And he looked down at Scotty and Alan in his own arms, and then across at Susan, in Roberta's arms. Next he said, almost in a whisper, "I never knew how much I hurt you. Yes, of course, I'll do whatever you want me to."

With enormous relief, through smiles and tears, every member of the team rushed to Jeff's side. They hugged him, me, each other. They couldn't believe how smoothly it went—exactly as they had rehearsed, but better. And then they left for the airport and Jeff's noon flight to the treatment center.

Reality plus love are hard to beat.

12

Compliance

Most planned interventions work almost exactly like Jeff's. Most chemically dependent persons agree to seek treatment without initially knowing what kind of treatment their intervention team has in mind. Once they know, they still agree. Further, like Jeff, most chemically dependent persons agree to treatment without hearing the consequences they would face if they refused.

Are you surprised? Don't be. The planned intervention process is a *powerful* motivating procedure; besides, chemically dependent persons really want help, at least on some level.

Addicted persons suffer greatly, and they all want out of that suffering. They all want relief, but they know no other way of seeking relief than through the use of chemicals. They can be told of other ways, but they do not *know* other ways. They all want help, but they do not know how to ask for the help they need. Planned interventions are successful, in large measure, for the very simple reason that they do for the dependent what he cannot do for himself.

As you'll recall, the chemically dependent person's defenses tell him the world is all messed up and that he's not only okay, but superior to others; and his defenses, used rigidly and repeatedly, are his means for protecting this distorted image. The more defended he becomes, the more invested he is in his image; and the more invested, the greater his difficulty in asking for the help he needs. In time, protecting his image is almost as important as using alcohol or drugs; consequently, the chemically dependent person can go to the grave far more easily than he can ask for help. The planned intervention allows the chemically dependent person to seek help *without* asking for it. It acknowledges a need he feels underneath his defenses, but a need that he cannot admit because of his defenses. For those of you who've never suffered a double bind of this order, I hope you never will. Death truly can look attractive in the face of such a bind.

Concerned persons have a need to know that dependents want relief and that they are doing the right thing by addressing that want. Consequently, when preparing families and friends for planned interventions, we always discuss the dependent's *cries for help*.

The chemically dependent person's pain is so great that periodically, for brief moments, it sneaks through his defensive barrier in plaintive pleas for help. Unfortunately, his cries for help are often so circumspect and then so quickly covered by his defenses that families and friends have difficulty either recognizing or effectively responding to them.

One dependent told his wife, "You won't have to worry about me when I'm fifty because I'll be dead by then." He was forty-nine at the time. Not hearing his plea for help, his wife pointed out that he was too young to die. Margaret said repeatedly, when both drunk and alcohol free, "No one cares about me." Jim couldn't understand why she kept saying that because he told her repeatedly that he did care. Taking her literally, he missed her cries for help.

Jeff, when hung over, often told Susan he thought he was dying. Usually she thought he was exaggerating; sometimes she perceived the cry for help and offered to call a doctor or AA; in turn, he denied needing help. He had told two other members of his intervention team, months before, that he needed help and that his drinking was out of control; yet, when they responded to his cries for help, he told them he could handle it alone.

One teenager packed a suitcase and left it in plain sight in her room. When no one took notice, she planted it outside her mother's door. In response to her mother's question about the suitcase, she said, "So I'll be ready when it's time to go to the hospital." Until then, treatment had never been discussed, but when her mother offered to make arrangements for immediate admission, her daughter said, "Fuck off! I'm not going to any hospital."

Even when heard, cries for help are hard to answer. The alcoholic's defenses are too powerful; more often than not, they thwart our efforts. Like family members, I often cannot answer the cries, which is another reason why I had no desire to see Jeff prior to the intervention. I knew that even if he sneaked out a cry for help in my presence, the odds were stacked on the side of his defenses and that they would have thwarted me, alone, as surely as they had thwarted others.

Sometimes I can work my way through the defenses by myself, but not usually. I will tell you about one successful venture because I want to validate what I trust are your growing beliefs that defenses should not be taken at face value and that chemically dependent persons desperately want help.

Nancy, a friend of mine, had once been hospitalized for chemical dependency but a few months later decided she could safely return to drinking. When I saw her, sometimes she looked pretty good, other times she didn't look very good at all, and every time she denied any need for help. Then one evening she called and spoke about how great her life was going—she had been promoted and was now a vice president at her bank; she and Joe were getting a lot of help in marriage counseling, and so on. The next thing, out of the blue, she asked, "If an alcoholic needs detoxification once, does he need it every time he stops drinking?"

There's our cry for help, and I answered it. "Pack your bags, Nance, I'm coming over to take you to the hospital."

"What're you talking about? I just asked a simple question. I don't need your help. Besides, if I needed help, I'd ask Joe," she protested.

"Good, then we'll have coffee. I'll be over," I insisted. Upon my arrival, she fell into my arms and said, "Thank God, Ruth, I knew if I asked, you would help me." *That's asking!*

The next thing I knew, her little Yorkshire terrier was jumping all over me—jumping feebly! It was literally starving, and it was caked with Nancy's vomitus. I usually think of those little dogs as overgrown caterpillars, but this one had lost its metallic sheen and was so weak its energy for jumping soon gave out.

Nancy's Christmas decorations were still up, and it was May. Joe was not around; he had left her shortly before Christmas. Not only had she not been promoted, she had been fired months ago. Empty vodka bottles were strewn all over, and so were clothes and upturned furniture. Yecch! And she was telling me how great her life was! When I finally made it into her bedroom to pack her bags for the hospital, I searched for her jewelry, thinking I would take it with me to keep it safe. But Nancy had no idea where her jewelry was; she guessed that she had been robbed "once or twice."

We finally made it to the hospital, and Nancy got well and is still well, but unfortunately I couldn't get the hospital to admit that poor little Yorkie, so I took it home with me. After devouring some food, it attacked my son's great big boxer. Nancy got well; she was dying and sneaked out a cry for help, yet her defenses made her insist that she was well, in need of no one.

We don't have to expect that we alone can circumnavigate these defenses and answer the chemically dependent person's cries for help. But it is helpful to know, when undertaking an intervention, that what we're doing is something he wants, at least on some level.

In essence, planned interventions respect the dependent's need to protect his image. It allows him to seek treatment and *to save face* at the same time. Even though the reality of his chemical use is described clearly and specifically, at no time is the chemically dependent person asked to admit that he needs treatment; instead, his family and friends admit his need for him. Therefore, he can accept treatment not, God forbid, because he *needs it,* but because *they think he needs it.* He can keep his image intact all the way to AA or to the treatment center.

One of the functions of the counselor comes into play at the end of the intervention when the last team member asks the dependent if he will seek help. Until then everything is highly choreographed; at the end, the dependent is once again free to talk, and among other things, power struggles may develop and must be avoided. Some dependents seem to want to accept treatment but feel unable to do so and will set up a verbal struggle, an argument. It is then up to the counselor to help the group avoid that struggle and to help pave the way toward making it possible for the dependent to accept treatment. Often that way can be paved when the counselor or a team member hits upon a way for the dependent to save face. Sometimes it's short and sweet. One young man said, "I can't go to treatment in Minnesota."

"Why?" I asked.

"I don't have a parka," he said.

"Take mine," I offered. And he did.

Another man asked me, "Where'd you get that accent? Are you Canadian?" I told him that while part of my family is Canadian, I was raised in this country. He then said, giving me another chance to catch on to his face-saving clue, "So, you're part Canadian! Do you think I need treatment?"

"No," I replied, "I don't *think* you need treatment. I *know* you need treatment."

"Well," humphed he, "one thing I've always said: 'When Canadians speak, people should listen.' So, if you think I need treatment, I guess I'd better listen."

Saving face, obviously, doesn't have to make much sense,

but it is often an important ingredient in the success of both planned interventions and reversals. Margaret, you will recall, accepted detoxification and AA so she could be of help to Carla. Carla accepted AA and NA, along with out-patient counseling, because it *looked* as if she were making her own treatment decisions.

Saving face may happen a few hours or days after the planned intervention. Peter went to treatment when his wife, rather than he, acknowledged his need the following day. Another dependent refused treatment at the intervention; then, as he and his family were on their way home, they passed the airport from which he was to have departed for the treatment center, and he said, "Hey, there's La Guardia! Let's stop for lunch." For those of you who are not familiar with La Guardia, *no one* eats there unless there is no other choice, and even then one has to be pretty hungry. So, they all stopped at La Guardia for lunch, as if that were a normal thing to do. Once inside the terminal, he said, "Hell, as long as I'm here, I might as well get on the plane."

Another woman said she couldn't go for treatment, and when her husband asked why, she said, "Because I have an appointment at the beauty parlor tomorrow." So she kept her appointment and then went to treatment. Sometimes dependents say, "I won't go to a treatment center, but I will stop drinking and go to AA." In many cases this is a viable alternative, as long as the dependent agrees to enter a treatment center if she resumes drinking or using drugs.

Saving face is as important to dependents as it is to many Japanese—for different reasons, perhaps, but the significance is as great.

Planned interventions work! Most go exactly as planned, or better, because they are *well planned*—every facet of the dependent's illness is considered, and little is left to chance.

First of all, planned interventions are not done if the person has been drinking or taking drugs during the several hours immediately preceding the intervention. The intervenee needs to be chemically free; thus most of our interventions are done early in the morning. If the chemically dependent person appears intoxicated or stoned at the intervention, the process is put off to a later date. If the person is an around-the-clock user, then different options are discussed in advance to make sure a drug-free period occurs between the last usage and the intervention. This can be a real problem, especially with pill takers and cocaine users; nevertheless it is a surmountable problem and one that is carefully addressed in the intervention preparation.

At the intervention, one of the first things to happen is that the chemically dependent person is asked to listen to the team members; consequently, he is locked into an agreement of silence. If he interrupts at any point, the counselor or any member of the team reminds him of his agreement to listen. Having to remain silent immobilizes many of the chemically dependent person's defenses. He cannot, outwardly at least, deny, joke, minimize, blame, or rationalize—he can only listen. Sometimes I think an intervention works for the very simple reason that the dependent, for once, does not have access to his usual defensive tactics. AAers have a saying, "Take the cotton out of your ears and put it in your mouth." The truth is, not much good can happen until the dependent shuts up and listens.

Next, at the intervention, the dependent is presented with data related to his chemical use from several persons, not just one person. It's relatively easy for an addicted person to cast aside what one person says, but it is extremely difficult for him to ignore data from many.

Another dynamic associated with the group presentation has to do with the data itself. Alcohol- or drug-related incidents are described: the actual, concrete, factual events. Opinions, judgments and generalizations are avoided. Facts hit home, while opinions and judgments elevate the dependent's defenses, making him want to strike back, and generalizations are too vague to have any meaning at an intervention. Potentially frightening or pejorative words are avoided, such as hospital, junkie, alcoholic, etc. And anger is withheld. Intervention is a means for helping a sick person; it is not the means for venting the family's anger. While such anger may well be justified and a strong part of the family member's makeup, expression of that anger at the intervention is not appropriate. Among other things, the anger would only make the dependent feel a need to protect himself. We want to lower his defenses at the intervention, not raise them.

Another dynamic associated with the group presentation is that the team freely express their feelings of pain associated with the chemical-related incidents. Rather than *reciting* their feelings, we ask the team to *relive* the pain, and thus show the *feelings*. Sharing of feelings in this manner modifies the dependent's defenses. It's the rare dependent, and Peter was one of them, who can sit statuelike while his family members, particularly his children, are in tears.

Also, at the intervention the chemically dependent person is confronted by a united, well-prepared team who are all working in concert with one another. Up to this point, the dependent often has his family and friends divided and working at cross purposes with each other, which is one of the reasons his tyranny has worked so well. Now they are together and they've gained a power that he has lost.

The team members all sit at the intervention with their lists of incidents right in front of them. First, they need their lists; they are so nervous that, without them, they would forget much of their data. Even more important, we want the dependent to know that the team have done their homework, that they are well prepared. The lists help to show the dependent that his family and friends are taking the whole business very seriously and, as a result, are an invitation for him to take it seriously as well.

Another dynamic that makes the intervention a powerful process has to do with the makeup of the group itself. Peter's intervention team was an exception; most include people outside the nuclear family who are significant to the dependent—siblings, parents, grandparents, aunts, uncles, cousins, friends, neighbors, teachers, colleagues, minister—whoever cares, has knowledge about the chemical use, perceives a problem with that use, and is willing to help. The average team contains eight to ten persons, but can contain many more. Persons outside the nuclear family add a new element. Dependents feel free to say and do anything in front of their spouse and children, while in front of outsiders they tend to be on their best behavior. Thus, not only are outsiders needed for their data to show the extent of the problem, they are also desirable to help keep the dependent in line, so to speak.

Another reason why interventions work seems to be the result of a change in the co-dependent's attitudinal posture. As I mentioned earlier, because of her newly rebuilt boundaries, the co-dependent is no longer locked into enabling; thus she no longer feels compelled to manipulate the dependent. She has gained sufficient emotional strength to be able to do what *she* has to do and to let go of the dependent's response. *With* her new boundaries, she can extend herself out to him; but *because* of those boundaries, she no longer has to hang on to him. Consequently, at a planned intervention, the co-dependent can sanely offer a clear choice, which the dependent can either accept or refuse. Before, when locked into enabling and its associated manipulative behavior, she was charged with a lot of submissive, negative emotions, and the dependent could not hear a clear choice; he could only perceive a threat or that he had to do something to make her feel better. Either way, he could only feel manipulated.

At planned interventions, dependents who *refuse* treatment hear the consequences attached to their refusals. While they may not like what they hear, they nevertheless *can* hear and *believe* the consequences simply because the co-dependent is no longer manipulating. Now she has truly let go. His response is his response. Either way, she'll survive and he knows it, for the first time. Thus, in many cases, the dependent's "no" quickly becomes a "yes."

Sometimes interventions work because the dependent wants to get everyone off his back or because he wants to please his family and friends. Sometimes they succeed because for the first time the dependent perceives that he can get well; and sometimes because the dependent actually sees some of his illness and recognizes, at least partially, his need for treatment.

But, finally, interventions are successful because they *allow the dependent to feel worthy.* Addiction is degrading to the person in every possible way, and when someone feels less than human, he is not apt to have enough self-esteem to feel worthy of treatment.

The planned intervention is a very loving process. The chemically dependent person's dignity is protected throughout, and members of the team repeatedly express care and love for him. He is told by all team members how valuable he is to them personally and how much they like to be with him when he is chemically free. His chemical use is the culprit, not his person. He is not attacked, nor is he judged. The reality of his chemical use is confronted, but he is loved. Just by being there the team show how much they care, and a typical response at the intervention is, "I never knew how much you cared." Dependents reporting back to us after the intervention give many reasons why their intervention worked, but the one most commonly reported is, "They made me feel worthy of treatment."

If there are no chemical dependency therapists or centers in your community that help families with interventions, you can still do one. But first, have you *consistently* performed your reversals for several weeks? Have you become active in your self-help group? Are you slowly, but surely, shifting your focus off the dependent onto yourself? My experience, as well as that of many of my colleagues, shows that if you get out of your former enabling posture and also perform reversals repeatedly, the chances are *excellent* that the dependent will then seek treatment on his own.

If not, you can do an intervention without professional assistance; but first make sure you have made all the above personal changes. Then, rather than attending a series of lectures for increased knowledge about chemical dependency and the intervention process, as you would do if professional help were available, have your team of concerned persons read this book in advance of your rehearsal. You might also read Louis Krupnick and Elizabeth Krupnick's book, *From Despair to Decision*, which addresses planned interventions specifically and will serve as a good handbook for your team.[6] Rather than having an alcohol/drug counselor, select someone on your team from outside your immediate family to act as your guide—perhaps a member of the clergy, an older brother, or an AA friend.

Prior to your rehearsal have each member of your team prepare his or her list of specific chemical-related incidents and the feelings associated with each incident. Use five or so sentences, at most, to describe the incident—what, when, where; and use one word or so to describe the feeling—"and I felt *sad*," or "*mad*," or "*scared*," or whatever.

Then meet as a team for several hours and go through a dry run of the intervention, addressing an empty chair in place of the dependent. Have each team member follow this simple three-part formula for his presentation: (1) a statement of why the team member is present, for example, "I'm here today because I love you and I'm worried about your drinking (or drug use)." (2) recital of each incident and feeling, paying special attention to reliving some of the pain associated with each incident; and (3) upon completing the list of incidents, an expression of the team member's wish for the dependent to seek help. The last person to present is the only one who asks a question and, at the end of her presentation, she asks, "Will you get help?"

You've just read about the dynamics of a planned intervention that contribute to its success. You have the formula. You can do it. I know you can.

Your goal, like other families, is to get the dependent to agree to accept treatment, and most times interventions meet this goal. Chemically dependent persons agree to seek treatment for any or all the reasons I've described or for reasons

6. Louis Krupnick and Elizabeth Krupnick, *From Despair to Decision* (Minneapolis, Minnesota: CompCare Publications, 1985). pp. 55–94.

unknown. Most times they agree to seek treatment for all the wrong reasons, for reasons that have nothing or very little to do with their perceived need for treatment, and that's okay. We're looking for compliance, not miracles.

It does not matter why a chemically dependent person agrees to seek treatment. Treatment outcome is not affected by the chemically dependent person's reason for seeking treatment.

Those worn-out sayings—"You can't help an alcoholic until he wants help" or "Addicted people have to 'hit bottom'"—are *shibboleths*, inaccurate and dangerous. If we buried those sayings, we wouldn't have to bury so many chemically dependent persons.

There are several stages to the recovery process, and compliance is the first of those stages. With compliance, treatment can begin; with treatment, recovery can begin.

13

Jeff in Treatment

She really carried on with that business about the shakes,"
Jeff thought as he left the lecture given to the patients on the
detoxification unit. He was certain the nurse had overstated
her case, especially as she insisted that tremors were a symptom of late-stage alcoholism. "I've had the shakes for years,"
Jeff muttered to himself as he headed back to his room.
"What's the big deal? Who doesn't shake after a night of heavy
drinking?"

Jeff was completing his third day in detox and was scheduled
for transfer to the primary care unit the next day. Before his
admission he had been fearful about entering the treatment
center, thinking he might be heading for a scene out of *One*

NOTE: *I have chosen to present Jeff's experience in treatment as if I had access to
his thoughts and actions as well as the actions of his fellow patients and staff. In
reality I have pieced his experience together from his reports once he returned to
me for recovery support therapy. Since I was once a counselor in a treatment
center similar to Jeff's, I also drew from my recollections to create the following
treatment experience composite.*

Flew Over the Cuckoo's Nest, and was relieved to find that the center was not like the movie at all. "No Nurse Ratcheds! No locked doors! Everyone was on a first-name basis, and they all went out of their way to help me. I was feeling like the dregs of humanity, but that's not how the staff treated me. They were very kind and far friendlier than I expected."

Jeff received medicine during his first two days to ease his withdrawal from alcohol and, as he felt comfortable, he was able to walk about as he wished. "A couple of people in detox were really sick and had to stay in bed, but most of us attended lectures and hung around with the nurses or watched T.V. We also started on some of the books and pamphlets that we were given to read."

But now, preparing for his transfer, Jeff began to think he didn't need any further treatment. After his physical the previous morning, the doctor had told him he had an enlarged liver due to his drinking. With that information as well as everything he remembered from his intervention, Jeff felt he had learned enough. It was obvious to him that he had to stop drinking, and he had every intention of doing just that. He felt ready to go home and couldn't see why he had to waste any more time in treatment.

Hoping to get support for his view, he told Kathy, the nurse who had given the afternoon lecture, how well he felt and that he had made a decision to stop drinking.

"Stopping doesn't seem to be much of a problem for you, Jeff," she replied. "You mentioned this afternoon that you have stopped drinking several times in the past. It seems to me as if you need treatment so you can learn how to stay stopped. That seems to be your real problem."

"What kind of TLC is that? Didn't they teach you about sympathy in nursing school?" Jeff joked, and they both laughed. But Jeff was ticked off. He was sure that now that he knew the facts, he would never drink again. And now that he felt well physically, he sensed an urgency to get home to prove to everyone that there was no reason for any further concern. More than anything, he wanted to put the past behind him— immediately!

When he called Susan to tell her he was coming home, he fully expected she would be excited about his early return. Instead, she seemed stunned and began to cry. "Susan, for chrissakes, I'm fine," Jeff exclaimed. "What are you crying for? You should be happy to know that I'm not as sick as everyone thought, and that I'm never going to drink again."

"I'll be happy, Jeff, if you get treated and get well," Susan replied as she recovered from her shock. "But I'm certainly not happy to hear that you are thinking of leaving treatment."

"I've had all the treatment I need, Suzie. This place has been great, and I'm glad you made me come here. Now I know for sure that I can never drink again. There are some real sickies here, Sue, and I've learned from seeing them what alcohol can do. I'll never drink again, sweetie, no siree, no more booze for me ever again. Listen, what I want you to do is meet me at the airport tomorrow. I'll check out the flights and call you right back. It will be great, Sue, you'll see."

"Jeff, nothing will be great without treatment and a lot of work," Susan answered. "I just think you should know that the boys and I are continuing in treatment. You can do whatever you want to do, but we're going to get well even if you don't."

"What the hell is that supposed to mean?" Jeff asked.

"Well, if you leave treatment, I guess it means we will get well without you," Susan replied softly.

"I can't believe this," Jeff shouted into the phone, "You're actually threatening me, aren't you?"

"No, Jeff, I'm just very sad," Susan explained. "I had truly hoped we could all get well together. If you refuse treatment, I don't see how we can do that."

"I'm not refusing treatment," Jeff insisted. "I don't *need* treatment; there's a difference."

"Do as you wish, Jeff," Susan said as she hung up the phone.

"She hung up on me! She cut me off! Who the hell does she think she is?" Jeff muttered as he left the booth. Later that evening, he decided to stay at the treatment center a few more days. "I'll show her how sick everyone else is; then she'll agree that I shouldn't be here."

The next morning Jeff transferred to the rehabilitation unit and attended his first group therapy session. "Welcome to our group, Jeff. Would you care to tell us a little about yourself?" asked a man sitting across from him. There were eight patients and a counselor in the group, all seated in a tight circle, and Jeff decided he might as well break the ice, not that he intended to be there for long, but so they would leave him alone.

"Sure thing," Jeff replied with much bravado. "I'd be happy to tell you about me. My name is Jeff Martin. I'm from New York and this is one of my busiest seasons. I head the northeast region for my company and we're just about ready to get our fall sales underway. Frankly, I'm not too happy about being here when I know how much I'm needed back at the office."

"Jeff, my name is Bonnie," said an attractive woman sitting next to him. "I'm happy to meet you and to hear about your job. It sounds as if you hold an important position in your company and I'm sure it is a busy time for you, but I wonder if you would tell us why you're here."

"That's a good question," Jeff replied. "I've been wondering the same thing myself."

"Do you have a problem with chemicals?" Bonnie persisted.

"What do you mean by chemicals?" Jeff asked with more than a touch of arrogance.

"Alcohol and other mood-altering drugs," Bonnie replied.

"I used coke at one time, but I haven't touched it in years, so the answer is no . . . no problem with chemicals," Jeff coolly responded, obviously uncomfortable as he sat rigidly upright in his chair.

"How about alcohol?" asked a man sitting across from him.

"Well, I'm sure my wife thinks I drank too much and I'm sure I did from time to time, but that's all behind me now. Besides, my wife has problems of her own and she's never been able to understand the pressures I'm under at work. Even now she refuses to see that this is my busiest season. You'd think she'd realize that the longer I stay here, the harder it will be for me when I get back," Jeff complained.

"You haven't told us about you, Jeff," Bonnie persisted. "I'm hearing a lot about your job, but not about you or why you're here."

"I wonder if we could move on?" asked Dan, a distinguished-looking man Jeff had met earlier that morning when he was transferred to the primary care unit. "Jeff, three weeks ago I was doing exactly what you're doing . . . defending myself by concentrating on all the outside factors in my life, particularly my job and my wife. But that's not where it's at for me anymore. I'm from New York also, Jeff, and if we were to compare job pressures, I guess mine could probably match yours. I'm in the insurance business—the head of our home office as a matter of fact—but I've learned in these past three weeks that my illness, my chemical dependency, is my most important problem, not my job. So I really want to talk about my illness and I need time today, group, if that's okay with all of you?" Dan inquired as he shifted his attention from Jeff to the others.

"Sure, Dan, go ahead," several of the group's members said at once.

"Well as you know, my family is here now for family treatment," Dan continued. "I'm going to see them for the first time this afternoon and, well, I'm a little scared."

"Can you share your fear with us, Dan?" asked Bob, the group counselor.

"Yes, but it's not easy for me. I've been working on my Fourth Step, listing all the things I've done that have hurt me and others. It's not a pretty list," Dan said softly as he leaned over, covering his forehead with one hand.[7]

After a few moments of silence, someone gently asked from across the circle, "What are you feeling, Dan?"

"How can they love me?" Dan asked as he continued looking toward the floor. "I'm afraid they don't love me. Oh! God!" he moaned as his shoulders started to heave with his sobs. "I'm afraid . . . afraid to see them . . . afraid to look them in the eye . . . afraid they will tell me they don't want me home again . . . afraid they hate me."

Two of the group members put their arms around Dan, and in a few moments he continued through his tears, "I was never

7. The AA Fourth Step is: *Made a searching and fearless moral inventory of ourselves.*

there when my kids needed me. I kept promising them that I'd do things with them, and then I'd drink instead. I never built them up. I called them names and put them down all the time. Nothing they ever did was good enough for me. And I blamed them for everything. When my daughter first got her driver's license and skidded on the ice, hitting a tree and damaging the car, I screamed at her for hours in a drunken rage. She was already upset. She needed my support, not my drunken attack. God! I'll remember her crying and pleading with me to leave her alone that night for the rest of my life.

"Another time," Dan continued, "I punched my son and threw him across the kitchen. Why? Because he was trying to stop me from hitting his mother . . . my wife. Can you believe I hit him for protecting her from me?" Dan sobbed, shaking his head and unable to continue. Several others in the group were in tears as well, feeling Dan's pain along with him and remembering how they, too, had hurt the ones they loved.

After a few moments, Dan said, "I'm so ashamed. I've given them every reason to hate me," and then he raised his head and looked around at the group with a startled expression on his face. "I've never really looked at that before," he continued, no longer in tears. "I've done hateful things, why shouldn't they hate me? They really do have a right to hate me, don't they?"

"I guess they probably do," answered one of the group members.

"This may sound crazy to you," Dan smiled, "but just knowing they have a right to hate me somehow makes me feel better."

"Dan," Bonnie said, "you did a lot of hateful things, just like the rest of us, and I'm sure your family does have some hate in them about that, but that doesn't necessarily mean they've given up on you. And I just want you to know that I see a lot of good in you, too, Dan."

"Thanks, Bonnie," Dan replied. "Maybe I can use whatever is good in me to let my family feel whatever they feel. I can see now that I've always told them how they should feel. Perhaps this week I can let them be whatever they feel like being. Maybe that's what the expression 'Let Go and Let God' means."

"How does it feel to realize you don't have to control everything, Dan?" asked Bob.

"Neat . . . peaceful . . . good," Dan replied with a huge smile. "I'm still a little scared about seeing my family this afternoon but, you know, now it's going to be okay," Dan said.

"I feel good about you, Dan," Bob said. "Being able to share your pain with us shows a lot of progress. You've worked hard this morning, and it sounds to me as if you are going to be able to tune in to your family in a different way than in the past. Thank you for sharing with us."

As the group broke, they stood in their circle, arms clasped behind each other's backs, and said the Serenity Prayer: *God grant me the serenity to accept the things I cannot change, the courage to change the things I can, and the wisdom to know the difference.*

Many of the members then hugged Dan and thanked him for sharing. Jeff, however, immediately retreated to his room, full of disgust and confusion. He felt like he had just experienced the worst hour and a half of his life. He thought his intervention had been hard to endure, but the group was even worse.

He was furious that no one would listen to what he had to say. Jeff overlooked the many female patients who were equally involved in their careers. He didn't expect them to be able to understand his business pressures, but he felt that at least they could stay out of the conversation, and he resented Bonnie's intrusive questions. He thought Dan was an absolute wimp; it didn't matter to him that Dan ranked above him on the corporate hierarchy. "With a crybaby like that as the head of the home office, his company's probably just a two-bit operation. Jesus! I thought I was going to bolt right out of the room when he started to cry. A grown man, blubbering like a baby. And *he* had the nerve to tell *me* that job pressures aren't important!"

Jeff also felt that if he had needed prayers he would have

stayed home and gone to church. "This is sophisticated treatment? It's more like Sunday school campfire days." But more than anything, he hated the group hug. He didn't want to touch *anyone* and he didn't want *anyone* to touch him. Throughout the hug, he had stood rigid. He wanted to keep his arms to his sides, but he also didn't want to draw attention to himself by being different, so he placed his hands lightly on the backs of the people on either side of him. He felt as if their arms encircling him were burning right through his back. He didn't see how he was going to be able to get through *two* group therapy sessions a day.

Jeff could not grasp the healing that had occurred in his group that morning, but he knew well that things had not gone as he wished. While no one seemed to care very much about the responses he gave, everyone but Jeff seemed to think Dan's behavior was something to be admired.

As usual he felt out of kilter—unique—different from everyone else. And, as usual, albeit unknowingly, he defended himself by belittling others. He believed, beyond any doubt, that he was the only normal person in the group.

Yet, he kept thinking of something Dan had said. Dan had knocked his son across the room, and so had Jeff—for the same reason, to stop his son from protecting his mother from his father's attack. Even Jeff could see there was clearly something wrong with that, and he didn't like being reminded of the incident at all. He also remembered his sons and their tears at the intervention. While on one level he blamed Susan for causing them to cry by dragging them into the intervention, on another level, he was beginning to see that he, like Dan, had hurt his children on other occasions long before the intervention took place.

While pondering such thoughts, Jeff made a decision to stay in treatment. Even though he hated the group therapy, he never wanted his sons to say that he didn't love them; and he feared they might say that if he left treatment—so for them he'd stay.

But Jeff still felt strongly that the past is past, and he could see no point in dredging it up as Dan had done in that morning's group. "Watering last year's lilies is not for me," he told himself, and he became determined to be better prepared for future groups.

In between lectures, meals, and a meeting with his counselor, Jeff stayed in his room drawing up a list of all his responsibilities as a regional manager. Before going to bed, he felt ready to present a good case for himself when next called upon in group. But the group, busy with other matters, left him alone for several sessions; throughout each, Jeff remained tense, on guard against the moment when they would turn to him.

Meanwhile, he attended lectures and movies about chemical dependency and began to socialize with the other patients in his free time, finding to his great surprise that he actually liked the very people, like Dan, whom he had previously put down. He was surprised, too, to find himself laughing and enjoying this new camaraderie. He was impressed also with the staff, thinking they were really on their toes. While he respected their professionalism, mostly he liked the fact that they did not put themselves on a pedestal in relationship to the patients. Some of the staff were recovering chemically dependent persons, some were not, and Jeff couldn't tell the difference, which somehow made him feel relieved.

Toward the end of his first week, Jeff took a battery of psychological tests and met again with his counselor, Jill, who asked him to trace his drinking and drug use back as far as he could remember. Jeff felt he took an honest look at his chemical use and was particularly pleased to be able to talk about his marijuana and cocaine use. He was proud that he had stopped using those drugs and was sure Jill would be able to see that he could now do the same thing with alcohol. He was even hoping she would suggest that he didn't need any further treatment. "I've learned my lesson," he told her. "I know I have to stop drinking and if I could stop using those drugs, I assure you I won't have any trouble stopping the alcohol."

Jill replied by asking, "What will you use instead?"

"What do you mean, what will I use instead?" Jeff answered, miffed at her response.

"Jeff, from what you've told me, your drinking picked up considerably when you stopped using cocaine. It's quite clear to me that you replaced cocaine with alcohol. What are you going to use to replace the alcohol if you stop drinking?"

"Now, wait a minute! You're jumping to some pretty hasty conclusions here. My drinking had nothing to do with the coke."

"You could say that, perhaps, if you had not increased your drinking, but as you yourself say you increased your alcohol consumption after you stopped using cocaine, I suggest that you make a link between those two things. Let's close now, Jeff," Jill continued, "and in our next meeting we'll review the data that we receive from your wife and others who have some knowledge about your chemical use."

Nothing was going the way Jeff wished. His group seemed to be ignoring him; they never asked for his opinions and seemed intent on dredging up the past, or else they wallowed around in a lot of murky feelings. Jeff remained tense, afraid they would expect him to do the same at any moment.

And he felt Bonnie was getting to be a real pest. He liked hanging around with others in the lounge, but Bonnie was a nosy little busybody, asking him how his kids felt about his drinking and commenting on how hard everything must have been for his wife.

Jeff's life in treatment didn't improve when he next met with his counselor. "We've got all this data on your chemical use from Susan, Jeff," Jill explained, "and you're not denying any of it, but it doesn't seem to me that you're connecting it with the problems in your life.

"Let's start with your family," she suggested. "Tomorrow, I'd like you to share some of this data with your group. Tell them exactly how your alcohol, cocaine, and marijuana use interfered in your ability to be a husband and father. And, Jeff, your group's going to want to know how this data makes you feel."

Shortly after he started upon his assignment, Bob, one of the group counselors, interrupted, "Jeff, you're describing the chemical incidents well, but you're not telling us how you feel. Try taking them one at a time. Start over, and this time tell us how each incident made you feel."

Jeff then described how he had yelled at Susan after he had passed out at the luncheon with his colleagues. "I blamed Susan and, well, I guess that's not being a good husband."

"Maybe we can help you, Jeff," offered one of the group members sitting across from him. "Just sit back and relax, close your eyes if it will help, take yourself back to that moment when you're dumping on Susan. Tell us what happened."

"I yelled at her," Jeff said. "I told her it was all her fault, that I never would have had to drink like that if she hadn't made me handle Tad's problems at school. Then she screamed back at me and I walked out and got drunk."

"How does that make you feel?" Bonnie asked.

"It was stupid on my part," Jeff replied.

"That's an opinion, not a feeling, Jeff." Bob prompted.

"Oh?" asked Jeff, "what do you mean by feeling?"

"Sad, mad, glad, ashamed . . . any of those kinds of things," Bonnie explained. "You dumped on Susan when it was really your fault to begin with. How does that make you feel?"

"Well, lousy, I guess," Jeff replied. And so it went with each incident. Jeff minimized the consequences and either passed a value judgment on his behavior or named a feeling without showing any emotion.

Bob said, "That's okay for now, Jeff. You've told us *some* things about your chemical use and that's more than you were willing to do last week, but you haven't added anything to our knowledge of your chemical use that your wife had not already listed. You didn't really give us any more than you had to, did you? Also you're keeping your feelings locked up. I know that many of the things you've told us—Tad's exposure to the taunts of his friends about your drinking, and being drunk at your youngest son's birthday party—must be very painful for you, but you haven't shared that pain with us. Jeff, if you want to make better progress in treatment, you'll have to start dealing with your feelings."

Jeff was confused. He knew the group wanted more, but he

didn't know exactly what they wanted; besides he was determined that *he* wasn't going to fall apart. "I suppose you want me to cry like Dan last week or get angry and shout like Liz over there. Why does everything have to be negative?" he asked angrily.

"What are you feeling right now?" asked Liz, who had raised her voice in anger several times in recent group sessions.

"Okay."

"Really?" she asked. "You're shouting and your fists are clenched. You don't look okay, you look as if you are angry."

"I'm *not* angry! Jesus! Get off my back, will you!" demanded Jeff angrily.

Bob said, "It may well be that you're not feeling your anger, Jeff, but the reality is you're acting as if you are angry. Perhaps instead of feeling your anger, you are using hostility as a defense, as a way of keeping us away from you."

"Whatever you say, you're the expert," Jeff replied, dripping with sarcasm.

But life did not improve one iota for Jeff the rest of the week. At one of the groups, when a new patient was introduced and spoke of his job pressures and his wife's problems rather than his drinking, Bob asked, "Jeff, is there anything you'd like to say to Bill? You were saying those same things when you first joined this group."

"Yeah! He's in for it," Jeff answered, and then he turned to Bill and said, "I agree with everything you're saying, but they won't. I think we *should* talk about real problems. I've got a job to face, just like you, when I get out of here, but you'll find this group isn't very interested in the real world."

"I think Bob was hoping some kind of light bulb had gone off in your head, but I see it hasn't," Liz said sadly.

At another time, Jeff's roommate Jim asked, "When are you going to give up fighting, Jeff?"

"What do you mean fighting? I've got a right to state my opinion," Jeff replied.

"That's what I mean. Why don't you just let go, you'd be a whole lot more comfortable."

Jeff answered, "Listen, you do things your way, I'll do things mine, okay?"

"Yeah," Jim drawled laconically, "except it seems to me that if you had a way that worked, you wouldn't be here."

One morning, while on his way to get a cup of coffee, Jeff passed Liz and her husband and children in the lounge. They were embracing and wiping their eyes. Jeff got his coffee and went immediately to the phone. "Susan, cancel everything. I don't want you and Alan coming out here, and I mean it. You don't know what goes on in this place, and I'm telling you right now, I don't want you coming out here."

"Wow!" Susan replied, taken aback. "Jeff, I love you, I really do but, Jeff, you're ordering me around as if I were your slave. That hurts, Jeff. I'm your wife, not your slave; please don't order me to do things."

"All right, I won't order you, I'll ask you. Don't come out here," Jeff ordered.

"This is very hard for me to say, Jeff, but even if you asked me, I'd still go to family treatment. Alan and I need help, Jeff, and we're going out there to get help for ourselves."

Suddenly perceiving a possible explanation for Susan's behavior, Jeff asked, "You still seeing Ruth Maxwell?"

"Funny you should ask, Jeff," Susan answered, "I am, and just yesterday Ruth said that you might not want us out there."

"Ruth said—big deal—what does she do, say 'Abracadabra' as she passes her hands over the crystal ball? How much is all of *that* costing us? You ever stop to consider the cost of things? Now listen! You come out here, I leave. Got that?"

"Jeff, this is so difficult. I love you more than I can tell you, but Alan and I are going to attend family week. I hope you'll stay in treatment, but we're going even if you leave."

"Okay, you're asking for it," Jeff warned as he crashed the phone into the receiver.

Bob opened the afternoon group by saying, "Jeff, Jill just told me that your wife called reporting that you're threatening to leave treatment if she comes out here for family week. Is that true?"

"Yes, except it's no threat. If she comes, I leave," Jeff replied sullenly.

"Want to talk about it?" asked Jim, his roommate.

"No!"

"Well, I'm going to ask you to talk about it, Jeff," Bob said. "Alcoholics always think they can manage everything by themselves, which is one of the reasons why their lives are all messed up. We're going to give you a chance to *not* mess up your life any more than it already is. How come you don't want Susan and Alan here?"

Jeff replied angrily, "You don't have any fucking right to mess up my kid. He's been through enough, and I'm not going to let him go through any more."

"My kids are here right now, Jeff," Liz eagerly explained. "Why, we all met this morning and it was wonderful. We hugged and laughed and cried. Oh! Goodness, Jeff, I felt so close to them. It was so good to see my kids relaxed. They were always on guard with me, they'd clam up or leave the room in order to get away from me. Now they're hugging me, and they're letting me hug them. They haven't been *hurt* this week, they've been *helped*."

Jeff answered, still surly, "I saw that scene! It sure didn't look so hot to me. I don't know where you get off thinking it's good to have kids cry, but I'm not going to bring that down on *my* kid."

Jim quietly asked, "How're you going to stop it? Won't your wife and Alan be coming here for family week even if you leave?"

"What'd you mean—uh—I don't know if they will or not," Jeff answered, looking as if he had not thought of that possibility.

Bob asked, "Do you really think you can go on tyrannizing your wife forever? She's been getting help, Jeff. She did the intervention on you, remember? Your wife has changed, and I think you'd be wise to assume she'll be here for family week, no matter what you do. So I think you might want to consider Jim's question. What good will it do for you to leave, since that won't stop Susan from coming here?"

"I don't know," Jeff answered.

"I don't think you're afraid to have your son cry. It seems to me that you're afraid of breaking down yourself," announced Liz from across the circle.

"Bullshit!" replied Jeff, true to form, and the group went on to other topics, leaving Jeff in his conflicted state.

Later that evening at an informal patient gathering following a movie they had all seen about an alcoholic mother of young children, Liz started to cry as she told of how she had done many of the same things as the mother in the movie. From across the room, Jeff started to cry softly as he listened. When the man next to him attempted to offer comfort, Jeff got up and quickly retreated to his room before anyone else could see him.

He paced, he took a long shower, but he could not stop crying. All he could think was that nothing was going the way he wanted. Everyone seemed to be bucking him. No one understood him. He felt utterly alone and was overwhelmed with anxiety and sadness, but he didn't know why. He went to the window and looked out onto a bright night with a full moon and scattered clouds. To calm himself as he watched the clouds pass quickly by, Jeff started to say the Serenity Prayer, over and over. *God, grant me the serenity to accept the things I cannot change, the courage to change the things I can, and the wisdom to know the difference.*

Suddenly, he sobbed aloud, "Oh! My God! There's an order! The clouds are all moving in order! I've been bucking the order! There *is* a God! Oh! God! Help me. I *am* an alcoholic! I can't change that. I'm an alcoholic! Please, God, help me, I don't want to die." Then Jeff felt a great sense of peace, calmer than he could ever remember feeling. And he knew that somehow everything was now going to be okay.

When Jim returned to their room, Jeff said, "Jim, I want to tell you something. I'm an alcoholic. I know that now. I don't think I'll ever be able to explain what happened to me this evening, but I want you to know that I really am an alcoholic and I'm sorry for mouthing off at you and, well, I guess I'm not fighting anymore."

"Beautiful!" Jim answered with a big smile and embrace. "I don't have to hear any more than that. I'm really glad for you, Jeff. I don't mind telling you that I was worried about you. Besides being on your case these two weeks, I've also been praying for you."

Jeff's final two weeks were busy. He worked actively in group, sharing his feelings, both good and bad. He wrote out his Fourth Step and was responsible for showing the new patients around. "It was amazing to me how far I'd come. Those new guys would enter the unit talking about their jobs, and there I was, the hotshot regional manager, telling them that jobs weren't important."

Jeff had reentry counseling during his final week and was again amazed at the changes he had made. "Where once I couldn't wait to get out of there, I now wanted to stay longer. I was not at all worried about being able to stay sober when I was first admitted; now I had some fears about facing the drinking world. I had gotten in touch with the magnitude of my illness, and I wasn't at all sure I would be able to make it. The discharge counseling was great. It helped me work through some of those fears."

Jeff also took his Fifth Step—*Admitted to God, to ourselves, and to another human being the exact nature of our wrongs*—during his final week. "It was like I left all the pain in the pastoral counselor's office. I told him about everything in my past, and I accepted fully that I alone had done all those hurtful things. I didn't play anything down. All those feelings of shame, guilt, and remorse that I had been carrying around for so many years went away. I began to see that I felt like that because I had gone against my own values and against society's values. It was good to know I *had* values; I thought I had lost them. When I finished I was drained, but I felt good, hopeful about my life and eager to see Susan and to return to my family."

14

Chemical Dependency Treatment

The chemically dependent person entering treatment perceives that he has one basic task—to get out, unchanged, as soon as possible.

Chemical dependency treatment assumes quite a different task—to provide the atmosphere and guidance that help the dependent become concerned enough about his illness to develop a way of life that works.

Chemical dependency treatment is different from the traditional medical model of treatment in which, generally speaking: patients tend to be in a passive-submissive relationship with a dominant fixer; chemical dependency is viewed as a secondary illness—a symptom of psychological disturbance; and where treatment has a past/causal orientation and/or consists of long-term tranquilizers and/or deterrent medications. The chemical dependency treatment model is also quite different from the therapeutic drug communities that grew out of the inner-city "opium wars" of the sixties and from various forms of aversion therapy where manipulation and conditioning predominate.

Detoxification, ridding the body of mood-altering chemicals, is done within the medical model by most treatment centers. Vital signs are monitored and medicines in decreasing doses are given during the first two to three days to counteract dangerous and/or uncomfortable physiological withdrawal reactions. Contrary to popular belief, detoxification is a relatively easy and safe procedure under medical supervision. Also contrary to popular belief, detoxification itself is not treatment for chemical dependency; instead it is a precursor to treatment.

The chemical dependency treatment model, either outpatient or residential, is a blend of professional behavioral science and AA principles. One of its most important features is that it requires the patient to fix himself. This model assumes that only the dependent can do it, and treatment is the catalyst to help him do it. Among other things this means his role in treatment is active, and his recovery is achieved only through his thinking, feeling, and behavior.

Residential treatment, usually of three to five weeks' duration, is the most intense and comprehensive form of chemical dependency treatment and, as it contains the principles of both AA and out-patient counseling, I will describe the task of treatment as it unfolds in a residential setting. Later, as we follow our families in recovery, we will see more of the workings of the self-help groups and out-patient counseling.

Meanwhile, because AA is such an integral component in chemical dependency treatment, you may be interested in learning the Twelve Steps of Alcoholics Anonymous upon which the self-help programs are based:

1. (We) admitted we were powerless over alcohol—that our lives had become unmanageable.
2. Came to believe that a Power greater than ourselves could restore us to sanity.

3. Made a decision to turn our will and our lives over to the care of God, as we understood Him.
4. Made a searching and fearless moral inventory of ourselves.
5. Admitted to God, to ourselves, and to another human being the exact nature of our wrongs.
6. Were entirely ready to have God remove all these defects of character.
7. Humbly asked Him to remove our shortcomings.
8. Made a list of all persons we had harmed, and became willing to make amends to them all.
9. Made direct amends to such people whenever possible, except when to do so would injure them or others.
10. Continued to take personal inventory, and when we were wrong promptly admitted it.
11. Sought through prayer and meditation to improve our conscious contact with God as we understood Him, praying only for knowledge of His will for us and the power to carry that out.
12. Having had a spiritual awakening as the result of these steps, we tried to carry this message to alcoholics, and to practice these principles in all our affairs.

Now, back to the task of treatment—to provide the atmosphere and guidance that help the dependent become concerned enough about his illness to develop a way of life that works.

Upon admission to a treatment center, if a chart existed to measure self-esteem, the chemically dependent person would not be able to muster enough of a sense of self-worth to make it onto the chart. He may cover well with his omnipotent, superior, holier-than-thou demeanor, but deep inside (and sometimes not so deep) he feels lower than the lowest—less than human.

Thus, the treatment atmosphere is designed to enhance the dependent's sense of worthiness and is created in part by attractive, comfortable, clean surroundings; by sophisticated therapeutic processes; by a high degree of professionalism among a multidisciplined staff who, in attitude and actions, let the dependent know that it is okay to be sick—that being sick does not diminish him as a valuable, worthy human being; and in part by less tangible transcendental concepts.

The chemically dependent person's defenses are dishonest. They tell him lies—that he is well when he is ill. Also, as we have seen, his major defenses are among the most primitive and immature and therefore do not respond to reason. Consequently, the atmosphere is both honest and confrontive—and sometimes it's painful! The truth often hurts. In a no-nonsense, direct, but receivable manner, the staff and peers confront the chemically dependent person with reality—concrete, specific facts related to his illness.

Kathy, the nurse, confronted Jeff when she withheld sympathy and pointed out to him that he had a problem with being able to stay stopped. Jill, the counselor, confronted Jeff when she asked what chemical he would use to replace alcohol, citing his own data to show a history of chemical substitution. Jim, the roommate, confronted Jeff when he pointed out to him that he didn't seem to have a way of doing things that worked. On an out-patient basis, I confronted Carla repeatedly by suspending my belief in her version of her life while showing her, over and over, the concrete, specific facts related to her chemical use.

Chemically dependent persons suffer an illness that carries the burden of stigma. As addiction is degrading to the person, so too is society's moralistic and judgmental attitude about his illness. Thus, the involved person is doubly diminished. Unfortunately, the problems of stigma go further; our culture is far too ambivalent about alcoholism and other addictions just to pass moral judgments. Our culture also tolerates chemical dependency and in turn enables as significantly as do families. In fact our culture's enabling is, to a very large degree, responsible for the family's enabling.

One facet of cultural enabling that I did not cover when I spoke of family enabling is that in our rejection of the dependent's *behavior*, we reject the *dependent* as well. We do not like the behavior we see in him so we reject *him* for that behavior and then we compound the problem by tolerating both him and his behavior, as if they were one and the same.

Rejection plus tolerance, a reflection of society's ambivalence toward alcohol and drug addiction, keeps us from being able to have enough respect for the involved person to invest the time and energy to find out how to handle him effectively. Instead we ignore him, punish him, look the other way, preach at him, feel pity toward him, moralize about him, and so on. Then, we make matters worse by tolerating him. While we castigate, we neither insist upon nor assist with change. Thus, we virtually compel the chemically dependent person to get out of his pain the only way he knows how, by further chemical use. We also, of course, compel the family to enter a conspiracy of silence, so no one will know.

The atmosphere of treatment also makes a judgment, but it's positive—opposite to the one made by our culture. The therapeutic atmosphere says, "Not only do we think you are deserving and in need of treatment, we believe you *can* and *will* get well. We're going to give you the time and space to feel your sickness, so that you can get well. All you have to do is work, and we'll be right here with you for as long as it takes. Welcome! You're in the right place!"

To sum up, the therapeutic atmosphere *does* include care, concern, confrontation, honesty, and acceptance; the therapeutic atmosphere *does not* include sympathy, pity, moralizing, accusation, condemnation, punitiveness, or rejection. The former atmosphere exists in chemical dependency treatment centers, in AA, and the AA-modeled self-help organizations. The latter atmosphere exists almost everywhere else. With the former, the chemically dependent person can get well; with the latter he can stay sick.

It's amazing, almost unfathomable, but everyone who knows the dependent is concerned about his illness; everyone *but* the dependent. Even though addiction is the dominant reality in his life, it is virtually the only reality about which the chemically dependent person has little or no concern. Incredible!

The denial system of chemical dependency, which is formed by his whole repertory of defenses—denial, projection, repression, minimization, rationalization, intellectualization, and so on—causes a massive delusion wherein the chemically dependent person is rendered incapable of perceiving his condition with any degree of accuracy. As long as this denial system remains intact, the chemically dependent person cannot feel concern with doing anything constructive about his illness. Thus, part of the task of treatment is to penetrate this denial system, for only then can the patient reach the level of personal concern for his illness that will motivate him for change.

Patients in a treatment center, throughout their stay, are exposed to increasing amounts of information about chemical dependency in general and in their particular case. The information, cognitive and affective, head and heart, is conveyed in several ways—through lectures and movies, three times each day in most places; reading and written assignments; presentations of their own chemical histories and the results of various psychological tests; group therapy, usually twice each day; individual counseling; AA meetings; and peer interaction.

I'm often astounded by how meaningful didactic information is for chemically dependent persons. An alumnus of one of the treatment centers who is now actively engaged in one of our recovery support growth groups says that everything finally came clear to him as he was listening to a lecture on defenses and hidden pain. "I saw myself right on that blackboard—clear as day."

One of the things we do, besides our work with chemically dependent persons and their families, is help communities and schools design and implement chemical awareness programs to address the problems of adolescent alcohol/drug use, abuse, and dependency. Recently, in a special course for troubled students, one of the kids announced that he had started attending AA. When the teacher asked why, he replied, "Well, you taught the symptoms of addiction last week and they all fit, so I decided I'd better get some treatment for my-self."

Ah! If it were only always that easy! By the time chemically dependent persons land in a treatment center, their denial system tends to be firmly established and, while didactic education is important, other processes are needed.

To bring the patient's illness closer to home, within the first few days the counselor or case manager will conduct one or more individual sessions with him to obtain his chemical history—partly for the edification of the staff so they can determine if chemical dependency, in fact, exists and partly for the edification of the patient so he can see a broader picture of his illness.

Chemically dependent persons tend to view their chemical history—that part they remember—as if they were half-heartedly viewing a tennis match, looking at the strokes now and then, but totally unaware of the score. Having their history laid out before them can be an eye-opener. Another troubled student in a similar course in a different school also joined AA, saying, "When you asked me to fill out that chemical history form, I didn't fill it *out*, I filled it *up*! There wasn't enough paper for me, so I decided I needed some help."

But usually *much* more is needed. While their chemical history may represent the beginning of insight, most patients are not interested during their first week or so in seeing any data beyond their own, often limited, listing. And few tie their chemical use to actual problems in their lives. Therefore, many treatment centers ask the patient to relate his chemical history to his group. Because dependents are not at all used to talking specifically about their chemical use or the associated consequences, this is a difficult assignment indeed. As with Jeff, in the early days of treatment it is not uncommon for patients to report the chemical incidents, minimize the consequences, and remain aloof from their feelings. Still, they learn something very important—that *their* way of handling their chemical histories is not enough, not nearly enough. For other patients, this verbal presentation can be the exact avenue needed to "unrepress" additional data; or it can be an avenue into their buried feelings.

During the second week, data comes in from the patient's significant other people, the results are obtained from his various tests, and then the patient is presented with a far broader picture of his own illness. By this point, patients are usually experiencing a gradual reduction of their denial system, not only because of the increased flow of data specific to their illness and the continuing lectures and movies, but because of two additional components that also have been on-going since admission—patient interaction and group therapy.

Healing occurs when one dependent tells his story (chemical history) to another dependent. I don't know why this is so, I only know that it is so. There doesn't seem to be a scientific explanation for it. Bill Wilson, the founder of AA, knew about the potency of this healing fifty years ago. Many people to this day tend to minimize its importance.

Each year at various conferences I meet personnel from chemical dependency centers from all over the United States, and I am invariably impressed by the high caliber of their expertise. With all due modesty, the people with whom I work are also pretty good. Nevertheless, patient interaction may well have more of an impact than staff/patient interaction.

When the listening dependent hears the story of another person's chemical use, a story different from but similar to his own, he appears to be able to incorporate what he hears in such a way that he can "see" his own story, either in part or in toto, perhaps for the first time. Then the listener's denial system is finally penetrated. This kind of extraordinary healing identification can help the chemically dependent person become *very* concerned about his illness, and it can help him get well and stay well.

Recalling his experience of crying when he heard Liz talk after the movie about her experiences as a drunk mother, Jeff says, "I don't know what happened to me, but all I could think about were my sons crying as they huddled next to me at the intervention and, God, I felt so sad. Liz was reaching me; I didn't want her to, but she did, and that was the beginning of the end of my active addiction—right there with little ole Liz telling her story."

Patients in treatment, particularly those who've gained insight and are less defended, not only speak fully of their own chemical histories, they also zero in on the chemical histories and defensive behavior of the newer patients. They know well what questions to ask, they are not conned, yet they are sensitive to the need to be caring and accepting. Because each day patients spend several hours together in structured activities and several additional hours together in unstructured gatherings, *treatment goes on nearly nonstop every waking hour!*

And then there's group. *Ah! Group!* I just have to say that word and images of smiling faces flash before my eyes along with the words, "Yeah, group!" as if it were some kind of strange, intense memorable mixed-feeling experience—which it is.

Patients initially often call group the worst part of treatment. More than any other therapeutic process, group therapy threatens the chemically dependent person's aloneness—his terribly painful, but accustomed, psychic isolation. Dependents, as their addiction progresses and their sense of self-worth diminishes, come to believe that being affected personally by others on any kind of deep level will only add to their pain. As a result, they tend to relate to other people with minimal emotional involvement, as if other people were objects. Family members are often quick to point this out. "He's friendlier to our dog than to me," or "He cares more about his computer than our kids," or "She never cares what I think, as if I were incapable of thought."

In group the chemically dependent persons tend to feel that people are moving in on them, and their reaction is often one of panic. Thus, they shore themselves up to ward others off. They sit rigidly upright in their chairs with their arms folded and their teeth clenched, as if protecting their bodies will protect their aloneness. They stay up all night rehearsing what they're going to say in group the next day, as if guarding their words will keep others at a distance. In group, *all* their defenses go into high gear.

Later these same patients who call group the worst part of treatment, call it the best. When they are finally able to break out of their isolation, they discover something wondrous: the group's means of close personal interaction makes them feel "whole," "worthy," "high," "productive," "part of the human race." Then they can't wait to get to group, they don't want the sessions to end, and they remember each other warmly, lovingly for the rest of their lives.

Technically, the group members provide a mirror for each other. When they describe what they see each other doing— "You *look* angry; your teeth are clenched; your face is red; and you are shouting!"—they *illuminate* each other's defenses and provide themselves with the opportunity to see what it is they might want to change.

Technically also, the group members are expected to level, to get out of their *head* and into their *heart,* and to share with each other whatever it is that they are feeling. Then they change! Carl Rogers is right: sharing feelings does change the person.

Finally we come to yet another feature of chemical dependency treatment—spirituality. Positive, transcendental interaction permeates both the atmosphere of a chemical dependency treatment center and the treatment components themselves.

In many ways chemical dependency is a matter of power versus powerlessness. In active addiction, when they are under, as well as when they are *not* under, the influence of chemicals, chemically dependent persons are powerless. *They do not have the ability to manage their lives constructively.* They have lost free will and have become compelled, driven by all the forces of their addiction—their psychophysiological *need* for a chemical; loss of self-esteem; high level of hostility and defiance; buried negative feelings of shame, guilt, and self-pity; each of their many defenses and resulting denial system; and their psychic aloneness.

By themselves they are powerless; yet in active addiction, they feel omnipotent, in need of no one or no power beyond themselves. The dependent is his own *God*! Can you imagine choosing an addicted person to be *your* God? That's what they choose for themselves.

Chemical dependency treatment centers and AA as well are not concerned with religion; they are, however, concerned about the chemically dependent person's Godlike stance, for they know he will not be able to get well until he perceives that *he is not God and that he needs help from outside himself.*

The chemically dependent person faces a painful dilemma, and every day that he is in treatment he is brought ever closer to perceiving this dilemma, which states, "*Only YOU can do it and ONLY you can not do it.*" When face to face with such a conflict, the dependent slowly but surely (or suddenly) perceives that he has a choice. He can go on fighting or he can give up.

But then the whole matter becomes even more difficult and the dilemma felt even more forcefully because here too he is powerless! While he may believe he is choosing to keep up the fight, he really isn't—he's compelled by forces beyond his control. In the same way, he cannot will himself to give up. The process of surrender is not conscious; it's an unconscious psychic conversion, poorly understood, but incredibly powerful.

Surrender certainly has something to do with the dependent's ability to perceive the double bind, which in turn has something to do with a reduction in his denial system. Surrender seems to emanate not from psychic comfort, but from increased psychic pain. At the same time it does seem to be enhanced by the loving, safe, spiritual environment of the treatment setting wherein the patient learns: *intellectually* in lectures and elsewhere about power from without, about power that is transcendental to the person; *emotionally* in groups, patient interaction, staff interaction, and elsewhere that he truly does feel better and stronger *each time* he reaches outside himself; and *spiritually* that prayer and meditation can provide comfort and strength, even though he may not believe in God, in praying, or in meditating.

Of those patients who surrender, most do so gradually; little by little, they come to see their powerlessness and, little by little, they give up. We saw this in Jeff's group when Dan described his fears about seeing his family and, by the end of group, perceived and accepted the fact that he did not have the power to control how his family felt. Dan then could go on to perceive more of his powerlessness and to give up his control in other areas as well. Occasionally, patients experience a sudden, total surrender, as Jeff experienced it as he stared at the passing clouds while feeling overwhelmed by psychic pain. Either way, slowly or suddenly, the act of surrender produces dramatic changes in the person, which can be clearly seen by others.

Surrender, which, as you know, is altogether different from submission or compliance (both of which are accompanied by a begrudging "yes" on the outside and a defiant "no" on the inside) produces a switch from negative emotions to positive emotions: from resentment to gratitude; from grandiosity to humility; from anxiety and tension to serenity; from feeling alone to feeling connected; from feeling omnipotent to feeling a need for help.

Surrender represents a crumbling of the denial system, allowing the chemically dependent person to gain insight into the magnitude of his illness so that he sees it and *accepts* it in its totality. Thus, with surrender, the dependent, for the first time, becomes fully concerned about his own illness; only then do we see a shift in his priorities. With surrender, rather than being third, tenth or forty-sixth on his list, *getting well now becomes his number one concern.* Which leads us to the remaining section of the treatment task—helping him develop a way of life that works.

Follow-up studies of treated chemically dependent persons provide *empirical* support for two things many of us have long known. Now there's proof! Chemically dependent persons who demonstrate a sustained improvement in their ability to work, love and play: (1) remain abstinent from all mood-altering chemicals, and (2) attend AA (or NA and so on) regularly. Following treatment, chemically dependent persons who do not remain abstinent tend not to experience a sustained lifestyle improvement. Chemically dependent persons who do not attend AA regularly are at high risk for resumed chemical use.

As regular AA attendence seems important to both abstinence and an improved lifestyle, are there any predictors? Can we tell who is most likely to attend AA regularly? Yes, that, too, has been studied. J. Clark Laundergan, in his book *Easy Does It*, which describes a remarkably thorough follow-up study of patients treated at the Hazelden Foundation in Minnesota, reports that the chemically dependent persons who were able to break their psychic isolation—to relate on a personal, feeling, level with their peers in the group setting and with a Higher Power—were the most likely to attend AA regularly upon discharge.[8] Conversely, those who had trouble relating in a group setting or in developing a means of maintaining contact with a power greater than themselves were least likely to attend AA and were most likely to suffer increased social and psychological dysfunction.

Consequently, helping chemically dependent persons develop relational skills, interpersonal and spiritual, is as important as helping them break their denial system. Actually, as we have seen, treatment is provided in this direction beginning at admission and continues throughout the chemically dependent person's stay.

Further assistance is provided when the patient takes his Fifth Step—*We admitted to God, to ourselves, and to another human being, the exact nature of our wrongs*—with a member of the clergy during his final week in treatment. AA's Fifth Step is a marvelous opportunity for the chemically dependent

8. J. Clark Laundergan, *Easy Does It* (Center City, Minnesota: Hazelden Educational Services, 1982). pp. 89–138.

person to finally bring about a resolution to the terrible struggle he's had between his values and his behavior—the very struggle that has been the source of his great well of negative feelings, particularly guilt, shame, and remorse. The truth is that none of us can relate closely to any person or to any power outside ourselves if we do not feel worthy, and how worthy can we feel if we're riddled with guilt, shame, and remorse?

It is not at all unusual in a treatment center for a patient to hold out—fighting everyone and everything, passively or actively—right up to the bitter end, and then, finally, during the Fifth Step be able to become freed from the psychic wars raging within his denial system. The Fifth Step is often equally pivotal for dependents in AA who've never received any treatment other than AA. Even for those chemically dependent persons who already have penetrated their denial systems, the Fifth Step is important.

Not being a recitation of sins, the Fifth Step calls for the dependent to share his past behavior as well as associated feelings with another person. It does not seem sufficient just to write about the behavior and feelings, nor is it sufficient to speak only of the behavior; conflict resolution comes about best through the sharing of both behavior and feelings with another human being. Because value/behavior conflict is in many ways a moral conflict for the chemically dependent person, in a treatment center the acceptance and guidance of a trained member of the clergy can be particularly helpful to the dependent as he takes his Fifth Step.

Conventional psychotherapy is not designed to address feelings of shame. It handles guilt well, but not shame; and there's a world of difference between these two feelings. Both tend to exist in reaction to the outer world—important people, society's values, and our own behavior. But guilt results from perceiving that we have done something wrong, something that goes against our own values as well as those of society and other people. Shame is more a feeling of falling short, of somehow not making it, or not living up to either our own values or those of society and others.

I've often heard people say that Alcoholics Anonymous is a "divinely inspired" program, and the more I know about the program, the more I think it is; for several reasons, not the least of which is the fact that AA addresses shame as well as guilt.

In addition to the Fifth Step, both AA and the AA-based chemical dependency treatment centers, through other steps as well as philosophy, assist the alcoholic in recognizing and *accepting* his imperfection—his essential limitation as a human being, which, of course, is a difficult concept for anyone to accept. However, once accepted, the concept of personal finitude reduces shame for having fallen so short. Then chemically dependent persons can aim for progress rather than perfection; they need be less demanding of self and others; and then, of course, they can relate more honestly and openly with both people and powers outside themselves.

All kinds of special assignments are given to individual patients who continue to experience relational difficulties. They may be asked to read additional material on meditation or to attend special classes or counseling sessions with the spiritual counselor. They may be asked to take a walk in the woods to seek beauty, or to bring three interpersonal problems that they are currently facing in the center to every group session for a week. They may be asked to wear a blindfold for twenty-four hours, relying on others for help. They may be asked to talk for at least five minutes in each group about what friendship means to them specifically, or they may be asked to *not* talk at all for two days and two nights. (I once gave that particular assignment to an incredibly gregarious and gifted comedienne who had all the patients following her about enthralled with her performances, none of which had anything to do with relating closely with people. She nearly went bananas without her powerful performing defense, but she sure got the message.) If the patient continues to experience relational problems, extended treatment may be recommended.

During the final week of treatment, further assistance for developing a way of life that works is provided as the patient prepares to reenter the world—our "better living through chemicals" world. He may roleplay with a counselor and/or peers his first day back on the job or in school, his first business double martini luncheon meeting, his first cocktail or coke party, or his reunion with his family and members of his intervention team.

As he will have attended several AA meetings by his final week, he'll be knowledgeable about the workings of the self-help groups. He will now receive assistance on how *he* can best work his self-help program once he gets home. Finally, he will review all his discharge plans with his counselor. All the insight in the world and all the skills at relating will be of no avail unless put into action. Therefore, the chemically dependent person, prior to discharge, develops and makes a commitment to a plan of action for living once he leaves the treatment center, which may well include involvement in a recovery support growth group in addition to AA, daily prayer and/or meditation, *listening* to each member of his family, fun family activities, and so on. If they are to be effective, all such plans of action will, of course, be based on the commitment to remaining abstinent from *all* mood-altering chemicals.

On his last day of treatment, often at a ceremony in his group or elsewhere, he will hear from his counselor and peers what it is they find special about him (their perceptions of both his strengths and weaknesses), and he will talk about what treatment has meant to him. He may receive a medallion or some other carefully thought-out memento, and then he will say good-bye, amidst tears and hugs.

15

Susan in Treatment

"Hi! How are you feeling, Susan?" I asked at our first session following the intervention.

"He got there safely. It's hard to believe, but he's finally in treatment," she replied as she settled into her chair.

"Susan, are you aware of what happened just now? I asked you how *you* are feeling and you told me about Jeff."

"Oh, I know, but I guess part of me never believed he'd really get there. I had visions of him getting drunk on the plane and then refusing to go to the treatment center once he landed . . ."

"Susan, you're *still* talking about Jeff. I care about *you*. Jeff's being taken care of. How are *you* feeling?"

"I'm all right," she answered, looking disappointed, as if we were avoiding what she considered important.

"Tell me about your two days since the intervention. How has it been for you?"

"Oh, I don't know. Maybe it hasn't been as good as I thought it would be."

"In what way?" I persisted.

"I guess I don't feel the relief I thought I'd feel," she replied, making no effort at any further elaboration.

"Something I'm noticing here, Susan, is that when you talk about Jeff you have lots of words, but I feel like a dentist right now—like I'm pulling the words out of your mouth. Is what's happening with Jeff more important than what's happening with you?"

"It's the focus again, isn't it?" Susan asked. "In my head I know it makes sense to focus on myself, but it's obvious that I still don't accept that completely. I keep thinking that everything will be all right if only he gets well."

Throughout her preparation for the intervention, Susan had to focus on both Jeff and herself. It was quite natural that she would once again find herself preoccupied with Jeff, but I knew it would not be a lasting preoccupation. None of us gets well overnight; even without the intervention, it is natural for the co-dependent to move back and forth between being preoccupied with and emotionally detached from the chemically dependent person. The switch from illness to wellness represents a state of transition, in which there is frequent movement both forward and backward. Susan's reluctance to discuss her feelings indicated that she had slipped backward for the moment. Hoping to help her bring her focus back to herself once again, I said, "Jeff's in treatment, Susan, and he's probably beginning to feel better, but it doesn't sound to me as if you've been all that much better these past two days. It hasn't been as good as you thought it would be. What *has* it been like for you?"

"Oh, I don't know, but you're right. It hasn't been so good. The boys have been jumpy, getting into fights with each other, and I've been pretty jumpy, too. I'm screaming at them as much now as ever, maybe even more. I keep wandering around, like I can't get settled on anything. I haven't slept well either. Oh, damn it, I guess I don't fell very well."

"Do you think you might be scared?"

"Yes, I do think I've been afraid," she said, once again coming to life, "and that's what I've been trying to tell you. I really was scared that Jeff wouldn't get to the treatment center. You don't know Jeff like I do. He could very easily have changed planes and been right back here . . ."

"But he isn't here, he's there, Susan," I interrupted, "and you aren't feeling relief, are you?"

"No, I'm not," she agreed.

"Jeff's been there for two days, and you and the boys have been on edge, jumpy, scared for two days. I don't think your fears have anything to do with Jeff. He's there, you're here . . . scared. Your fears arc coming from within you, not from Jeff. And that's why we have to talk about you, not Jeff. Very frankly, you have good reason to feel afraid, which has nothing to do with Jeff."

"What do you mean?" Susan asked.

"Well, for one thing, change of any kind is scary. Jeff's away now. He's in treatment, and that's an enormous change. You might have some concerns about that. You're used to his being sick. Now, you don't know what to expect."

"That's right. I keep wondering what's going to happen next. Now what am I up against? I didn't like him sick, but you're right, at least I knew what to expect," she said.

"I know," I said. "There's always comfort in the status quo. Even though what we have may not be good, at least we *know* what we have. I'd be surprised if you *didn't* feel ill at east now, simply because *now* you don't *know* what you have."

With further discussion, Susan was able to share her other discomforts, namely guilt and fear of retaliation. Guilt because she was not sure she had done the right thing. She knew the intervention was needed, but it seemed "wrong"—so different from her usual way of reacting to Jeff. Enabling had been comfortable in many ways, and Susan talked about how it had been easier to acquiesce than to confront Jeff, but then she also spoke of the increased illness and pain associated with her former enabling. In turn, she began to feel "right" about having done the intervention. "At least now I've done everything I can do to help Jeff save his life—or at least save him from further illness—and I know he wouldn't have kept his job much longer."

But Susan still had some fears. While her reversals in actuality represented significant changes, Susan felt they were minor compared to the planned intervention. She felt she had "pulled the rug right out from under Jeff." Finally she was able to see that she now feared bigger retaliation because the intervention was bigger.

"What's the very worst thing that could happen to you now?" I asked.

"Well, Jeff might call and start shouting on the phone or something," she replied.

"You know, Susan, Jeff's not locked up out there. Forget about his *calling*. He can leave any time he wants. He might have already left. What if he's home by the time you get back there this afternoon?"

"Oh, my God!"

"If that were to be true, what's the worst thing that could happen?" I asked. "Chemically dependent persons tend to follow their own past behavior. What's the very worst thing you could expect from Jeff?"

"He might go on a rampage. He would shout and he might throw furniture. He might attack me in the middle of the night and try to kill me. Oh, I can't stand to think about it. It's just too horrible," she said as she put her hands over her face.

"Has Jeff ever done anything like that in the past, Susan?"

"No . . . no, he hasn't," she answered, her hands still over her face.

"Did your father?" I asked. But Susan didn't answer. She took her hands away from her face and looked at me, her eyes wide and startled, and once again she covered her face. Then she bent over in sobs, crying the tears from long ago. After a while she spoke of some of the things that happened when her father drank and of how afraid she had been as a child.

Most children can just grow up. Children of alcoholics are always deprived, at least emotionally, and they are usually brutalized one way or another. *Their* primary concerns have to do with survival, not maturation. As is so often the case, while listening to Susan's strikingly traumatic childhood, I was impressed first of all that she had survived and secondly that she had survived so well.

I assured Susan that we would help her further with her feelings from her childhood, and I asked if she thought some of her present fears about retaliation might be leftover fears from her father's behavior. Susan thought that was probably the case and that the worst she would have to face from Jeff would be his shouting and arguing, which she knew she could handle. Separating out her childhood fears of her father, she could see that Jeff was different, far less violent. She said if Jeff did become physically abusive, she could call the police or run to the neighbors, but she believed such violence would be out of character for Jeff.

Upon leaving my office, she said that she now felt comfortable about having done the intervention. She also seemed committed to her own recovery once again and able to let Jeff do his own thing. As a result, when Jeff called Susan the following evening to say he was coming home and needed no more treatment, Susan did not succumb to his manipulations.

In further sessions prior to family week, the boys discussed their fears about having done the intervention. While Susan and the boys remained concerned about Jeff's progress in treatment, it became easier for them to keep their focus on themselves, on their feelings, needs, and wants. Because it is not at all unusual for chemically dependent persons to ask their family to stay home rather than attend family week, that was, of course, an issue we discussed in one of our meetings. After Jeff's call ordering Susan not to attend family treatment, Susan said she had some fears that Jeff might carry out his threat of leaving treatment, but that she had reached a point of *almost* not caring. She had made a very real commitment to herself and to her own recovery. "If Jeff isn't willing to do the same for himself, then that's his problem. Right now, I'm not going to make it mine."

Susan arranged for her mother to stay with Tad and Scotty,

who were too young for the treatment center's family program. Meanwhile, both she and Alan had to write out and submit in advance of going to the treatment center a detailed questionnaire describing, among other things, their experiences with chemical issues from the present back to their grandparents.

Then, Susan and Alan entered the family week treatment program, where they once again did some backtracking. While they had made significant steps in shifting their focus from Jeff onto themselves, the closer they got to Jeff physically, the easier it became to return once again to their old ways.

Throughout their first day of treatment, both became increasingly uncomfortable. They were disappointed to find that it really *was* true that they would not see Jeff until the end of the week. Looking at the week's schedule, Susan was put off to see that very little attention would be given to the chemically dependent person's illness and treatment. She was even more annoyed to find that she couldn't get a progress report on Jeff. He had sounded great during recent phone calls, as if he had really changed, but no one would tell her if this was so. Susan's focus was still misplaced. She had made progress, but it was still easier for her to concentrate on Jeff than on herself.

When all the co-dependents were asked to take their own chemical histories the first thing their first morning in treatment, Susan thought, "What a waste of time! Neither of us uses chemicals." Later that afternoon when the family patients, about twenty altogether, shared their chemical use, Susan gasped when Alan talked about how he had used both alcohol and marijuana. "My God! He had always been so perfect. I couldn't believe what I was hearing. He had just had his eleventh birthday—he was still a child! I didn't want to hear it. I couldn't stand the thought of *more* chemical problems in my family, and I was angry with Alan. But I couldn't say anything to him since at that point we were to receive, not comment on each other's data."

Even before then, Susan was beginning to wish she'd left Alan home. Earlier, when they had done a roleplay of sorts—a sculpture—of a typical dependent family, Alan had volunteered to play the son of a dependent father. Several members of their group, having selected roles they wished to play, arranged themselves, with the help of the counselors, into the positions that would *show* family relationships, attitudes, and feelings. But they didn't talk; instead they sculpted themselves.

The woman playing the wife, feeling downtrodden and burdened, knelt on the floor, stretching out one arm with an accusing finger aimed at her husband, who was standing on a chair looking down at her with his fists clenched menacingly. The wife's other arm and accusing finger were pointed toward a teenage girl, the rebellious child, who stood on a chair apart from Dad with her fists clenched and directed toward both Mom and Dad. Alan stood next to the mother with his back toward her. He had one hand raised—palm out—at the father and the other—palm out—at the rebellious sister, as if warding off both. Another child sat apart from the whole group, her back toward them all. Two others were in various other accusing, protective positions; and they then stayed in that arrangement for several minutes, allowing the rest of the group a chance to *see* a typical chemically dependent family present itself, while the participants had a chance to experience what their position felt like in that family.

Susan felt the mid-morning lecture on the survival roles that are often developed in chemically dependent families fit her family altogether too well, and, while she was not a participant in the sculpture, she says, "Just looking at it really threw me. Alan started to cry almost as soon as he stood in his position. I felt so sorry for him . . . and so guilty. I had never realized how much I had counted on him to help me until I actually saw him in that *assistant* position next to the mother. I was also shocked to see that he had his back toward her as if he rejected her, while coming to her defense. I don't know *how* I felt about the fact that he was standing while she was kneeling, as if he felt stronger or superior to her. But I was most shocked to see that his pain was as great as mine. I guess I thought I had protected my kids more than I really had. Afterward when I tried to hug Alan, he pushed me away. That hurt—really hurt. He was angry with *me*, and I had tried so hard to make everything right.

"After lunch they had a game—a game! They had games all week. They were very big on games and I hated them in the beginning. I thought they were a waste of time. That first game had something to do with trust, or at least I think it did. We were supposed to close our eyes while standing, one at a time, and allow ourselves to fall backward and be caught by others. Some of them could do it, but I sure couldn't—which probably made some kind of statement on my willingness to trust."

Later one of the counselors described the group process so that everyone would know what was expected in group throughout the rest of the week. Afterward, to practice what they had learned, they were divided into three groups: the *fact* group, *opinion* group, and *feeling* group. Susan landed in the *feeling* group and when given the task to share a simple example of the *feeling* of love, Susan said, "I love honesty," only to hear from others that she had stated a value, a judgment (opinion), rather than *sharing* love.

She says, "My only comfort was that I was not alone; each of us in the feeling group had trouble. Actually it was very helpful for me to see that I had given out a lot of judgments in the past when I really believed I was sharing my feelings. But I still didn't like the family treatment as I saw it unfold."

After dinner the children were given an assignment to write an *open letter* to each of their parents, saying *whatever* they wanted their parents to know, but had never been able to say before. All the others were to prepare a resentment list, itemizing all the things they could think of that they resented in their lives, both as children and as adults. The letters and lists were then to be shared the next day in groups where the family members would be separated from each other. Each group, of course, was committed to confidentiality, to keeping everything that was said in group *in* the group. Thus, each person would have a safe place to talk about things that he might not be able to say directly to the persons involved.

Dear Mom,

I hate it when you fight with Dad. PLEASE DONT
SCREAM. I HATE the screams. Do you know I sit
in my closet? Did you ever sit in a closet? Do you
know that THE SCREAMS GET IN THE CLOSET.
Please dont brag about my grades. I dont like it
when you brag about me. DONT EVER BRAG
ABOUT ALAN. I dont want to help you fix prob-
lems. DONT MAKE ME HATE DAD. I LOVE MY
DAD. DONT MAKE DAD DRINK. DONT MAKE
DAD DIE

Alan

Dear Daddy,

Why did you throw my trophy? I won my trophy for
YOU. You scare me when you are drunk. *PLEASE
DONT DRINK ANYMORE.* PLEASE DONT DIE
DADDY. DONT DIE. I am scared.

Your obedient son,
Alan

There were seven persons in Alan's group, including two
children close to his age and one boy several years older. Alan
had had a terrible time the evening before. He had so much to
write to both parents, but a great *need* not to write anything at
all. Then he wrote exactly what he had to say most of all. He
could hardly believe it in group when the other kids talked
about not wanting to write their letters and when he heard
that their letters said some of the same things he wrote, and
some things he had not written, but had thought about.

As they read their letters, several members of the group began to cry. It felt good to Alan to be held closely by the older
boy as he read his letters. A couple of the adults followed the
children's example, sharing their pain, as they told of their resentments. Two claimed not to have any resentments but were
not believed by the others.

Alan felt a whole lot better after group, as if a large burden had been lifted from his shoulders. Carrying all his fears, all his pain, inside for so long had taken so much energy! Now he felt freed of that burden, but something else happened as well. He could see that they *all* had suffered, young and old alike, just like he had suffered. And he could see that they *all* had done everything they could to make the alcoholic stop drinking and that they *all* had failed, just like he had failed. *He didn't feel like a failure any longer! He didn't feel alone any longer!* After group he hugged his mom.

Susan also felt much better after her group. Like Alan, she had taken a risk and shared her pain as she told of her resentments. Also like Alan, she had gained insight into the pain of others and had left a lot of her pain behind. Both she and Alan began to feel close to the other families.

She even enjoyed the game they all played before lunch— one that most of them enjoyed and played several times during the rest of the week—the Knot Game, where they all got into different kinds of positions, held hands, and then tried to get themselves untangled from this great knot without letting go of each other's hands. "The whole thing was silly, but it gave us a wonderful chance to see our 'tangled' relationships, our own 'knots,' and how none of us was truly free. It also felt good to laugh."

After lunch, they returned to their individual chemical histories and gave feedback in the cases that presented problems. Rather than lecturing or expressing her anger to Alan, as she surely would have done the day before, Susan was able to tell Alan how much she loved him and how scared she was about his chemical use. He, in turn, was able to tell her he had used pot and alcohol because he was angry and afraid, but that now he didn't feel that way any longer. They hugged each other, not needing to say anything more.

Both the co-dependents and the staff thought one of the men, the father of a chemically dependent son then in treatment, had a serious drinking problem. His wife and daughter were able to add to his chemical history; the day before they would have maintained his imposed *conspiracy of silence.* At everyone's suggestion, he transferred out of family treatment and into treatment for chemical dependency.

Next they attended a lecture on the features of functional and dysfunctional families. Once again, Susan and Alan could see how disturbed they had become as a family unit, *where no one nurtured and no one blossomed.* As they listened they began to see what they wanted to change.

The rest of that day, as well as much of their time on following days, was spent in group work, where sculpting was often used to help individuals connect emotionally with conflicts, particularly relational conflicts, that became evident in the treatment environment or that appeared in the detailed questionnaires they had submitted prior to admission.

According to Susan, "The nice thing about sculpting was that it not only let us see the messes in our lives, it also helped us put things together the way we wanted them to be. In one of my sculptures, I wanted to do some more work on my relationship with Alan, so I took him out of the assistant role that he had put himself in the first day and placed him on the chair alongside me. Then I crossed his ankles, brought his knees up into the lotus position, and had him sit with his feet up on the chair; something the old *serious* Alan would *never* have done. Then I got real close and put one arm around his shoulders, my other hand on one of his knees, and I looked at him and smiled. Oh! I also put a smile on his face."

When the sculpture was over, after they had stayed in those positions for a few moments, Susan talked about how the sculpture showed Alan that she didn't need an assistant any longer, and that he didn't have to be so grown-up and perfect; she liked and loved him as a child. She said she felt good in that sculptured relationship with Alan, and several of the other patients spoke of how it felt good as they watched. Alan said he wanted to *show* how it felt to him by doing his own sculpture.

"You know what he did?" Susan asked, "I'll never forget it as long as I live. He made the *same* sculpture, except he put me into the same lotus position as he was in. Then he put one hand on my knee, and with his other hand *he held onto my arm* that he had placed around his shoulder. Then, he had us both smile, but I burst into tears I was so happy—*so happy he wanted me close* and we hugged each other for a long, long time." Susan said she was moved to hear Alan say that his sculpture *also* meant she didn't have to be serious and proper all the time either. They both could have fun.

And so it went for the rest of the week, lectures here and there, but mostly group work, games, and assignments of various kinds each evening.

By Thursday, most of the activities concerned change—changes made and changes needed. Each person developed his own short- and long-term goals and roleplayed or sculpted some of the actions he would take to meet his goals. Both Susan and Alan, among other things, included further assistance as part of their planning. For Alan, this decision represented a major change; prior to admission he had resisted seeing me and refused to become involved in the chemical awareness program in his school. Now he made a commitment to that program, to Alateen, and to family work with me. Both Susan and Alan also made very specific plans to add fun and silliness to their lives. Alan said he was going to start the whole thing off by getting on the plane the next day with a great big two-scoop ice cream cone covered with sprinkles!

Early on their last day, prior to their group, Susan and Alan met with Jeff for the first time since their intervention. They were nervous, but none of them wanted a counselor present. None felt the need for help or a neutral person to act as a buffer. Susan and Alan, of course, were aware of the changes they each had made, but were not sure of Jeff's; and, Jeff, sure of his own, was not sure of theirs. When they met, they felt in tune; far calmer, far more comfortable, far closer than they had ever been before.

Later they went back to their respective sites to complete their treatment experience. Like Jeff, Susan and Alan had become very close to their fellow patients and now had to say good-bye. They, too, received a medallion for the successful completion of their treatment; but their good-bye ceremony was a little different. All the members of the family week program, counselors included, taped a poster-size sheet of paper onto their backs, and then they all scurried about writing messages to each other on the sheets of paper, putting in words their feelings about the other person, giving each other something very special to take home from each of them, and having *fun* in the process. Amidst hugs and tears, they then said good-bye.

That afternoon, if you had been at the airport, you would have seen a man, a woman, and a child, arms linked and laughing, licking two-scoop ice cream cones covered with sprinkles.

16

Co-Dependency Treatment

Family members entering treatment perceive that they have one basic task: to find out enough about the illness to be able to help the chemically dependent person stay off alcohol and/or drugs.

Even Susan and Alan, who had learned so much about chemical dependency and their own maladaptive reactions, were intent upon concentrating on Jeff's illness. While they had made significant changes, no one suffering from this illness gets well within weeks; thus Susan and Alan, like other concerned persons entering treatment, were to a large extent still trapped in the belief that if Jeff got well, they'd be well or, conversely, if he didn't get well, they couldn't be well.

As recently as ten years ago, family treatment specific to chemical dependency (other than Al-Anon and Alateen) meant working with the spouse rather than the whole family and was designed primarily to help the spouse help the dependent. Thus, in years past, the treatment center's perceived task was the same as the family's; in turn, both the chemically dependent person and the co-dependents were shortchanged, to say the least.

While increased success in the treatment of chemically dependent persons was being achieved, the needs of the co-dependents were ignored. Without treatment specific to their maladaptations, co-dependents tend to want life to return to the way it used to be before chemicals became a problem. Recovering chemically dependent persons, on the other hand, fear returning to that point; for them that's where it all started, and they feel a great need, a survival need, in fact, to move on to new modes of functioning.

Only in the past decade have we looked more specifically at how the trauma of living with a dependent affects others, and today we know the maladaptive responses of family members do not go away without treatment. They are long-lasting and not only survive the dependent's recovery, but are passed on to succeeding generations as well. Thus, today most chemical dependency treatment centers are designed to help co-dependents recognize and modify their maladaptive responses to chemical dependency.

Most commonly, both centers—those treating chemically dependent persons and co-dependents—are separate divisions with separate staffs located within the same complex. Generally, family treatment is residential and between five and seven days' duration. But because family treatment is relatively new, it does not contain the same degree of uniformity as does the treatment of chemically dependent persons, and often some family members are cheated, such as former spouses and adult children of alcoholics, especially if the dependent is no longer alive or involved with the family. While most dependents will experience the same treatment format as Jeff, the co-dependents who do receive treatment may well follow formats different from the one Susan and Alan experienced. In some centers, co-dependents join the chemically dependent person's therapy group once each day or two or three times during their stay. Other centers do not treat the co-dependents at the same time the chemically dependent person is in treatment. Still others do not have the co-dependents join the dependent's therapy group, but have them connect with the dependent on other occasions or just prior to discharge.

Whatever the format, each year chemical dependency treatment centers seem to be increasing their services for family members and are becoming more adept at keeping the focus on the illness of the co-dependents rather than the dependent. Thus, by and large, treatment centers today assume it is their task to provide the atmosphere and guidance that allows the co-dependent to become concerned enough about his illness to develop a way of life that works.

Like the chemically dependent person, family members suffer a drastic loss in self-esteem, feeling about as worthy as gnats. Each is as full of feelings of guilt, shame, inadequacy, self-pity and resentment as the dependent. Having learned well the lessons taught by society's negative view of chemical dependency as well as their own repeated failures in facing the tyranny, the family members are compelled to use defenses repeatedly and rigidly that bring some comfort but destroy their ability to function fully and to evaluate themselves accurately. Thus, the family treatment atmosphere, like the chemical dependency treatment atmosphere, is composed of concern, care, confrontation, honesty, and acceptance. This atmosphere is once again created by cheerful, clean, and comfortable surroundings; a high degree of professionalism among a multidisciplined staff who extend themselves emotionally to families; sophisticated therapeutic techniques; as well as less tangible transcendental concepts.

The atmosphere of family treatment makes a judgment, stating first that adapting to illness is maladaptive, and second that the maladaptive response itself reflects a primary illness. In other words, the family members, like the dependent, have developed a primary illness in response to forces beyond their knowledge and control. Thus, the therapeutic atmosphere, while maintaining the attitude that illness does not diminish one's inherent value as a worthy human being, does caringly, but adamantly, refuse to focus on any illness other than the family member's primary illness.

Susan and Alan, of course, encountered this atmosphere within the first moments of their admission to family treatment. None of the staff knew how Jeff was doing, or if they did, they did not share their knowledge with Susan and Alan. Instead, they conveyed the message that Jeff's recovery was not essential to Susan's and Alan's recovery. Everything the staff did and said was designed to lead Susan's and Alan's focus away from Jeff onto themselves, knowing their ability to grow emotionally and to improve their functioning was dependent upon them, not Jeff.

The sadism of the tyranny of chemical dependency has been likened to that suffered by inmates of concentration camps, because nowhere else does such consistent, long-term personal cruelty exist. Consequently, the atmosphere of family treatment is respectful of the defenses used by family members, despite the fact that their use of those defenses causes their dysfunction. First, last, and always the therapeutic atmosphere acknowledges that each individual in the family is a *survivor* and that the maladaptive responses have helped him or her survive; without defenses co-dependents could not have survived.

The therapeutic atmosphere validates the person's inherent survival strengths and in no way trivializes the traumatic experiences. Instead, it acknowledges the impact of those experiences upon the person's integrity while it provides the nourishment, understanding, and acceptance survivors need.

The therapeutic atmosphere is also one of hope. Dysfunction is addressed as a means of illuminating what one might wish to change, the inherent message being that change is not only possible, but in fact expected. In most centers, several of the staff are themselves recovered members of chemically dependent families and thus demonstrate proof that more rewarding ways of life are possible.

I don't know of anyone in his right mind who would conduct a treatment program for thirty or so dependents, all entering treatment at the same time and all solidly entrenched in their denial systems. Instead, dependents are phased into ongoing programs where a good portion of the other chemically dependent patients have moved out of their denial systems and into early recovery, and thus can assist with the newer patients. I can't think of anything worse than managing a treatment unit, giving a lecture, or facilitating group therapy where every participant thinks he shouldn't be there, has all the answers, believes he knows more than the staff, has no problems, is better than others, wants instant gratification, demands perfection, is full of blame, hurtful moral judgments and criticism, and defends himself with anger. No way! Dependents quickly ally their defenses with similar defenses in others. If all were locked into their similar denial systems at the same time, it is very likely that the treatment staff would be demolished before treatment could begin. Yet family treatment programs begin with thirty or so co-dependents all starting treatment at the same time, all of whom are more or less locked into systems of denial.

One often hears that family members and the chemically dependent person suffer the same illness. It's true there are many similarities. Members of the family are often as preoccupied with the dependent as the dependent is with chemicals. Both families and chemically dependent persons suffer great losses of self-esteem and bury their feelings of inadequacy, guilt, shame, fear, hurt, anger and self-pity behind defensive walls. Both are out of touch with the true nature of their illnesses; the denial systems resulting from their defenses lead them to believe they are okay or soon would be if the other were not sick. Both are locked into compelled, reactive thinking and behavior. Nevertheless, their illnesses are not the same; as their defenses differ, so do their illnesses.

Generally family members do not progress as far down the hierarchy of defenses as do chemically dependent persons; thus, they suffer less severe pathology. While family members have defensive walls, their walls seem constructed of plywood, easy to penetrate, while chemically dependent persons construct defensive walls of reinforced concrete, difficult to knock down. When it comes to perceiving their condition, it's as if family members have blurred vision and impaired hearing, while chemically dependent persons seem blind and deaf.

The neurotic and mature defenses used by most family members respond to reason more readily than the primitive and immature defenses used by dependents. Family members, closer to their pain, are more easily motivated for personal change; chemically dependent persons, further removed from both reality and their pain, tend to be motivated only for change in others. Family members are other-absorbed; dependents are self-absorbed. Family members tend to be indecisive; dependents tend to make quick, impulsive decisions. Family members are self-blaming; dependents are other-blaming.

A primary task of treatment of both chemically dependent persons and their families is to penetrate the denial systems. In co-dependents the denial system is, in essence, a false belief—an illusion that somehow, some way, some day they are going to strike upon the magic formula that will permit them to get the dependent well, so their problems will be solved. It is only an exposure of the falsity of this belief that allows co-dependents to become concerned enough about their own illness to develop a more fruitful way of life.

One of the first things that happens in virtually all the centers is that co-dependents are asked to examine their own chemical use with the help of the staff. It is not at all unusual for a spouse, parent, or child to medicate him- or herself in order to avoid the pain of living in a chemically dependent family, or to use chemicals in rebellion or as a means of showing the dependent how to use properly, or to be chemically dependent as well. Because family members automatically compare their use to the grossly harmful use of the chemically dependent person with whom they are involved, their own chemical use will often appear harmless to them, even when it isn't. Thus, without assistance, family members are unable to evaluate their own use accurately. Also, because treatment requires some clear thinking and feeling, both of which are impeded by chemical use, virtually all centers require family members to remain chemically free during their stay.

Recently, at the beginning of a newly formed young people's Children of Alcoholics group, I asked if all were remaining chemically free. Two of the eight teenagers, none of whom had received residential co-dependency treatment, said they had never used and had no intention of using. The remaining six members all looked at me as if surprised, even though their chemical use and our requirement of remaining chemically free had been thoroughly covered with each in advance of joining the group. Their responses made me realize how right we are to insist upon abstinence.

One said, "You're kidding!" Another, a fifteen-year-old, said, "I'll look pretty silly in a bar ordering Perrier." Another asked, "If I can't commit suicide and I can't get stoned, what can I do?" Another said, "My dad's always drunk, my boyfriend left me, my mom's a mess, and you think I'm giving up speed? Forget it!" And she was quickly seconded by the remaining two users.

All, in comparing their use to that of their addicted parent, were convinced that they would never become like their addicted parent and that their use was insignificant. Needless to say, this session went well beyond our scheduled one and a half hours, and it was only after several weeks of remaining chemically free that each was able to see how meaningful a role chemicals had played in their lives. Their treatment, of course, could not really begin until this issue had been addressed.

Fortunately, unless addicted, family members are close to their pain and desirous of change so they quite readily see the reasonableness of remaining chemically free during their treatment. As a result, their need for abstinence is a hurdle they usually quickly overcome; if not, they are then evaluated for chemical dependency.

Residential co-dependency treatment is of short duration compared to the treatment of chemically dependent persons. To speed the treatment process and because co-dependents are capable of operating on a feeling level, their treatment usually contains a large number of affective (experiential) components. While lectures and reading assignments are given, a major part of each treatment day is spent in large groups for various kinds of roleplays and small groups for the sharing of feelings and mirroring or seeing oneself through the feedback of others.

As with Susan and Alan, the first days in treatment are devoted mostly to helping families see and feel what is. As none of us can change until we first see what it is about ourselves we wish to change, co-dependents are helped to investigate and clearly perceive their own specific maladaptive responses as well as the dysfunctional interaction of the family as a unit or system.

Initially, though they're relatively close to the surface, most co-dependents will have difficulty in expressing their feelings. Instead, they tend to ask questions, pass judgments, give opinions and advice, or they describe events. Because co-dependents tend to be riddled with indecisiveness and feel optionless—without any means of behavior other than the painful, compelled reactions they've learned so well and have used so long—many feel a great need for direction and, in fact, respond well to the direction inherent in both their small and large groups, where they are shown all sorts of options and are encouraged and supported in attempts at new behavior.

One young woman in Susan's feeling group described a scene with her fiancé, then in treatment for chemical dependency, when he complained about her sarcasm, and she asked the group, "What else could I have said?" Rather than attempting to solve her problem by giving advice, another member of the group asked what she was feeling when she was being sarcastic, and she replied, "Scared, I guess. You mean I could have told him how I was feeling? Oh wow! I never thought of that. You mean tell him the truth? Yecch!" And she thus received guidance, scary perhaps, but guidance nevertheless.

A young husband of a dependent, who was also the son of an alcoholic, seemed stuck in the caretaker role he had filled for much of his life. Susan reported that he was placed standing in the center of all the people in his life who perpetually made demands upon him. These people, played by Susan and other co-dependents, circled around him, drawing closer to him as they shouted their demands. He, of course, felt increasingly threatened as they drew nearer. When the counselor standing next to him asked if he liked the position he was in, he said no. She then asked if he wanted to get out of that position, and he said yes, but didn't move. She asked again if he liked his position and he again said no; this time the counselor suggested he walk away from the people circling about him, which he did. Later he told Susan that before the roving sculpture, he had never realized he had a choice; that he, in fact, did not have to be a caretaker.

Co-dependency treatment, modeled after both the Al-Anon program and behavioral science, rather than delving into the whys, pays attention to the existing reality of what is and what can be. Thus, while the first treatment days are centered on dysfunction, co-dependents are also shown ways out of that dysfunction from the onset of treatment. And, because family members are responsible for changing themselves, as are chemically dependent persons, their role in treatment is active, and counselors are guides, rather than fixers.

The roleplays, games, and assignments given during the early part of family week are designed to help family members first to see and then to begin to resolve some of their conflicted issues. For example, as I've said, co-dependents are always used and abused by the chemically dependent person, and part of their early recovery requires facing and sharing some of their associated feelings. Susan's first assignment to write and share her resentments was, of course, designed to help her get more of these feelings into the open. Later, in a sculpting roleplay, she was able to address and alter the unhealthy caretaker alliance she had unwittingly established with Alan.

While it is valuable for increased insight and emotional growth to share painful feelings, it is not always necessary, or even desirable, to share those feelings with the involved person. Some residential co-dependency treatment centers believe it works best if the co-dependents share their pain with those not emotionally involved, for then the feelings can be shared more fully while the involved person is spared needless hurt. Consequently, during their residential treatment, Susan and Alan resolved many of their painful feelings with their peers and were each more comfortable emotionally when they finally met with Jeff.

In other centers, co-dependents are encouraged to share some of their pain attached to the dependent's chemical use with the dependent during his afternoon (usually) group therapy session. He, in turn, shares his pain associated with the co-dependents' behavior with the co-dependents. Throughout, special care is paid to sharing the feelings beneath anger, rather than sharing the anger itself. With this method, as with the method used in Susan's center, the co-dependents and the dependent come to a new and more comfortable emotional balance.

Is one method better than another? Frankly, I don't know. Both prove to be rewarding for the short term, while neither proves lasting without continued treatment once the participants return home. No matter what the method of sharing and, thereby the resolution of some of the painful feelings, I prefer the residential family treatment programs where co-dependents concentrate mostly on themselves, which very frankly means spending *far* more time with their peers in their own therapy than with the dependent in joint therapy. As you'll see when we discuss early and long-term recovery, sustained nurturing interactions with members of the chemically dependent family are about the *last* thing to occur. Intimacy with others depends first upon becoming intimate with oneself; thus I favor and recommend the treatment programs that concentrate on increased personal insight rather than a restoration of healthy familial relationships, which at best can only be superficial at the beginning of treatment.

One of the issues that keeps popping up time and time again in the early days of residential co-dependency treatment has to do with fixing others. It is a result of the co-dependents' great sense of powerlessness and belief in a magic formula for curing the dependent and all their problems. People who feel powerless tend to look for magic formulas, and they tend to manipulate others. Another issue always present at the start of treatment has to do with the co-dependents' absorption with what others are thinking, feeling, and doing; that they gear themselves to others rather than themselves. Consequently, most of the early group work addresses the underlying pain associated with powerlessness and not feeling whole.

In Susan's peer group, whenever anyone cried, Susan jumped up, gave the person tissues and on one occasion even wiped away the tears. "Boy did they call me on that, and then for two days, every time anyone cried, they'd look at me and ask how I was feeling. Horrible! That's how I was feeling. I couldn't stand their pain. I wanted it to go away. I soon found out, of course, that my fixing of others was just a way to avoid my own pain. By my second night, I just couldn't run from it anymore. I had gotten a lot of my pain with Jeff out here with you, but the pain of my dad's alcoholism came charging forth and I cried throughout group and half the night. But somehow sticking with it and not running from it made me feel a whole lot better."

Susan had also learned a great deal about letting go, about not being Jeff's fixer, before entering family treatment, but says she really didn't grasp it entirely until she found herself in the Knot Game. "We all struggled to get untangled, but, of course, we couldn't as long as we kept clinging to each other. God! That was like a blow in the stomach. Suddenly, I knew I had to let go—really let go—not only of fixing Jeff, but of fixing anyone other than myself. For the first time I really saw that I had to be a separate person and not an extension of Jeff."

By her third day Susan and most of the other family members accepted that they had to look at themselves and take care of themselves before they could do anything for anyone else. They were then ready to move on to the remaining treatment task—developing a way of life that works.

The treatment format of occasional lectures, but mostly large and small group work, continues throughout the remainder of treatment, but now the content switches from what is to what can be and what will be, in other words, to changes made and changes still to be made. Initially, family members are asked what they don't like about their lives; now they are asked to consider their needs and wants, and what they are willing to do to get them fulfilled.

As we saw, Alan did not want to be Susan's assistant. The burden of helping her was too heavy, and much too painful. But Alan also had to think about what he wanted instead. He was eleven, but acting like a grown-up. His group asked him if that was what he really wanted to be, and he said no but then admitted there were some payoffs to acting like an adult. With guidance, he was able to look at more of the pain behind the pressures, many of which were self-imposed, of being what he wasn't, and only then could he share his fears of failure and deep sense of inadequacy. Finally, he was asked to write out a permission prescription for himself in which, among other things, he was to allow himself to fail at something at least once a week and to do at least one silly, but fun, thing every day for the next three months.

In essence, having chosen to be a kid, Alan was asked to give himself permission to be a kid—not perfect, just an okay kid—which he did. Had you been at the airport that day to see Alan licking away at his two-scoop, sprinkle-covered ice cream cone, you would have felt you were seeing a miracle. The old Alan would have had a dixie cup, and been properly seated with napkin and spoon.

Susan came to see that in the past she had attempted to have her needs met by pleasing others. In effect, she posed impossible tasks for others while she set herself up for perpetual disappointment. During family week she had a lot of trouble recognizing her needs and found it virtually impossible to express them directly once she did recognize them. For example, it was only with much help that she was finally able to tell members of her group that she wanted some alone time. In the beginning, when they asked her to join them for walks, or coffee, or whatever, she replied, "Do you think we have time?" or "I don't think the coffee's made yet." By the end of the week, she was finally able to say, "No, thanks anyway. I want to be by myself for a while."

So, Susan was asked to draw up a list of ten specific needs or wants, as well as her specific plans for openly expressing and meeting her needs and wants. She was encouraged to re-evaluate her list weekly and to keep a record of her accomplishments as well as the areas requiring further work.

Because family members are used to pain, not fun, games are often played right up to the very last moment of treatment. The purpose of the games, of course, is twofold: to increase insight into one's condition and also for the pure fun of it all. Both Susan and Alan will surely treasure their final game—perhaps for years to come—of everyone writing messages to each other on the large sheets of paper attached to their backs. The message Susan liked best was that several people said she was a "great risk-taker"; she had felt like such a nebbish for so long. Alan felt good when someone wrote, "You're a silly kid—and I love you a whole lot."

17

Out
of
Illness

Early recovery is often exciting, but rarely easy.

Getting well requires change, and change of any kind is stressful. Everyone in the chemically dependent family will feel a strong pull to return to former ways. The family system will also resist change; it, too, will exert a strong pull to return to its former equilibrium. It won't matter that the past was destructive, supportive of illness rather than wellness. What will matter is that the past is *known* and therefore *predictable*, albeit destructive. The pull to return to the known will be powerful for each individual and for the family itself.

Let's look at the chemically dependent family system for a moment. While in the field of chemical dependency individuals are addressed before the family, the forces of the family system can prevent sustained individual growth, and its rules perpetuate individual illness.

Every family is a system, something larger than the sum of its individual members. Sharon Wegscheider, in her book, *An-*

other Chance, likens the family to a mobile, with interdependent parts flexibly balanced. If one part moves, the entire mobile moves. It now has an energy of its own, causing movement in all its parts, and its energy will be used to restore balance, the same balance it once had.

In the beginning of this book I listed three rules set by the chemically dependent person as he progresses into his illness—*he's the most important person in the family; he's always right;* and *his chemical use is not his primary problem*—which represent a change in one member of the family causing, in turn, a jarring of the entire family system. Then every member of the family jumps around following the energy of the system, which is aimed toward equilibrium. But the dependent's change is too great; the family mobile cannot restore its former balance; instead it forces change upon its individual parts, resulting in a new balance, a new equilibrium way out of kilter, but an equilibrium nevertheless. Now whenever shifts occur in any family member, the system's energy will be directed toward restoring the new, out-of-kilter equilibrium.

The changes forced upon every member of the family, including the dependent, by the system's demand for equilibrium are governed by a new group of family rules, closely related to the dependent's original three—*don't rock the boat; don't talk about problems; don't feel, don't be selfish,* and *don't play.* Only by following these new family rules can equilibrium be restored to the family system. But, by following these rules, the individuals become increasingly maladaptive and the family system becomes increasingly dysfunctional. And, not long after following these rules, the energies of both the individuals and the family system become directed toward maintaining the status quo, albeit maladaptive and dysfunctional. Both the individuals and the system develop a momentum toward illness; both will resist change.

In the past fifteen years of working with chemically dependent persons and their families, if I've learned nothing else, I've learned that human beings have an enormous capacity for change. Dependents and co-dependents change: they recover.

They rise above the energies within themselves and within their family systems, which are directed toward illness and resistant to change. Their courage, strength, and wisdom boggle the mind.

To begin her recovery and to motivate the dependent to seek help, the co-dependent makes a *big* change. She breaks the dependent's three rules that started her craziness. She recognizes that she can no longer tolerate his illness, and has a need for change. She puts her need for change over his demands, she sees that he's not right at all, and that his primary problem is his addiction. Then, while helping herself, she, most times, is also able to help him. But she makes further changes as well; *enormous* changes. To continue her recovery, she breaks the family rules that have perpetuated her maladaptive response.

To become self-motivated, the dependent also makes a *big* change. He breaks his own rules. He sees that he's not God, and, in fact, is crazy, albeit a unique form of crazy, and chemical dependency is his primary problem. But he makes further changes as well—*enormous* changes. To continue his recovery, he breaks the same family rules governing his wife that have perpetuated his maladaptive response.

What happens if only one of these persons continues the voyage to recovery? All hell breaks loose, that's what happens. The energies of both the other person and the family system will be directed toward maintaining the status quo. The maladaptive response of the person left behind, the one not on the voyage to health, will become exaggerated and the family rules, as they are broken, will become more rigidly enforced. The nonrecovering person and the system's momentum toward illness will increase, not decrease. If either the dependent or the co-dependent suffers a relapse, it is often because he or she could find little space for recovery and considerable resistance against it within the family.

More than anything in the world the dependent and the co-dependent truly do want the other to change but, unless they are working on their own recovery, they will try to prevent that change from causing any change in themselves or their family, which is an impossible task. *Change in one demands change in the other.* Chemical dependency is a family affair, in both illness and wellness. Recovery for one does not create recovery for the other. Recovery for each person is dependent upon each person addressing his or her own maladaptive behavior pattern. Recovery for the family is dependent upon the return to health by each member, so the former dysfunctional system can be replaced by one that supports health.

The first order of business in early recovery is to seek help, to not treat this illness yourself. If you have not already done so, join Al-Anon or Parents Anonymous and seek professional counseling specific to chemical dependency, if it is available in your community. You do not treat any other major illness by yourself, I trust; and you shouldn't treat this one either.

As you've no doubt gathered, I don't care at all *why* people seek help, I only care that they do. But I'm dealing with an illness for which the treatment is so powerful and so attractive that it reaches people even if they don't want to be reached. I worked for a number of years as a psychiatric nurse in charge of the male admissions unit at the New York State Psychiatric Institute at the Columbia-Presbyterian Medical Center in New York City, and I've observed conventional psychiatric treatment from near and far since. I've got news for you. The power and appeal of conventional psychiatric treatment, even very good psychiatric treatment, just does not compare to the power and appeal of chemical dependency treatment in all its forms—the self-help groups, in- and out-patient primary care, and recovery support counseling (sometimes called aftercare or growth groups). Consequently, aware of the unique motivating nature of chemical dependency treatment and the need for involving each individual in the family in treatment, I go to any lengths to secure their compliance, be they dependent or co-dependent.

Now there's no way anyone in his right mind could or should label Jim and Virginia "sick." They, like most persons we work with in the field of chemical dependency, suffer a maladaptive pattern of thinking, feeling, and acting that overlies a solid core of mental/emotional health. I believe dependents and co-dependents respond so well to treatment and get so well because underneath their trauma and defensive maladaptation to that trauma, they are healthy, which, in all fairness to conventional psychiatric treatment, plays a role in allowing chemical dependency treatment to have its unique power and appeal—with basic health one can do more.

Virginia was in favor of joining Al-Anon and one of our recovery support groups; there were things about herself she wished to change. However, she did not wish to risk Jim's displeasure; therefore she based her decision upon entering treatment upon Jim's decision. Jim resisted the idea of treatment; there was nothing about himself he wished to change, nor did he feel there was any reason for Virginia to change. Lynn, Carla, and Margaret were all in treatment. In his mind his problems were solved. I knew they were about to begin.

There are several issues that are addressed in early recovery; one of them, as I mentioned, is the breaking of the family's dysfunctional rules. In all likelihood, Margaret, no longer living with Jim's nuclear family, could break her own family rules without causing significant disruption to Jim and Virginia. But what about their daughters, deeply ensconced in their nuclear family? When those two kids started breaking the dysfunctional family rules, all hell really would break loose. Without personal change, Jim and Virginia risked increased personal maladaptations and greater family chaos. And without their personal change, their daughters faced a higher risk of relapse.

Don't rock the boat is the guardian of all the other family rules. In healthy families, the guardian rule is, *It's okay to be different, to change and grow; your family's behind you all the way.* In Jim's family, as well as Susan's, as well as all chemically dependent families to one degree or another, *don't rock the boat* is the overriding family rule, which requires the sacrifice of individuality in order to maintain family harmony and imposes punishment if the rule is broken.

All the members of Jim's family repeatedly sacrificed their

own rational self-interests in favor of family peace. Look at the price Virginia paid: contentment in heaven, if ever. We know the price Lynn and Carla paid, but how about Jim? Look at his enormous control of self and others. It may have hidden his inner conflicts from others, but not from himself. All that control was not creating serenity for Jim, not by a long shot.

Conflicts often occur between individual needs and the system's needs. To get well Lynn and Carla would frequently have to *rock the boat,* to put their own needs before the system's needs; otherwise they were going to stay ill. One hopes they would not be meeting their own needs at the personal expense of others, but at times they surely would be doing it at the expense of family harmony. Even if Jim understood *in theory* why it was necessary for the girls to disrupt family peace from time to time, do you think he'd allow it? Of course not. He was too motivated by forces from within, which were beyond intellect. He'd try to go along with their changes, but he'd seethe inside and sooner or later he'd respond punitively. And so would Virginia, all in the name of family peace.

To get well, Lynn and Carla were also going to have to *talk about problems*—openly and without the use of messengers. Lynn had already broken this rule, and she paid a price. On several occasions she told both Virginia and Jim some of the things she knew about Carla's chemical use. On each occasion, they ignored what she said and put her down for maligning her sister. Lynn, in turn, felt guilty, like she'd done something wrong, so she stopped talking about Carla's chemical problems. Later, in a session with me, Jim and Virginia criticized Lynn for not telling them what she knew. Unless Jim and Virginia changed, how could they avoid repeating this repressive pattern in the future?

A problem Carla faced early in her recovery evolved around playing tennis with her dad. Both were excellent players, but Carla told her recovery support group that she couldn't stand playing with her father. "I like to relax and enjoy the game, but he won't let me. He plays for blood. For him tennis is work, and he gets angry if I don't take it as seriously as he does."

Carla had been handling this problem indirectly, by giving all kinds of "phony" excuses for not being able to play, "but I don't like myself when I do that." With the help of her group, she roleplayed various options for stating her problem openly without criticizing her dad. But Jim responded angrily, telling Carla she would never get anyplace in life with her "frivolous" attitude. Then Carla was hurt and walked out of the room, banging the door behind her. This annoyed Jim more, so he grounded her; and Carla said she felt like smoking pot "just to show him."

When the *don't talk about problems* rule is strong in a family, messengers are used. Jim repeatedly asked Virginia to speak to his mother about her drinking. Virginia often asked Lynn to tell Jim about Carla's most recent crisis—"He gets disgusted with me, but he'll listen to you." Carla often asked both Lynn and Virginia to "get Dad off my back." Lynn regularly appealed to Virginia to solicit her father's approval of her. The problems associated with using messengers are great. Unhealthy alliances are often established between various family members, creating partnerships against others. The messages, often loaded with hidden meaning, always come out garbled and increase, rather than decrease, family chaos. At the same time, the messengers become victims, caught between people who are unable to address their own problems openly. Besides assuming the burdens of others, they run the risk of rejection on either side; damned if they do and damned if they don't. The pain of being a messenger can be unbearable. To get well, Lynn and Carla would have to stop being and using messengers, which would actually increase their parents' need for messengers. In turn, Jim and Virginia might unknowingly ally themselves against their daughters.

Another ironclad rule in virtually all chemically dependent families is *don't feel*. At first, every time I asked anyone in Jim's family how he or she felt, the person gave an opinion. They devalued feelings so much they each seemed to shut down and not feel. Yet, Jim had ulcers; Virginia suffered migraines and insomnia; Lynn was depressed and Carla hurt and both had attempted to medicate their pain; chemicals worked for one for a while but not for the other; one became addicted, one did not; but both used chemicals originally to alleviate emotional distress. Everyone had feelings in the family, but no one was allowed to *experience* those feelings. To get well, to know themselves, Carla and Lynn would have to experience their feelings. What would that do to Jim and Virginia, both deathly afraid of *feeling* feelings?

Virginia and Jim each came from a childhood in which play was not allowed. Virginia's family was overly involved with our culture's work ethic; her parents valued productivity over just about everything else. Jim's family was so direly threatened that all work and no play seemed essential to survival. Both had always taken everything very seriously. As Carla said, "even their play is work." It was as though the child within them died before it ever learned to play. And now no one else could play either. None of them could even "do nothing." They had to be productively employed at all times. Without play and play's down time, they never had the chance to re-create themselves; at best, their lives could only be lives of endurance. To get well, though nearly adults, Carla and Lynn would need to connect with their child within. Without personal change, Jim and Virginia would have to reject their daughters' "child" as they rejected their own "child."

Don't be selfish, the last dysfunctional family rule, means *pleasing others*. Now this is a fine, upstanding rule. Unfortunately, it is an *inhuman* rule. It simply is not possible, even if it were desirable, always to put the needs of others before one's own. This rule, strongly enforced in chemically dependent family systems, leaves all the members feeling guilty, as if they're doing something wrong, which makes them try harder to please, so they fail harder. In time, some members of the family will give up and distance themselves in one way or another, while others will become so involved in pleasing the rest that they'll become caretakers, with their identity and self-worth dependent upon how well they please other people. Jim was a caretaker of the highest order and like all caretakers, he deeply resented the fact that no one seemed to appreciate everything he did for them.

We'll look at this *don't be selfish* rule much more closely as we see Susan in her recovery, but it was a strong rule in Jim's family as well. Both girls were immediately labeled "selfish" whenever they did anything that displeased others. And all labeled themselves "selfish" if they even thought of displeasing someone. Lynn was "selfish" when she wanted to be alone; Carla for not wanting to play tennis with Jim; Virginia for secretly resenting Jim's frequent unexpected dinner guests; Jim for putting his work before his family.

Don't be selfish is an impossible and undesirable rule. It results in harsh and destructive judgments. To get well, Lynn and Carla would have to be selfish from time to time, and that would be very hard for Jim and Virginia to take, and very hard for the girls to do within a family where it was so wrong to be selfish.

I didn't explain all of this to Jim when I encountered his resistance, though the issue of rule-breaking, along with other early recovery issues, was certainly on my mind. I figured Jim was so well defended intellectually that lengthy explanations would be like water off a duck's back. Instead, knowing that Jim was a rule follower, I simply told him of our policy of not treating teenagers in isolation, that we strongly insist on their parents' participation in our recovery programs. Unable or unwilling to break our rule, Jim agreed to join one of our adult child of alcoholic recovery support groups, while Virginia joined a co-dependent parent recovery support group that met the same evening. Additionally, Virginia agreed to attend Al-Anon and Jim an ACA (Adult Children of Alcoholics) self-help group, both of which met in a neighboring community.

Next, I asked them to consider their goals—what they each wanted to change about themselves. Jim, needless to say, was a bit nonplussed; he, after all, had just told me he saw nothing he wished to change. I gave them material to read on family rules in chemical dependency and asked them to consider which dysfunctional rules they recognized and would like to start breaking. They, like their daughters and mother, then entered their voyage out of illness into wellness, apart from each other at first, and later together.

Notice the separations? Everyone in a separate group? The reality is that you can forget about togetherness in early recovery. You'll be getting *yourself* together first. Before achieving intimacy with others, you'll become intimate with yourself. In early recovery from chemical dependency, the guiding principle is distance before closeness.

Gaining emotional distance from each other and from your family does not mean you're going to ignore them or neglect your responsibilities, but it does mean securing *enough* emotional detachment to throw some sand on the fires that have burned you all so badly, so your old wounds can heal without too many new ones being formed. Take care of whatever needs your care, but secure *enough* emotional distance to have the energy for personal change. Pay attention to others, but secure *enough* emotional distance for self-focus, so that you can clearly differentiate yourself from others.

While early recovery is characterized by emotional distancing from family members and from the family itself, early recovery is also characterized by a connectedness to new persons outside the family, to peers in recovery. I can't begin to describe the excitement dependents and co-dependents experience when they meet with others in their various support groups and discover they are not alone, that they are not unique in their misery, and that there is hope for them. Dependents and co-dependents are often stunned to find that everything that's happened to them has happened to others. They are relieved beyond words to know they can get well. And they feel good, just plain good — simply by being, their fellow sufferers validate their self-worth. Consequently, early recovery is very often accompanied by great excitement.

Susan and Jeff, upon their discharge from residential primary treatment, joined our recovery support groups—Susan, a co-dependent spouse group and Jeff, a chemical dependent group—and Alan, Tad, and Scotty enrolled in COA (Children of Alcoholics) groups offered in their school. We decided to hold family sessions as needed for assistance with conflict resolution. Meanwhile, Susan and Jeff agreed to attend Al-Anon and AA on a regular basis.

Initially each entered a honeymoon period, what Al-Anoners and AAers often refer to as the "pink cloud." They each experienced tremendous relief; their old scorching fires seemed squelched and they weren't hurting each other any longer. The conflicts and problems related to Jeff's drinking seemed over, and they seemed to float on good feelings and great expectations for their future. Jeff said he was so overjoyed with his newfound sobriety that he was "literally skipping down the street."

While they floated, they each also ignored any conflicted feelings. As hard as they wanted to trust Jeff's new sobriety, Susan and the boys were full of fear that it would not last. They secretly worried over the number of AA meetings Jeff attended and did all kinds of special things for him so he would "stay happy." Jeff ignored the conflict that arose when AA members suggested that he attend "ninety meetings in ninety days," rather than the three a week he and his counselors at the treatment center had agreed upon. Awakening one morning from a dream of having resumed drinking, Jeff felt afraid, not at all sure he'd be able to stay sober, but he did not discuss his fears with Susan, knowing she was already worried about him. So while they floated during their honeymoon period, they also walked on eggs—each trying extra hard to keep peace and avoid conflicts.

The major issue in the early months of recovery is chemical abstinence. Dependents and co-dependents do start breaking the dysfunctional family rules in order to meet their rational self-interests, but most of their energies hover around the issue of chemical abstinence. Their old behavior patterns are deeply ingrained. The dependent is used to using; the co-dependent is used to his using; his chemical use has become the dominant focus in both their lives. *And this focus does not go away overnight.* In early recovery when he is not using chemicals and when she is not focusing solely upon him, they are each behaving in ways that are not yet *natural*. New adaptive behaviors are not yet developed; therefore it is *natural* in the early months of recovery to have chemicals, then the ab-. sence of chemicals, as a dominant life focus. While both the dependent and the co-dependent will be involved in developing new adaptive behavior patterns, each also will be concerned about trust and each will have many questions related to chemical use.

Co-dependents often report that they feel bad about themselves because they don't trust what's happening—chemical abstinence seems so unreal. Dependents often get angry because their abstinence is not immediately trusted. The truth is, neither *should* trust chemical abstinence in the beginning. It's still too new, and trust of anything is not *a given*; trust is earned, and that takes time and effort. Give yourselves permission to *suspend* trust in the early months of recovery; it will come in time, if earned.

The questions most frequently asked by co-dependents are: what do I do about all the liquor in the house? How's he going to handle returning to work and facing those three-martini lunches? How's he going to handle returning to school where all his friends drink or use drugs? What about cocktail parties? or keg parties? What can I do to help him? How many AA meetings is enough? What about my own use? Should I stop drinking? What happens if he returns to alcohol or drugs? What do I do then?

First things first. Regarding any questions related to your own chemical use, for your own sake, you should evaluate your use. Many of you may have become so turned off that you've stopped using chemicals. Many of you will still be using—how do you know it's not a problem? Comparing your use to his use certainly won't give you your answer. I always ask co-dependent clients to abstain from all chemical use for the first three months we work together. You might want to ask the same of yourself. You can only gauge its importance *in absentia*. Either way, if you continue using or resume using chemicals after an evaluation period, and wonder how the dependent feels about that, you'll have to ask him. Don't assume anything. Your chemical use may or may not bother him. Only he knows, and you can only know by asking.

Regarding any questions about how he's handling either his treatment or his abstinence in his life apart from your life together, *back off*. His treatment is his responsibility, not yours. How he copes with chemical using situations when he's not with you is his business, not yours. If he wants to talk to you about either, he will. If he does not talk to you about either, don't pry. Stay out. Remember, many of your questions are also his, and he knows whom best to ask—his chemically dependent peers.

Regarding any questions you may have about how you should handle chemical situations involved in your lives together, *don't assume anything*. The most common mistake co-dependents, friends, and colleagues make is to assume they know what's best for him or how he'd like things handled. You don't know. Only he knows. So ask him. Is he comfortable with alcohol in the house? Does he feel ready to return to work full time immediately? Does he prefer you to serve or not to serve alcohol at dinner parties? Does he wish you to accept or to decline invitations from your mutual friends who may be heavy users? There is no right answer to any of these questions. Only he knows what's right for him, and he'll respect you for asking, as you'll respect him by asking.

In answer to the most frequently asked question—How can you help?—first, always take care of getting well yourself. It is through your return to health that you can help him the most. Second, recognize that his recovery is solely his responsibility. The greatest disservice you can do is to assume responsibility for his treatment for him. There's a simple natural law that operates here—the more you move into his treatment territory, the more he'll move away from it. So, if you want him involved in his treatment, you'd be wise to stay out of it completely. Third, examine your attitude toward his recovery. What are your expectations? Whatever they are, they'll be conveyed through your attitude.

It's my experience that people meet realistic expectations,

theirs and others'. With the proper treatment, it is possible for chemically dependent persons to stay chemical-free. I expect the chemically dependent person to remain abstinent from all mood-altering chemicals. I don't take his abstinence for granted, not at all; not for a moment do I assume it's an easy or simple matter. I acknowledge that chemical freedom takes a lot of effort and is a remarkable accomplishment; nevertheless, I expect it. Occasionally in addiction literature I come across statements about relapses being a natural part of recovery, warning practitioners to expect their clients to return to chemicals. Not me. I don't buy that at all. Put yourself in the dependent's shoes, remembering that even if we don't articulate our expectations, we convey them in our attitudes. Who would you rather have help you—someone who expects you're going to be able to stay off chemicals or someone who expects you'll resume using alcohol or drugs? One expects success and the other failure. Which attitude feels best to you?

Ask yourself another question. What do you have to lose by expecting his success? That doesn't mean you take it for granted and count on it in the early months, but expecting it does show a faith in his ability to succeed. What do you have to lose by showing that faith? If you can adopt an attitude of good faith, a belief in his ability to remain chemical-free, you'll be doing the most important thing you can do for the dependent, other than getting well yourself.

Now for the *biggie*. What do I do if he returns to alcohol or drugs? First, because he relapses does not mean you have to relapse, so continue in your recovery no matter what he does. Keep your focus on you, on recognizing and meeting your own needs. You can help him best by getting as far away from your former maladaptive, enabling pattern as possible, which, in essence, means: resume your reversals and continue breaking all those dysfunctional rules. Remember, your health is no longer dependent on his.

Second, as his recovery was his responsibility, so is his relapse. With the former, the dependent reaps rewards; with the latter, he reaps painful consequences. If he returns to the use of alcohol or drugs, let him assume full responsibility for every single consequence resulting from his relapse. Do not rescue him; do not do anything to make his life less painful; let him *feel* and *face* the results of his own behavior.

Third, examine your expectations once again. What do you expect? Is this relapse the end of the world? Is this how it's going to be forever? I'll tell you my expectations. He blew it; now I expect him to do something about that. If he had made a prior commitment to another form of treatment if this one didn't work, I'd expect him to fulfill that commitment and, in fact, insist that he do so, with appropriate consequences for a refusal. If he had made no prior commitment, I'd now expect him to increase his treatment efforts. If you have expectations similar to mine, I can't guarantee the specific consequences he will experience as a result, but I can guarantee that you will not tolerate his chemical use and he will then more readily perceive his need to return to chemical abstinence.

Carla blew it. She drank alcohol one weekend during her fourth month of recovery. When I saw her a few days later, she said, "I don't know why I drank. I just wanted to drink. I woke up wanting a drink. I fought it all day, but that night I just said 'screw it.' All my friends were drinking, so I drank too."

I said, "You were doing so well and blew it. You must feel pretty lousy about that."

"Yeah . . . crappy," she agreed.

"What're you going to do about it?" I asked.

"*Do about it?* What's to do? It's over! I'm not drinking now . . . I only drank that one night," she replied indignantly.

"Nope. That's not the way it works, and you know it. You've been around AA and NA long enough to know it's the first drink or chemical that gets you drunk. Saturday night was your first drink, Carla. Even if you had drunk the whole keg, the keg was your first drink. Saturday night was the beginning of your downfall. You've begun the momentum back into continued chemical use. What're you going to do about that?"

"I'll do what I've done."

"No you won't," I replied. "First of all, what you've done was not enough or you wouldn't have drunk in the first place. So you've got to be thinking about more treatment, not the same or less. Secondly, you no longer meet the criteria for your recovery support group. Only people who don't use can be in that group, so you're out. You broke the rules, so no more group, not until you put a month of sobriety together again. So let's talk about *more* treatment. What are your ideas? How about a residential program?"

"Oh for crissake! Back to that. No—absolutely not. I'm not going into a treatment center," she announced angrily.

"So, come up with something," I insisted.

"Can't I just see you more often?"

"Carla," I answered, "I will continue seeing you, and we can increase our number of meetings, but only if you stay off chemicals and come up with a whole lot more than just me. What else will you do? How many AA and NA meetings will you get to each week? You haven't picked a sponsor yet; what are your plans about that? What else? Is there someone from your recovery support group who can be your buddy and help you through your first month of abstinence so you can make it back into group? Those are the areas I want you to consider."

"Okay!"

"*Okay what?* Carla, I need to tell you something. You're approaching your relapse as if it were insignificant. Your life's on the line and it just so happens that I like you a whole lot. I'll feel very sad if you go down the tubes. I'll really miss you. I've gotten used to you slumping around here. But that drinking last Saturday is not insignificant, and it didn't just happen for no good reason. Chemical dependency is a big disease and your efforts to maintain abstinence simply weren't big enough. I don't want to be part of your downfall so, unless you come up with a plan containing *big* efforts, I'm not going to see you anymore."

Carla came up with a reasonable recovery plan containing big efforts, which she, I, and her parents agreed upon with the stipulation that, if this new plan did not work, she would then enter a residential treatment program. To date, nearly two years have passed since Carla's relapse and she's away at school, chemical-free, without further relapses.

As a co-dependent, if the dependent returns to chemicals, increase your personal treatment efforts, spend time clarifying in your own mind what is and what is not acceptable to you. Remember the power of expectations; they'll affect you as much as him. If you expect abstinence and believe you have a right to insist upon his abstinence, as I did with Carla, then you will find that his chemical use is not acceptable to you and you won't accept it. If the dependent does not meet your expectations of abstinence, you might want to do, or repeat, the planned intervention. If that doesn't work, you may decide to separate yourself from him. If he falls, do not fall with him.

As the dependent moves into his recovery, he will start replacing his primitive and immature defense mechanisms with those higher on the scale. Many, like Jeff, move into the use of *reaction formation,* a neurotic defense.

Virtually overnight Jeff changed from being a person with a wife problem but absolutely no drinking problem, to a person who stopped drinking, cast aspersions on other drinkers, attended AA regularly, and openly announced that he was an alcoholic, in fact, a "grateful alcoholic." Before treatment, he assumed virtually no responsibilities in his family, other than providing an income. As he moved off his "pink cloud," he became the captain of the ship, shaping up one and all—disciplining the kids; haranguing them about their messy rooms; questioning them about their day at school, their homework, friends, and after-school activities; taking over complete management of the household repairs, maintenance, and finances from Susan; expressing along the way much dissatisfaction with the way she had formerly handled things.

From one extreme to the other—from drunkenness and denial to abstinence and admission, from acting irresponsibly to acting overly responsible. *Reaction formation!* The defense that quiets the passions that rage the strongest. The defense that causes problems for others, yet saves the dependent's life.

Reaction formation often leads to a rigid overdoing, especially in the dependent's approach to treatment. While Jeff overdid without discrimination, many dependents will neglect their home life and virtually adopt AA as their *whole* life. In such instances, the dependent seems to live for his self-help group. He attends daily meetings, spends his free time at home on the phone with self-help group members, and tells one and all that his treatment program is a "selfish" program, demanding that he meet his sobriety needs first, foremost, and sometimes exclusively. No matter how reaction formation is manifested, it usually results in an approach to abstinence that is as rigid as was the former approach to chemical use.

While reaction formation can be a real pain in the neck for people close to the dependent, it nevertheless is an ingenious defense. Consider little boys and girls as they approach puberty and start hormonal shifts and deep yearnings, usually unconscious, for the opposite sex. Zoom! As part of their normal emotional maturation, many move right into the defense of reaction formation. Those inner fires are scary and must be stifled. Suddenly little boys and girls will have nothing to do with each other. They can barely stand to speak to their former playmates. Now it's boy sports in all-boy gangs and girl twitters in all-girl cliques, and ne'er the two shall meet, at least for a year or so until they move out of reaction formation and swing back toward each other.

Reaction formation leads dependents in early recovery to think, feel, and act in direct opposition to their inner, unacknowledged urge for a chemical; consequently, it is an extremely valuable defense for chemically dependent persons. It can serve them very well indeed. Reaction formation not only stifles the dependent's inner urge for a chemical, it frees enormous energy, which is then directed toward not doing that which he'd most like to do. Thus, though this defense may rub others the wrong way, it does help the dependent to save his life.

Normally, reaction formation is not a healthful defense for adults. Instead of integrating one's psyche, it buries feelings and compels the user into rigid, reactive behavior and attitudes. Thus, while reaction formation is helpful during the early months of recovery, it is not a defense that will serve the dependent well for long. Fortunately, reaction formation tends to be a transition defense and, once the dependent's urge for the chemicals diminishes, as it will with abstinence, he will be able to leave *reaction formation* behind.

Susan, once deeply entrenched in the use of this defense herself and not yet completely out of it, had been the family's superdoer, and she secretly believed she could be Jeff's eventual savior. She resented and was frightened by Jeff's addiction and decreased functioning; yet when he was actively addicted, she knew he needed her, that he truly could not exist without her. With his dramatic move into sobriety, she felt left behind, even resentful that he was getting well without her help. She was also angry that Jeff was feeling good without having atoned for his past behavior—all those years of abuse. And she was stunned, awash with resentments, as Jeff took over all the responsibilities she had once handled so well, and which were now so difficult to relinquish. She felt at loose ends, not needed, and without value. She was furious when Jeff belittled her former means of doing all those chores he should have done but was incapable of doing. Needless to say, she was shocked by her new and unexpected feelings and began to feel guiltier than ever.

Formerly, Susan and the boys had enjoyed a lot of freedom; they didn't like Jeff's drinking, but it nevertheless meant, more often than not, that he was unaware of what they were doing. Now, in addition to feeling replaced and unnecessary, they felt supervised, constantly under his critical eye. The boys, remembering how undisciplined Jeff had been for so long, rebelled at his sudden disciplining of them. Secretly, each of them deeply resented Jeff's new sober behavior and thought life would be better if he returned to drinking. Then they wondered what kind of people they were for having such terrible thoughts.

In one of their early family sessions with me, Jeff opened the discussion by complaining that both Tad and Scotty seemed withdrawn and wouldn't enter conversations with him. When I asked for a specific example, Jeff described an incident of the evening before when he asked Tad about his day at school, and instead of answering, Tad left the dinner table. "When I followed him to his room, I found his door locked. I had to use some pretty harsh words before he let me in, but even then he refused to talk."

"Let's go back to the dinner table," I suggested. "Tell me as much as you can remember from the time you sat down to eat."

"Well, dinner is one of the few times we're all together," Jeff explained. "It's about our *only* time together as a family, so that's when I ask each of the boys about their day. But they just clam up. They're my sons. We're supposedly a family. I think I have a right to know what's going on in my own family, but they just sit there like lumps."

"Jeff, you're acting indignant right now, as if you're really hurting inside," I said. "And look at your whole family, not just Tad and Scotty. They've all moved way back into their chairs, drawn in upon themselves, as if they're hurting, too. What do you feel right now, Jeff, as you look at your family?"

"Annoyed! This is exactly what they're like at home."

"You're angry, Jeff. But we've talked before about how your anger is often used as a defense against more painful feelings. What are you feeling under that anger as you look at your family?"

"Scared, I guess. I feel like they're excluding me—shutting me out. And that makes me angry. I have a right to know what's going on."

"You really are scared, aren't you? For all the years of your chemical use, you *were* outside your family much of the time, weren't you—cut off from them emotionally?"

"Yes," he replied.

"And now you're still feeling cut off?"

"Yes."

"How do you feel about that?"

"Hurt, lonely, I guess. Yeah, lonely. It scares me."

"So you come on like a bulldozer driving everyone away?"

"Ah, damn!" He smiled, not without chagrin. "I'm doing the same thing I did in treatment, aren't I? I'm covering my fear with anger."

"Jeff, go easy on yourself. No one expects you to get well overnight," I explained. Then turning to Tad, I asked, "How're you feeling right now?"

"I'm still mad at him," Tad replied, scowling, but with his head bowed as if close to tears.

"A whole lot of questions can do that," I said. "They can be too much to handle. What would you like your dad to do instead?"

"Hug me," Tad said softly, at which point Jeff went over to the sofa next to Tad and held him in his arms as he wiped away a tear or two of his own. After more discussion, Jeff was surprised, but pleased, to hear that his family was as interested in his day as he was in theirs.

No matter what defenses are employed, familial interactions are often turbulent during early recovery. They have become used to *extreme positioning*: some overdid and others underdid, and some pursued and others distanced. Such extreme positioning does not go away overnight. In early recovery it is not at all unusual for members of the family to retreat to an old extreme on some days and to venture to the exact opposite extreme on other days.

Early recovery represents a state of transition. The family equilibrium is not at all settled; each family member is neither here nor there. They're not where they used to be, nor are they where they're going to be. All will feel uncomfortable with the stresses associated with their unsettled existence; all, like Jeff, will feel a strong need to change others to secure their own comfort.

Their self-help groups will be of great support during this turbulent period—helping them focus on changing themselves rather than others, letting them know that emotional pain is okay and that "this too shall pass." At the same time, professional counseling will assist them in recognizing their defensive behavior and underlying feelings. In turn, their increased insight will direct them toward more mutually nurturing interactions.

In summary, the primary task for the co-dependent in early recovery is to become self-focused. Some co-dependents will be able to do that within months, even if the dependent is not abstinent. Others will take much longer, even if the dependent is abstinent. If the co-dependent does not become self-focused, she will not take the voyage from illness to wellness. The primary task for the dependent in early recovery is to maintain his abstinence. If he does not remain free from alcohol and all other mood-altering drugs, he will not take the voyage from illness to wellness.

Early recovery is the opportunity for both to become *stabilized* in their respective self-focus and abstinence, both of which require emotional distance. To achieve these tasks, both will begin to break the dysfunctional family rules in order to recognize and meet some of their own wants and needs. Most personal and interpersonal conflicts are not resolved in early recovery; consequently both the co-dependent and dependent may experience associated stress. At the same time, they will find comfort and excitement as they work closely with others who have gone, or are going, through similar experiences.

If you are a co-dependent in early recovery and, aside from your jobs in and out of the home, it seems as if about all you're doing is concentrating on shifting your focus off the dependent onto yourself, *you're doing all that you should be doing right now.* If, aside from his jobs in and out of the home, it seems as if the dependent is concentrating almost solely upon maintaining his chemical freedom, *he's doing all that he should be doing right now.* Nothing else is needed right now.

If you're not feeling all that well yet, if you're nervous or depressed, *that's exactly what you should be feeling right now.* You may have learned as you've traveled through life that there's something wrong with having emotional pain. Now you must learn the opposite. Experiencing emotional pain is right. It means you're changing. You're having growing pains.

A few years ago, I heard Marty Mann, the first female member of Alcoholics Anonymous, tell a combined audience of AA and Al-Anon members, "We don't get well by Thursday. Until Thursday, we're going to have some pain."

It's not Thursday yet. Soon, but not yet.

18

Into Wellness

A number of years ago, while I was sitting in a meeting of employee-assistance program coordinators in California, my eyes were drawn repeatedly to a large chart on the wall of the conference room which showed several bands of primary colors, each separated by an inch or so of white space, paralleling each other as they curved down from the top of one corner of the canvas to the bottom center and then back up to the opposite corner. During a break I asked our conference host what this chart in the shape of a large U was all about, and he delightedly explained that the bands of color represented the chemically dependent person, the spouse, and their children as they descend into illness, join their respective self-help groups, and then ascend into health. I wished I hadn't asked. I felt like I was seeing one of those old movies with Jeannette MacDonald and Nelson Eddy holding hands as they marched off into the sunset—except my host's chart didn't even have his people holding hands as they marched up and away.

That chart bothered me a lot. It seemed to minimize the enormous courage and effort required to traverse the potholes and detours along the voyage into wellness, while, at the same time, it pointed to one of the gravest dangers members of the chemically dependent family face as they move out of illness—continued emotional separation rather than intimacy. The chart also underscored what I was perceiving as a major deficit in the continuum of chemical dependency care offered at that time, ten years ago. Daily I was seeing recovering chemically dependent persons and members of their families, active in their self-help groups and now abstinent and self-focused, but dissatisfied or distressed with their lives. While professional chemical dependency treatment was readily available for assistance with the tasks associated with moving out of illness, only isolated pockets of professional chemical dependency treatment was available for assistance with the tasks associated with moving into wellness. Professional help existed for the early months, while little professional help existed for the work toward health that can begin only after abstinence and self-focus are achieved and stabilized—work that is not necessarily performed best through the self-help groups alone.

Members of Alcoholics Anonymous and Al-Anon, as well as members of their corollary self-help groups, often have a great deal of antipathy for professional psychotherapy—for good reason. While some were misdiagnosed and grossly mistreated, others were accurately diagnosed but still grossly mistreated. To this day, few, if any, schools of medicine, nursing, psychology, and social work teach accurate or anywhere near full information on chemical dependency. Nevertheless, a new profession is growing, a new group of chemical dependency therapists drawn from widely varied backgrounds and disciplines, who have received specialized education and training in the treatment of chemical dependency. Today, while expansion is still needed, in addition to primary treatment, professional recovery support specific to chemical dependency also exists in many parts of the United States. Thus, members of AA and Al-Anon and their corollary groups who are finding themselves stuck on that plateau where their lives are a whole lot better, but not yet good enough, can seek and often find the professional help they need to go further in fulfilling their health potential. Those who have received primary treatment can also move right into long-term professional recovery support therapy as an adjunct to AA and Al-Anon.

I know that mental health is a great deal more than just not being ill; still, I am hard put to define it. Vaillant describes mental health as the ability to fully love, work, and play; and more specifically he cites six features of health, drawing from Marie Johoda's book, *Current Concepts of Positive Mental Health*. Mentally healthy persons are in touch with their own feelings and possess empathy for others; they are oriented toward the future and over time are fruitfully invested in life in the here and now; their inner worlds are at peace and provide them with resistance to stress; they possess a clearly differentiated identity, separate from others; they perceive reality without distortion and are able to recognize what suits their needs; they are masters of their environment, efficient in problem solving.[9] M. Scott Peck, in his popular book, *The Road Less Traveled*, takes mental health a step further. Equating mental growth with spiritual growth, Peck asserts that mental health, in addition to the features outlined above, requires an ever-continuing growth in the direction of becoming as one with God—of becoming ever more closely connected with a transcendent loving force.[10] If Peck has not already found acceptance in the world of chemical dependency, he soon will. Spiritual growth is the bedrock, the foundation from which all else proceeds in chemical dependency treatment.

In chemical dependency the spirit shrivels. Chemically dependent persons and their family members come to feel hopeless, helpless, totally alone, unloving, unaccepting, nontrust-

9. George E. Vaillant, *Adaptation to Life* (Boston: Little, Brown and Company, 1977). pp. 351–76.

10. M. Scott Peck, M.D., *The Road Less Traveled* (New York: Simon and Schuster, 1978). pp. 185–97, 280–313.

ing, and unforgiving. Their illnesses do not lend themselves to anything they try, from willpower and perseverance to conventional psychotherapy. Alcoholics Anonymous, and all the self-help groups modeled after AA, emphasize one's powerlessness and unmanageability, the turning of one's life over to the care of God as one understands Him, and the seeking of the knowledge of and the ability to practice God's will. Yet, even though chemically dependent persons and co-dependents frequently declare themselves to be spiritually bankrupt, many initially resist AA's spiritual emphasis, which no doubt violates their world view, their understanding of what life is all about.

And they are not alone. Mental health workers also frequently take exception to AA's spiritual emphasis, knowing AA shows good results but believing it to be a form of mass hypnosis or an inappropriate religious substitution for chemical dependency or co-dependency. No doubt AA's spiritual emphasis violates their world views as well. Mental health therapists can, perhaps, afford to continue through life with their world views intact, whatever they may be, but chemically dependent and co-dependent persons cannot. Because of the nature of their illness and their resulting spiritual bankruptcy, without spiritual growth chemically dependent and co-dependent persons are ultimately left with only willpower and perseverance, and continued painful and limited lives. Health care professionals may be profoundly disturbed by the idea of a loving and powerful force throughout one's inner and outer worlds that transcends comprehension, but they do their chemically dependent and co-dependent clients a gross disservice if they turn them away from a source of mastery and peace, as contained in AA's spiritual program.

Chemical dependency specialists, for the most part, are on their own continuing personal voyages to spiritual growth and are in tune with AA's spiritual emphasis. Having come to know the power inherent in the spirituality of AA and AA-modeled self-help groups, they tend to view their own work with considerable humility, thinking of it as an adjunct to the self-help groups, something like the icing on the cake, good but not all by itself. Thus, in recovery support therapy, while professional chemical dependency therapists help their clients illuminate defenses, experience feelings, and increase communication skills, they work within the spiritual framework of AA and secondarily to AA, Al-Anon, and the other self-help groups. In doing so, many of us consider ourselves blessed. We give, but are always replenished in such a way that we are enhanced. We help our clients grow, and find that we have grown.

Before following our families on their voyages into wellness, I would like to talk about controlled drinking. Once chemically dependent persons are stabilized in abstinence, the question of controlled drinking is often raised, most often by persons other than recovering dependents or co-dependents. "You mean you can *never* drink again?" Or, "She's been sober six months, can't she even have a glass of wine?" Or, "Okay, your addiction's behind you. You've learned your lesson. Now you'll be able to manage one or two drinks a day." Or, "Hey, you've got it licked, how about a beer?" And so on.

The idea of abstinence from marijuana, cocaine, heroin, and the other illicit drugs doesn't bother many people in our society. After all, those are not socially acceptable drugs in the first place. But the idea of abstinence from alcohol bothers many; it's an idea not tolerated well at all, as if abstinence were about the worst thing that's ever come down the pike. Using the rationale that controlled drinking will make it possible to reach an increased number of alcoholics, a whole lot of money has been poured into controlled drinking experiments. Rather than proving the possibility of controlled drinking for alcoholics, these have demonstrated the need for abstinence. But, like the ancients searching for the formula for gold, rather than heeding the results of these experiments, our society supports unreality by pouring more money, time, and energy into more experiments. So far, the formulas for gold and controlled drinking for alcoholics have not been found.

I don't think I have ever, not even once, heard it suggested that former cigarette smokers can safely return to controlled smoking. We all know that if the former smoker picks up a cigarette, the chances are great that he or she will soon be back to smoking as much as or more than she smoked in the past. Both cigarettes and alcohol are socially acceptable drugs, so what's the difference? Oh, I know the addictions are very different. Among other things, alcohol addiction contains a personality deterioration not found in nicotine addiction, but is not abstinence, once stabilized, the same for both addictions? Why do we support a smoker's need for life-long abstinence but question that same need in alcoholics? We don't spend money on controlled smoking experiments, using the rationale that controlled smoking will help us reach more smokers, so why do we assume that rationale has any basis in fact in alcoholism? I often feel like I'm back at work in the psychiatric hospital, surrounded by schizophrenic reasoning.

There are many former smokers who report no desire for a cigarette. And there are many who report that they would like to be able to smoke again, yet at the same time, they express gratitude or relief for being off cigarettes. Alcoholics are no different. In sobriety, many report no desire for a drink or any other mood-altering drug, while many think it would be nice to be able to drink or use drugs again, and they also express gratitude or relief for being off chemicals. But our society treats their abstinences differently. We support abstinence from all drugs, including nicotine, but not alcohol.

Perhaps we're still suffering from the fallout of our Prohibition era, and fear taking a strong stand on abstinence. Maybe what it boils down to is that many of us cannot fathom ourselves without alcohol and therefore are unable to recommend or support abstinence for others. Or, because smoking addicts nearly everyone while alcohol addicts relatively few, it is easier for us to overlook the actual alcohol addiction and to feel self-righteous toward alcoholics, certain they *could* control their drinking if only they *would*. Whatever our rationales behind our inadequate support of abstinence, the fact remains that once addicted to any mood-altering chemical, in order to be freed of their illness, chemically dependent persons must remain free from *all* mood-altering chemicals, including alcohol. Otherwise they're playing Russian roulette; they are an accident about to happen.

As discussed in the previous chapter, in the early weeks and months of recovery when chemical abstinence is achieved and the co-dependent and dependent become actively involved in Al-Anon, AA, or the corollary self-help groups, both move toward self-focus, acquire emotional distance from each other, develop support networks outside the family, and take steps toward meeting their own needs and assuming responsibility for their own problems. This new expansiveness plays a vital role in undercutting some of the hostility, resentment, and bitterness inherent in the chemical dependency relationship. Both the recovery support therapy and the self-help groups help each family member to settle down to a more comfortable, if tenuous, structure. The stabilization in self-focus and sobriety achieved in early recovery lays the groundwork for future change. As Claudia Bepko and JoAnn Krestan point out in their book, *The Responsibility Trap*, the actual functional and emotional organization of the family changes little during this period, yet individual healing occurs.[11] Distortion of reality is reduced, insight into self is increased, and a sense of emotional security begins to develop as personal boundaries are rebuilt; then new work can begin.

Susan, arriving a few minutes late for her recovery support group, quietly slipped into her chair, taking care not to interrupt the conversation in progress. After nearly an hour, she still had not entered the group discussion, gazing instead at the floor with her head bowed. One of the members asked, "Susan, you look so sad, and you're usually not this quiet. How're you feeling?"

"Okay," she replied, smiling briefly before returning her gaze to the floor.

11. Claudia Bepko with JoAnn Krestan, *The Responsibility Trap* (New York: The Free Press, A Division of Macmillan, Inc., 1985). p. 175–98.

"Wow, Susie, you don't look okay," exclaimed another member.

Susan started to cry, saying, "I guess I'm not okay." Without elaborating, she once again returned her gaze to the floor in front of her, only this time tears were flowing freely down her face.

"Can you talk about what's going on with you, Susan?" asked one of the counselors.

"Nothing. That's why this is so stupid. Nothing's going on; I just feel sad. It's like I'm sad all the time now. Last night was our anniversary and it was horrible. As usual I ruined everything. Jeff brought me a dozen roses when he came home from work, and like an idiot, I started crying when he handed them to me. He was happy—all ready to celebrate—and all I could do was cry. Jeff got angry and I don't blame him. He'd made reservations for us to have dinner at a lovely restaurant that we used to go to years ago, and I just couldn't get ready. He came into the bedroom to tell me we were late, and as he was helping me zip up my dress, I started to cry all over again, and the tears got on my dress. It was silk and I knew there'd be spots, and I didn't know what to do. I knew I had to change my dress and I knew I'd find another one to wear if I looked in my closet, but I didn't even look. I just stood there and cried. Then Jeff picked up the anniversary card I had given him and threw it at me; he told me to shove it and then he stormed out of the house. It's all so stupid. I should have been celebrating our anniversary and all I could do was cry. I feel so stupid."

"You don't sound stupid to me at all, Susan," one of the group members commented. "You sound sad—like you didn't feel like celebrating."

"But that's what's stupid. Jeff's been sober five months now. This was our first sober anniversary in years—ever."

"That alone could make someone feel sad, Susan. You've been married for a long time and you've never had a sober anniversary."

"I don't know. All I can think of is that it's all so stupid."

"Like there's something silly, or stupid, or wrong about feeling sad," suggested one of her peers.

"Yes," Susan nodded.

"Feelings aren't stupid, Susan. Feelings aren't supposed to make sense. Feelings just *are*. And you're feeling sad—very sad, aren't you?" asked another member.

"Yes, but why?" Susan asked.

"Let's let that *why* go for now," the counselor suggested. "When you're sad, Susan, it's natural not to want to celebrate. You're not feeling joyous right now so, of course, you wouldn't want to celebrate. It sounds to me like you're making very good progress here. You're sad and you're feeling your sadness. A few months ago, you would have swept those feelings under the rug and pretended everything was fine, right?"

Susan nodded her agreement and then said, "But this doesn't seem better. That wasn't right last night—to just cry when Jeff wanted to be happy."

"I agree with you," the counselor said. "It wasn't exactly an ideal interaction, but you'll get to your ideal relationship with Jeff with the kinds of changes you're making. You're allowing yourself to feel your feelings now, Susan, and that's a wonderfully good change for you. I'm going to ask you to do something. Let go of what you think your relationship with Jeff should be like. Trust that you are on your way to finding it, because you are. In the meantime, I'm going to ask you to give yourself permission to feel sad. You've always run from your sadness. Concentrate on letting yourself *feel* your sad feelings. They're real—sit with them—you need to *experience* them. Will you do that?"

Susan agreed and, with the group's support, over the next few weeks she spoke of and experienced the grief she felt over all the losses she had endured in her marriage—the years of health she felt she'd lost due to what she termed her "stupid" response to Jeff's addiction, the loss of healthy parenting she might have had with her children, the loss of love and companionship she had dreamed of having with Jeff, the loss of friendship she'd had over the years, the loss of feeling supercompetent, the loss of feeling righteous, the loss of feeling she didn't need anyone, the loss of being everyone's fixer—all the losses, all very real, that Susan had ignored until now. There were days when her depression was profound. She had trouble sleeping. She lost weight and she cried a lot. She couldn't seem to get her work done, and she wanted to drop out of group. Some of her Al-Anon friends told her she was crazy to put herself through so much pain. Others, having gone through it themselves, supported her, assuring her that God gives us all kinds of feelings to feel and he wouldn't give her more sadness than she could handle.

Gradually Susan started to feel better—angry, but better. She was literally fuming when she arrived over a half-hour late for group one evening. Breathing heavily with her lips tightly clenched, she tapped her fingers on the arm of her chair as she waited for a break in the discussion. She didn't have long to wait. Everyone in the group immediately picked up the angry vibrations she was sending forth.

"Do alcoholics *ever* get well?" she asked. "I mean that—I really want to know. Do they *really* get better, or is that just somebody's fantasy?"

"Wow! Where's the depression? What's going on with you?" asked one of the members of the group.

"I sat in that car for over thirty minutes waiting for Jeff to get his royal act together so we could get over here for group. And he got in the goddamned car like nothing was wrong. When I asked him if he knew what time it was, he asked what the hell was wrong with me. Jesus! He's late and he's dumping on me. Just now, as we were coming up the stairs, he said he couldn't see why I was so angry; that all I ever do is sit around anyway. That did it! I'm not going to take any more of his crap. I've had over twelve years of his crap and I'm not taking any more."

"You're feeling a lot of anger, aren't you?" another member asked.

"You're goddamned right I'm angry. I suppose you think I shouldn't be angry. How would you feel if your wife treated you like that?" Susan asked, bristling.

"Angry, just like you're angry," the group member responded. After a few moments of silence, he asked Susan to elaborate further on what happened to her as she waited in the car. "Thirty minutes is a long time to wait for someone. What was going on with you?"

"Well, first of all, I knew I was going to have to wait. I'm always ready for group before Jeff. We're frequently late getting here—as you know—and that's because Jeff's always late."

"How does that make you feel?"

"It makes me feel a lot of things. I'm taking this treatment seriously. I've made a commitment and that means being here on time."

"And Jeff's being late means he's not committed, not taking his treatment as seriously as you," the same group member said.

"That's right. It's his goddamned illness in the first place," Susan replied. "Why should I be the one to take treatment seriously? Why isn't he?"

"Not only did Jeff make you sick, he then tops it off by not taking treatment seriously. You're taking it seriously and he isn't, and he started it all," said another member, feeling what Susan was feeling.

"Exactly. And I'm tired of all that crap about calling his addiction an illness. I've had it with that word."

"Like calling it an illness is a way of excusing all the abusive behavior," said another member with empathy.

"I hate the whole business. You know that people actually *congratulate* him? We were with some old friends last week who know about Jeff's chemical dependency and they just fell all over themselves—they kept telling Jeff how great he is for not using and for being in AA. I wanted to vomit. How about me? No one ever talks about what I've had to go through!"

"You took all his abuse, he gets congratulated rather than punished, while you're ignored," said yet another member, experiencing Susan's feelings right along with her.

"He's never faced up to how painful his illness was for me. He's very cavalier about that—like it isn't all that important— and now he's cavalier about treatment—this is all so stupid, isn't it?" Susan suddenly asked. "I know he has an illness. I don't have any right to be angry about it."

"Oh, hey, back up, Susan," one of the counselors said. "One of our rules here is that we don't judge feelings—our own or those of anyone in the group. Now you are judging your own feelings. You'll notice that none of us judged your feelings. Feelings aren't good, bad, right, or wrong. Whatever you feel, you feel. We were all putting ourselves in your shoes just now, Susan, feeling your feelings right along with you. And, group, I think we all did a good job with that and you were doing a good job of expressing your anger, Susan, but right now I feel like I've just been kicked out of your shoes. Let's back up. Let's assume what you said before is true. I don't know if it is, but let's assume right now that you're taking your treatment more seriously than Jeff. How does that make you feel?"

"Angry . . . hurt . . . very hurt . . . used . . . like the same old stuff is happening over and over," she replied, her anger diminished.

After a few moments of silence one of the members asked, "Does Jeff know it's important to you to be on time for group, that you place a high value on being here promptly?"

"Of course he knows. I tell him that all the time. I remind him every Tuesday morning that we have group that night. He knows I'll have dinner ready early. I even put his change of clothes out on the bed, so he can get ready faster; oh, oh—I'm controlling him, aren't I?"

"That's what I was wondering, Suzie—if you were back to your old ways and had somehow set yourself up to be used. How come, if you want to be here on time, you're not getting yourself here on time?"

"All right, I know what you're saying, but that really doesn't make any sense. Yes, I could drive my own car over here, but that would mean our driving both cars. That's just throwing money down the drain, and Jeff would really flip if I did that," Susan explained.

"Well," the group member, an accountant, persisted, "if Jeff thinks it's a waste, he can get ready on time and ride with you.

But how much of a waste are we really talking about, and is that the real issue? You drive a compact, you live about ten miles from here, right? That's about a dollar sixty round-trip and—"

"Arnold, you're too much with all your figures," interrupted another member.

"Let's let him finish," suggested yet another. "I think he's onto something. I've been going through this same kind of scene with my husband and I think I've been doing the same kind of manipulating stuff as Susan. I'd like to hear where you're taking all this, Arnold. I've got a sneaky feeling that what applies to Susan applies to me."

"Go to it, Arnold," encouraged one of the counselors.

"Yeah, Arnie, go to it," Susan said, with a smile slowly expanding to a big grin, no longer feeling angry.

"I don't think the dollar sixty means beans to you. I know you pretty well by now," Arnie continued, "and I know you don't sit around doing nothing. In fact, you've always done too much for everyone else. But maybe Jeff had a point when you were coming up the stairs tonight. Maybe in a sense you are sitting around expecting Jeff to meet your needs rather than actively meeting them yourself, and then you get angry because he doesn't meet your needs the way you want them met."

Susan replied, "I don't know. Maybe you're right. I think you probably are right."

"What *are* you feeling right now, Susan?" asked the counselor.

"I'm feeling okay. In fact, I'm feeling good," she answered. "That was a powerless position I put myself in, wasn't it? You really helped me a lot, Arnie. You all helped me. I really feel good knowing I don't have to sit around and take Jeff's crap. That—you know—I can get myself here. That's really a nice feeling. Thanks."

"Thanks for letting us get close to you," Arnie replied.

"Some very important things have gone on here tonight," one of the counselors added. "Having experienced all that sadness is now really paying off for you, Susan. Now you are getting to some of that anger that you've had salted away all these years, and that will free you up to make a whole lot of changes, like the one you made here tonight, where you've chosen to regain some personal power and responsibility. But something else happened as well. The smoke was coming out of your ears when you walked in here tonight, Susan. You were fuming, you were so angry. And look what happened—the world didn't fall apart."

"Yeah, it didn't," Susan agreed.

"Can you take yourself back to when you walked in tonight? Did you have any fears about losing control when you were feeling all that anger?"

"Yes," Susan answered immediately. "I was ready to scream . . . to do something terrible . . . to just fall apart. It was horrible. I couldn't keep my anger in, but I was afraid to let it out. Maybe I thought it would never stop."

"You must have been terribly frightened."

"Frightened? That's not the word for it. I was in a panic! I was going to explode in a million pieces if you all hadn't stopped talking."

"But you didn't explode, did you? You didn't lose control. In fact, you talked about your anger. You shared it with us and then you started to feel better."

"That's right, but it was scary. I could barely contain myself in the car with Jeff on the way over here. What happens if this happens again—if I get that angry again and don't have this group to come to?"

"Well, the chances are that it's going to happen again, Susan, if you'll let it happen again. And that's what I'd like you to let yourself do; if you're angry, give yourself permission to experience your anger."

"Oh boy! What am I in for now?" Susan asked. "Whenever you ask any of us to give ourselves permission to do something, all hell breaks loose. I was depressed for weeks. What am I going to be now, a screaming meemie?"

"No, you're not going to be a screaming meemie. And your

life's going to be a whole lot better now. You're not going to have to suffer like you've suffered these past few weeks. But it is highly likely, if you allow it, that you will feel some anger every once in a while. From time to time you're apt to do things that recall buried anger from your past. Like tonight, the anger you felt as you waited for Jeff was so strong partly because it wasn't only tonight you were angry about. Waiting for Jeff was certainly annoying, but in reality it was also the trigger for all those other things you talked about feeling angry about. Now—tonight—your own actions of putting yourself in that powerless position set the stage for your anger. You might pull one of those numbers again from time to time, and Jeff or the boys or anyone might do something that triggers past as well as present anger in the same kind of way. If and when that happens, I'd like you to feel free to acknowledge and experience your anger. Okay?"

"Okay, I guess," Susan replied.

"Susan, you don't have to go around inviting anger or looking for it. I'm just asking that if it happens, if you get angry, that you *feel* angry."

"Okay. But if the group's not here, what do I do, call you?" she asked.

"Yes, please do call me," the counselor answered. "And if you can't get me, talk to anyone. You know just about everyone who works here."

"You can call me, Susan," offered Arnie, who was then promptly echoed by everyone else in the room.

"What else can she do?" asked the counselor.

"Well, I went through this same thing," said one of the members of the group who was about to complete her recovery support therapy. "And, for sure, when you're at the peak of your anger—when you're first learning how to feel anger— you're not going to be able to share it very well with the person you're angry at. I can handle my anger better now, but I couldn't in the beginning when I first started feeling it. I used to take walks. I'd just get up and leave and walk. I walked in the middle of the night and in the middle of the day. I walked and walked and walked; then when I felt calmer, I went home. Sometimes I talked about what was going on with my husband and sometimes I didn't. Now, I always do; but then I walked."

"How does that sound to you, Susan?" asked another member who had also been in the group much longer than Susan. "I walked a lot, too, but I didn't feel safe walking at night, so I grabbed a pillow and went out into the garage and screamed my head off into the pillow . . . kicked a few paint cans around sometimes . . . but mostly I screamed; then I'd feel better."

"I did those kinds of things, too," said another member. "It sounds crazy, but we do have to learn how to experience our feelings, rather than bury them. It's made me feel a whole lot better—more equipped to deal with the world. Remember, everyone, what I did? I took all your numbers. I walked, screamed, and everything else but, if I reached one of you, I was able to talk my anger out instead—just like you did tonight, Susan—and that helped the most."

"What do you think, Susan?" asked the counselor.

"Think or feel?" she asked.

"Both. I'd like to know where you're at on both levels—what you think about experiencing anger and managing it along the lines we've suggested and what you're feeling right now. Let's start with that. What are you feeling?"

"Kind of stunned, wondering if I would have joined this group if I'd known how much work was involved; a little shocked, shocked to know the depths of some of my feelings, shocked to have such feelings in the first place, but I guess I'm relieved also—yeah, relieved. I don't have that horrible sadness now, and that's an enormous relief, but—this is going to sound silly—I feel relieved because I feel alive. I think I'll kick newspapers. We've got about a year's worth all tied up in neat bundles alongside the wall in our garage. Maybe I'll go beat up on newspapers; uh, I'd also like all your phone numbers."

Everyone in a chemically dependent family suffers losses—loss of dreams, of wasted years, of what could have been, of established patterns of behavior that didn't work, but at least were known. Their losses may be different from Susan's, but they will be no less painful. Some may have lost their children's growing years, others may have lost cherished friends, some may have lost being sober when a parent was dying and in need of them. Whatever. Their losses are numerous and very real and their grief must be faced, experienced, or they will remain chronically depressed and without energy for growth, to one degree or another, for the rest of their lives.

Those who enter the voyage into wellness often find, once they are stabilized in the changes made in early recovery, that they now start feeling depressed. They don't actually *become* depressed. They *already are* depressed, and have been for years. They've just hidden their sadness from themselves with all their defensive behavior and, now that their use of defenses becomes less pronounced, their underlying sad feelings come forth. Now, to move further into recovery, they must *feel* their sad feelings. Burying hides the feelings; feeling the feelings gets rid of them. Because they will want to avoid experiencing the pain of their depression, they will need others to encourage them to *feel* sad, to even insist that they grieve, and then to hang in there with them as they suffer for as long as they suffer.

At this point many will feel a strong desire to drop out of treatment and some will actually do that. It takes courage—there's no other word for it—enormous courage to give up old established behavior that hides feelings when doing so increases personal pain, yet most of the dependents and co-dependents with whom I work do just that. Their courage seems without limits as they deliberately, knowingly, allow themselves to grieve, to face greater emotional discomfort.

We find it helpful to talk with people about the increased pain in advance. If chemically dependent, do they now feel ready to face emotional pain? Are they committed to abstinence, for chemicals will not be an acceptable option to escape from that pain. Whether they are dependent or co-dependent, we talk about the desire to leave treatment they may experience, so that it can be addressed more easily when and if it happens, so that the desire is discussed rather than put into action.

As the grieving process takes place, the great depth of sadness experienced can also make others want to flee or to get the person "fixed up" and out of pain. All of us would do well to remember that grief over loss is healthy—that, in fact, grieving is the *only* remedy for loss. The loss can never be replaced, but the pain of loss can be overcome, by experiencing it fully, and by no other means. It will be easier for us to share another's grief, of course, if we have first allowed ourselves to grieve over our own losses.

Grief is not something co-dependents and dependents willfully conjure up; it begins to well up automatically after abstinence and self-focus are stabilized. Then, no longer as rigidly defended, they have a choice. They can put the lid on it, submerge it once again, or they can let the sadness show itself. And then they have the choice of sticking with it, of feeling it, for as long as it is manifested. Getting well, while it addresses emotions, includes considerable conscious decision making. Our thoughts and feelings may be separate entities, but their impact upon each other is great.

Besides sadness, co-dependents and dependents submerge an incredible amount of anger during active addiction. We often think that it's only the co-dependent who suffers anger secondary to the hurts of unmet dependency needs and abuse. Actually, as we all know, it takes two to tango, and the hurts are not one-sided. In active addiction both the co-dependent and the dependent are out of touch with their feelings and are functioning within the framework of a grossly distorted perception of reality. As a result both are incapable of nurturing, of meeting one another's needs. And co-dependents are often as abusive as dependents. Driven beyond their endurance, they may strike back with screaming taunts, butcher knives, or an angry detachment, which is but a thinly veiled desire for revenge. "Let her get stoned, who cares, maybe this time she'll fall and break her neck." Dependents also suffer the degradation of the co-dependent's virtually constant manipulations. They both suffer years of great hurts and contain an enormous well of rage.

As the co-dependent and dependent experience the sadness

of the losses, they relive their past hurts and, slowly but surely, the sadness dissipates and feelings of anger start trickling to the surface. Then, once again, they have some decision-making to do. Are they going to allow themselves to experience the anger or are they going to shove it under the rug, pretend it isn't happening, and bury it once again? If they bury it, they've got that old can of worms back inside themselves, eating away, consuming their energy, and dictating spasmodic, reactive behavior. And their depression will return, for they've turned their anger back in upon themselves. If they choose to confront their own great rage, chunk by chunk, it will come forth, be experienced, and then dissipated. In time, their well of submerged anger will run dry.

If they choose the latter option, they once again demonstrate enormous courage, for anger is rarely a comfortable emotion and they are, once again, consciously allowing themselves to face greater discomfort. Sometimes, especially with co-dependents and dependents who are also children of alcoholic parents, anger is an emotion that the person has never allowed himself to feel. Or if anger has been expressed it was most likely in the form of a frightening, totally out-of-control tantrum. Thus anger is scary. It has spelled destruction to them in the past—they were the brunt of someone else's anger; or they suffered more pain as the result of their own destructive expressions of anger; or they've actually never expressed anger. Consequently, they fear anger, believing if they express it, they will lose and never regain control. As with the experiencing of their sad feelings, they will again require encouragement, acceptance, and support from their peers and counselors as they experience their anger. They will also profit enormously from the guidelines or techniques for safe expression of anger they receive in their support groups.

Besides dissipation of anger, the constructive experiencing of anger carries with it a sense of power. Anger is a form of energy; when constructively experienced—by talking it out, walking it out, whatever—the anger departs but the energy remains and can be used for further growth; new actions, feelings, and ideas, new opportunities. Thus, once anger is con-structively experienced, worked out, the person begins to feel alive in a new kind of way. She will feel recharged, empowered.

In the setting of the recovery support group, all sorts of per-sonal conflicts are addressed as they are raised. In addition to grief and past anger, co-dependents and dependents will face conflicts over, for example, upcoming retirement; coming out of the closet with one's homosexuality; career change; depen-dency needs; loss of job; the list is virtually endless. As with grief and past anger, most personal conflicts are not resolved in one or two sessions, though some are. Most will be recur-ring issues in the group over a period of time and many ses-sions.

In the setting of the recovery support group, the members first help each other with full expression of the emotions as-sociated with the conflict, pointing out any barriers to such expression, like Susan's defensive judging of her own feelings. Then, once the feelings are sorted out and altered by expres-sion and being understood on an emotional level by others, the precipitating incident can be examined more closely and ac-curately, with attention paid to the presenter's role in that incident. Next, with the greater insight gained from exam-ination, various options for handling the incident become ap-parent and are discussed. By the end of the process, the presen-ter comes to a new ownership of both her responsibility and her solution. With help, she fixes herself.

Where, you might ask, were Jeff and the boys when all of this was taking place with Susan? They were in their own sup-port groups, facing their own personal conflicts. As I've men-tioned, we encourage as many members of the family as pos-sible to become involved in their own treatment; thus several are often with us in separate groups at the same time. I find it absolutely fascinating. Each one of them can be involved in great personal undertakings—such as working through grief or past anger—that increase their individual discomfort without causing all that much disruption in their lives together as a family.

I've done a lot of looking at this fascinating phenomenon of a rise in individual discomfort being accompanied by only minimal or no rise in familial discomfort in the past six years of working with several members of a family at the same time. At first it didn't make sense to me, but now it does. Part of the answer to the riddle has to do with ownership. As each member faces personal conflicts, as we've seen, he or she becomes responsible for his own solution and does not dump on others. Usually, by the end of each session the members are no longer blaming their discomfort on others. They are no longer insisting that others change so they can be comfortable. They are no longer demanding that others take care of them. Thus, though they may go home without the total conflict resolved or perhaps with more discomfort, they go home knowing their conflict is theirs and no one else's.

Part of the answer to the riddle is simple and obvious. Their past familial lives were so disruptive and painful that any new disruptions occurring as a result of working through personal conflicts are insignificant in comparison. It's as if, not knowing peace or harmony, they've become inured to chaos. But part of the answer to the riddle has to do with the fact that there is still considerable emotional distance between the family members. In letting go of each other to some extent, they've given themselves *room*. Now when they experience feelings, they can do so with less entanglement of others. Another part of the answer has to do with the fact that each member of the family has become emotionally strengthened and can more easily tolerate the increased discomfort they perceive in others. In other words, their emotional strength allows them not to take the pain of others personally.

Yet another part of the answer has to do with the fact that the individuals are not only addressing personal conflicts at this point, they are also addressing interpersonal conflicts, and thus from the very onset are learning new ways to relate to others. As they achieve emotional distance and an increased sense of autonomy, they have begun the process of learning or relearning how to relate in ways that are mutually nurturing, first with peers in their groups and then with each other.

In addition to their self-help and recovery support groups, Jim, Virginia, Lynn, and Carla also met with me periodically for assistance with family communications. At the beginning of one such session, Carla announced that she did not want to attend the college in Massachusetts where she had been accepted; instead she wanted to study acting in New York City.

"That's absolutely out of the question," Jim responded immediately, registering shock at the very idea.

"You can't possibly mean that, Carla," Virginia exclaimed.

"You're crazy! You made it into Harvard and now you're not going?" Lynn asked. ·

"Of course she's going. I think it's time we moved on to another topic," Jim declared.

"Hi, Carla! You've really dropped a bomb, haven't you?" I smiled, and turning to the others, I said, "A bomb is a bomb. It's been dropped. You can't just ridicule it or ignore it. We've spent a lot of time in recent months exploring your feelings and how your behavior affects each other, but in a real crisis, like this bomb, your communication breaks down. You don't *listen.* You all react like puppets, jerking all over the place. You were the first to react today, Jim. So let's start with you. Carla said something and you didn't *hear* her . . ."

"I heard her perfectly well," Jim interrupted. "She said she wanted to attend acting classes in New York rather than going to Harvard. She's lucky, very lucky to be in that school. I'm certainly not going to entertain the idea of her giving up that kind of an opportunity. It's simply out of the question."

"That's what I mean," I explained. "You didn't listen . . . not fully. Tuning in to someone means hearing her feelings as well as her words. I'm not even sure you've heard Carla's words, Jim. Do you want to go on communicating in this limited manner or do you want to go further?"

"We're here to learn how to communicate more effectively of course, but I have grave concerns about where this is leading," Jim said.

"You want to know something? I'm not even going to get into your concerns, Jim—not right now. Let's just take this power struggle, and that's what it is, a power struggle, to its natural conclusion. Let's go, Carla, you're the expert at winning power struggles. You go into your Gandhi act, and I'll be your dad. Okay?"

"Yep," Carla replied.

"So drop your bomb again," I said. "You've just walked in here, and I'm your dad."

"I've decided I'm not going to Harvard. I want to study acting at NYU instead."

"That's absolutely out of the question!"

"Why?"

"You have made it into Harvard, young lady, by the skin of your teeth."

"I don't want to go to Harvard."

"That's ridiculous!"

"How do you know what's ridiculous for me?"

"I have a great deal more experience with the world than you have, young lady. And that puts me in a much better position than you to evaluate the wisdom of your decisions."

"You know what I want better than I do?" she asked.

"I know what's wise for you better than you."

"Doing what I don't want is wise?" she asked, incredulous.

"You obviously don't know what's wise, and I'm not going to carry this ridiculous conversation further. I will not entertain the notion of your rejecting an incredible opportunity like Harvard."

"Okay, but you'd be wise not to send the tuition payment."

"The decision has already been made. You selected Harvard, and that's where you're going."

"I've changed my mind, and that's *not* where I'm going."

"I won't hear of this, Carla. Besides New York is not a safe environment for you."

"Oh, for crissakes! Thousands of women my age go to NYU. People do live in New York, you know—millions of people."

"Well, it's not a healthy environment, and I won't hear of it. And I'd appreciate it if you didn't swear."

"Oh, Christ! So don't hear of it. Just don't say I didn't warn you. You're throwing your money away if you pay the tuition to Harvard."

"I'm certainly not paying for acting classes in New York City—or anywhere else for that matter."

"I'm not asking you to," Carla announced.

"What's that supposed to mean?"

"I'll pay for my own classes. You don't seem to understand, Dad. I'm eighteen. I can work. If you don't want to help, I can hang out with friends—get a job as a waitress and study acting part-time."

"That's impossible! Just the expense of commuting into New York every day would be more than you could earn as a waitress . . ."

"You really don't hear, do you, Dad?" Carla interrupted. "I'll live with friends. I've already been offered space in someone's pad. I won't be living at home. But you're right—money will be short, so I won't even be visiting."

"That's the natural conclusion to this power struggle, Jim," I went on, moving out of the roleplay. "Carla will get her way, just as she always has in the past when you've put your will against hers. Did that little roleplay seem real to you—like that's how the whole conversation might have gone?"

"Yes. That's the kind of thing that's happened in the past," Jim agreed.

"What are you feeling right now?" I asked.

"Angry—frustrated, like I don't have any influence—scared, but really angry, disappointed."

"How're you feeling, Carla? You've always won with this kind of thing, but it's not really winning, is it? You were acting like you were being backed into a corner, without options. How're you feeling right now?"

"Angry . . . so angry . . . I just wanted to hurt you," she replied.

"So angry that you were willing to hurt yourself?" I asked.

"Yeah, I guess so—but I'm not going to Harvard."

"Back off, Carla. You want your dad to back off, but you've

also got to get out of the power struggle. Do you like talking with your dad like that? Is that what you want?"

"No."

"Jim, I can appreciate your concerns about Carla's change of mind. Do you see that your gravest danger comes from handling this your old way—by entering and maintaining the power struggle, which just becomes more irrational the longer it lasts?"

"Yes, I guess I can see that."

"That *any* new approach might be better than your old approach," I suggested.

"Well, yes—if that's the way you put it," he replied.

"Is there any other way of putting it? Can *anything* be worse than these irrational power struggles?" I asked.

"No."

"Okay, then let's talk about a new way. I have an assignment for both of you. It's going to require that each of you let go of any decisions about college for at least two weeks," I said, and Jim and Carla each agreed that no action or decision regarding college was required at this time.

"Carla, you brought the topic up today, so we'll start with your expressing yourself to your dad throughout this week. And, Jim, your assignment will be to listen to Carla. Next week, we'll reverse it and have Carla listen to you as you express your ideas and feelings. This is the assignment: every time Carla speaks about any topic, you, Jim, are to restate what she's said to see if you've understood her correctly—listening to both her words and her feelings. Then, Carla, you are to correct your dad if he's not hearing you accurately. If you haven't heard her correctly, Jim, you are to keep restating what you've heard until you get it right. You can repeat her exact words or you can phrase her words differently, but you've got to repeat the *gist* of what she's saying to her satisfaction.

"Let's start now. Carla, you've just come into this meeting. We're beginning at the beginning. Tell us about your change of plans."

"I've decided I don't want to go to Harvard. I want to study acting at NYU instead."

"Why do you want to do that?" Jim asked.

"No, Jim," I interrupted. "That's a question, giving away *your* opinions and feelings. You're supposed to be tuning in to Carla, which means getting out of yourself. And you're not allowed to ask questions—only to restate what you hear her saying and feeling. Start over. Go ahead, Carla."

"I've decided I don't want to go to Harvard. I want to study acting in New York instead."

"You don't want to go to Harvard. You do want to study acting in New York."

"That's right," Carla agreed, with no further elaboration.

I prompted, "Carry it further, Carla. If you want your dad to understand you, you'll have to tell him where you're at."

"I chose Harvard because I knew that's what you wanted. But that's not what I want. I want to go to NYU and study acting."

"You chose Harvard because I wanted it. But you didn't want Harvard yourself. But surely you can take acting classes at Harvard."

"You're not hearing me correctly now," Carla said. "I didn't say anything about acting classes at Harvard."

"I can't say *anything* I want to say?" Jim asked, looking at me.

"No, you can't," I explained. "Your assignment is to put aside your own opinions or feelings. How can you listen to Carla if you're caught up in your own agenda? Get into Carla's words and feelings—and only Carla's. Take up where Carla left off wanting to go to NYU."

"You want to study acting at NYU," Jim began again.

"That's right," Carla agreed. "It's the best school of drama anywhere, and I want the best I can get. It won't even cost you as much."

"NYU has the best drama school and you want the best. And it won't cost me as much."

"Yes. I want to act, Dad. I want that more than anything."

"You want to study acting more than anything."

"And I think I can be good. You know I was good in the plays we put on at school," Carla continued.

"You believe you can be a good actress," Jim said, getting into the swing of it. "And you were good in the plays you've been in."

"Yes . . . really good. I want to be really good, a *great* actress. That's what I've always wanted."

"You've always wanted to be an actress, a great actress."

"Oh yes, Dad, ever since I was little."

"You've wanted to be an actress all your life."

"All my life! Oh, I'm so excited, Dad. I want to be on stage. I want to do all the classics."

"You're more interested in the stage than movies—to do the classics."

"And Tennessee Williams . . . Albee . . . Eugene O'Neill . . . all of them, Dad. I want it all."

"You want all the great plays, all of them."

"All of them, Dad! Oh God, I can't go on," Carla said, bursting into tears for the first time since I had known her. "It feels so good having you listen to me, Dad. I feel like hugging you," and she did.

After a few moments, I said, "You did a terrific job, Jim. How did it feel to you?"

"Well, actually it was quite fun, but I still have grave concerns . . ."

"I'm sure you have," I said. "But for the rest of this week your assignment is to let go of your concerns to tune in to Carla. Next week she'll be putting her own concerns aside and tuning in to you. I bet you found out some things about Carla today that you never knew before."

"Yes, that's certainly true."

"How does that make you feel?"

"Good, but guilty, sorry. I wish I had listened to her more in the past. I feel like I've been left out on a lot. But I feel closer now, like I know you better, Carla," he responded, turning to Carla and once again putting his arm around her.

"Maybe next week she can get to know you better, get closer to you," I suggested.

The secret to effective communication—the kind of communication that enhances and draws people closer—is the fine art of listening. The initial steps to the process of learning or relearning this fine art begin at the onset of recovery, when co-dependents and dependents gain insight into their own feelings. Then they begin to look at the impact of their behavior on others. Next, they begin to tune in to the feelings of others, to step into their shoes, so to speak, so they can *feel* the feelings of the other person and interrelate with empathy. In turn, the person receiving the empathy feels understood and becomes altered as a result of that understanding; consequently he or she can recognize expanded options and choose ways of behaving that best meet the needs of the self as well as others.

After further empathetic interaction with her family, Carla selected Harvard with the understanding that, after her first two years, if she was not getting what she wanted, she would transfer to NYU. It was a decision that satisfied them all. While Jim and Virginia certainly never would have chosen an acting career for Carla, they gained an appreciation for both the profession and Carla's desires. Carla said she chose Harvard for two reasons and admits she doesn't know which influenced her the most. After relating closely with her father, she found she *wanted* to please him. She also thought she would receive a good education in the theater at Harvard. Lynn was delighted; once Carla was "heard," Lynn found a new way to be "heard" herself.

There are two forms of enriching *listening* that occur in recovery: identification and empathy. Identification is a process of feeling the feelings of others *in relation* to one's self, while empathy is a process of feeling the feelings of others *without* relation to self. With identification, one listens in order to bring home, so to speak, what applies. With empathy one listens to move away from home, to become "as one with the other." Identification is possible with or without a clearly delineated sense of self and occurs at the outset and throughout recovery. Empathy, which requires a temporary giving up of oneself, becomes possible only after one has achieved a solid sense of self. After all, one cannot give up what one does not have.

Perhaps the best way to grasp this is to think first of the sense of wholeness, of feeling put together, and then to consider boundaries as the outer edge formed by that wholeness. Chemical dependency is considered a boundary-invasive illness because the defensive behavior of the chemically dependent person shatters the boundaries of those close to him, destroying their sense of wholeness. Consequently, being vulnerable and nonintegrated psychically, co-dependents unconsciously replace their natural boundaries with a shield composed of rigid defensive behavior and attitudes. Not only does this shield block the co-dependents from many of their own feelings, it keeps them from being able to extend themselves in empathy to others.

In recovery, the psyche of the co-dependent is reintegrated, permitting natural boundaries to be reestablished. Once again in touch with their feelings, co-dependents are no longer blocked by a defensive barrier. Empathy is possible as they become more readily able to give themselves up temporarily in order to get closer to others. They do not collapse their boundaries in the process. They keep themselves intact, separate, but now very close.

To listen to Carla, Jim had to put his judgments, ideas, and feelings aside. There's no way we can listen in empathy if we are riddled with our own emotions at the point we are trying to hear the other person; or if we are concentrating on what we're going to say next; or if we believe the other is way off base; or if we are eager for the person to see our view; or whatever. We can only listen in empathy when we put our own agenda aside, when we get out of our own way to give the other our *total* attention.

The recipient of empathy, of course, is strengthened. Carla felt understood and accepted by Jim for perhaps the first time when he empathized with her. Then she could better accept herself, but the reality is that much more than increased self-acceptance occurs, as important as that is. Empathy also alters the emotions of both persons. They both end up with emotions that are quite different from those with which they enter the empathetic experience. Empathy always results in an emotional shift in a welcome direction—from negative to positive; from painful or less pleasurable to less painful or more pleasurable feelings. Empathy creates a high—a nonchemical, self-enhancing high—which is one of the factors that makes recovery an exciting experience. Not only are the feelings moved in a welcome direction, one's horizons are expanded. Rather than feeling optionless, one discovers a multitude of options out of which behavior choices can then be made that meet one's own needs as well as those of others.

Chemically dependent family members, though not readily capable of giving empathy in early recovery, nevertheless receive it from others from virtually the first moment they walk into an Al-Anon, AA, or recovery support group. Later, when they begin to be able to extend empathy to their peers and their families, they begin to rejoice, to thank their Higher Power that they had to suffer from chemical dependency because now they have something wondrous, which many believe they would never have had if not for their illness.

The final work in recovery support groups will very often have to do with sexual conflicts, continuing difficulties with trust, or unfinished family of origin business.

Jim and Virginia, as they became emotionally intimate through empathetic listening, decided they wanted to become more intimate sexually, and sought sex therapy at a nearby hospital as they completed the couples support group they had joined the second year of their recovery. Stoics, the masters of suppression, are terrific; they really don't like their lives of quiet desperation, and as they move into wellness, they are apt to move all the way into wellness.

But being stoical in nature, they will often work very quietly in the recovery support group, which doesn't mean they don't talk but that they are apt to resolve their conflicts through their participation in helping peers work through conflicts. Their role in group is active, but their method of resolving personal conflicts in the group is often indirect. I like to think that I'm reasonably astute, but Jim was in one of my support groups in his first year of recovery and worked through his grief over his losses without my awareness. It was only when he was no longer depressed that we could see that he had been depressed. As he helped others relive their grief, he experienced his own privately.

Many persons who have a strong need for privacy will initially be threatened by the idea of group therapy, yet they are the very ones who can benefit most from the indirect processing that occurs with every member of the group as one person directly addresses a conflict. Groups are a powerful modality of treatment for co-dependents and dependents. Not only do members receive love, acceptance, understanding, valuable feedback, and guidance from several persons, but even when they are not working upon their conflicts directly, their conflicts are being worked upon by the indirect process inherent in every group.

Several years ago, rather than establishing separate groups, we offered recovery support groups for couples, often in conjunction with individual family counseling sessions, and not much happened. On the surface things looked okay. The family members seemed to be increasing their insight into themselves and each other but, after several months, we found that the same conflicts were being raised time and again. It became glaringly evident that personal change in depth was not being achieved, and improved intrafamilial interactions were not being sustained. So we departed from the standard practice at that time and offered separate recovery support groups to the family members in advance of couples group, often in conjunction with individual family counseling sessions. And then remarkable growth occurred—personal and familial.

The individuals need a *safe* environment in order to be able to face and resolve many of their personal conflicts. Susan, for example, might never have been able to address her great rage over past hurts in Jeff's presence. Family members need to be able to learn and then practice empathetic listening with their peers, those with whom they are less emotionally involved, before resolving interpersonal conflicts with each other. Jeff, accustomed to being emotionally detached from people, had much difficulty *hearing* even his peers, and required considerable personal work before being able to tune in to his family.

After nine months in their individual groups, Susan and Jeff joined a couples group where they continued personal conflict resolution while they addressed their interpersonal difficulties, one of which was trust. Jeff wanted Susan's trust. He thought he had earned it, but Susan did not yet seem ready to give it. While she was comfortable with his chemical abstinence, trusting that it would continue, she feared trusting Jeff with her emotions. For good reason as it turned out. In the couples group, virtually every time Susan shared negative feelings of any kind—fear, anxiety, sadness, or whatever—Jeff belittled her feelings. Even if her feelings were the result of a conflict that did not involve Jeff, he put her down for feeling what she felt. Yet he expressed hurt because she did not feel free to share her feelings with him. Jeff was, of course, confronted with this behavior in the couples group, along with the fact that, while he wanted Susan to share more openly with him, he did not share his innermost feelings with her.

Their break in these patterns of nontrust and trust-with-pain occurred during a vacation amidst the Aztec ruins of Mexico. After climbing to the top of a pyramid, Susan found herself paralyzed with fear of the height. She couldn't move, had trouble breathing, and was in such a panic that she couldn't even tell Jeff what was wrong. But Jeff knew what was wrong without being told. He reassured her, telling her that it was going to be okay, that he was going to hold her elbow tightly and guide her down the pyramid one step at a time. For the first time, he invited her trust in him without belittling her feelings; and Susan gave him her trust, feeling that she was literally putting her life in his hands. In turn, he became willing to take the risk of trusting Susan with his feelings. In time, empathetic communication—the mutual sharing—became a natural process and was, of course, extended to their sons. Then they, like Jim and his family, perceived the joys of intimate, nurturing communication.

Their final steps in the recovery support group involved Jeff's reconnecting with his family of origin. Emotional maturation always includes, at some point in our lives, a reevaluation of our parents in order to see them more accurately, even if they are no longer living. In so doing, we begin to perceive strength where we had seen weakness or sickness; or humanness or fallibility where we had seen perfection. In turn, with our more accurate view, we can internalize the wisdom, weaknesses, strengths and courage that we now recognize. While Susan had accomplished this task, which she had begun in primary care and then completed during her process of grieving, Jeff had yet to fully face his father. While he had shared his grief over his father's death and his guilt for being drunk when needed by his dad, Jeff felt he had never really said good-bye.

His recovery support group offered him that possibility, and Jeff accepted. Prepared to stay as late as needed, his group *staged* a psychodrama one evening to give Jeff the opportunity to reconnect with his father. With the lights low and with the group member selected by Jeff to play his father lying on the sofa, the stage was set for Jeff to visit his dying father in the hospital. The psychodrama began as Jeff and Susan entered the hospital room where the other members of the group, now playing the roles of the rest of his family, were gathered around his dad's bedside. At all times, the counselor leading the psychodrama remained at Jeff's side, either holding his arm or with his arm around Jeff's shoulders. After kissing his dad, saying a few words to him and then to his family, Jeff asked to be alone with his dad, and the group members backed away, resuming their seats in another part of the room. Sitting next to his father, holding his hand, Jeff spoke and sobbed for over an hour, describing their good times and their bad times; saying things he had always wanted to say. He ended by telling his dad how much he loved him and hearing from his dad how much he was loved in return, and telling his dad how sorry he was for causing him so much grief because of his alcoholism and being told that he was forgiven in return.

As strange as it may seem, reconnecting with our family of origin to complete the experience of being a child to our parents is possible even when our parents are no longer living. We can still, with our emotions, return to that relationship, often by methods far less dramatic than Jeff's—through introspection, for example, or by speaking of our parents with other relatives, in therapy, in a written but unmailed letter, or in the process of grief. Whatever our method, whether or not our parents still live, emotional maturation does include perceiving our parents accurately and then meeting them on our own terms, so to speak, where we leave the old "they're big, I'm little" immature relationship to move into one of self-mastery in order to relate to them as one adult to another. In the process, we incorporate or take into ourselves our parents' weaknesses and strengths; in so doing we become more accepting of our own weaknesses while we become empowered or enriched beyond ourselves, and our parents become immortal, living on within us.

Those who've observed the stages of life speak of man's expansion of self. Erikson describes mid-life generativity, where as part of man's maturation, he extends himself outward to concern for the species.[12] Vaillant, following the maturation of college students as they travel through life in his book, *Adaptation to Life*, reports that, as the men grew older, the Gods of their understanding became less important as surrogate consciences and more important as an invisible but trusted power behind the universe—the power Erikson describes as necessary for generativity. Peck, in the *The Road Less Traveled*, also points to a qualitative difference between the *belief* of childhood and the *faith* of adulthood, describing how the blind or

12. Erik Erikson, *Childhood and Society* (New York: W. W. Norton and Co., 1950). pp. 247–75.

superstitious belief of childhood often evolves into a lack of belief in the teenage and early adult years to a faith in the "reality of God" in maturity. Peck sees this spiritual growth as a journey from the microcosm of a child's world and view of life to the macrocosm of an ever-enlarging understanding of the reality of the cosmos and our role in it—a life-long journey toward being one with God.

Co-dependents and dependents have a lot of catching up to do spiritually as they leave their illness. Rather than being able to evolve into an enlarged spirituality enjoyed by others, they have been forced by their illness to regress spiritually, sometimes to no belief in any transcendent power and sometimes to a belief in a higher power but no trust or faith in that power; in other words to spiritual bankruptcy wherein they are all alone, filled with utter helplessness and hopelessness.

While AA and other programs neither endorse nor oppose any specific sect or religion, it steps guide co-dependents and dependents along the journey of spiritual growth: an increasing awareness of, trust in, and connectedness to a power greater than self. I hear, rather often, complaints about AA's religiosity, but AA is not in fact a religious organization. Ernest Kurtz describes in his book, *Not God*, how AA members are not required to practice any religious belief or to accept a single concept of deity.[13] Rather, AA members are encouraged to find a power greater than self, which can be construed in any manner the member wishes—the AA group itself, for example; or God, Christ, Buddha, and so forth; or abstract concepts of truth or love. Thereby, whether in the Western world, India, the Orient, or wherever, AA helps its members rise up out of the ashes of their spiritual destruction to a faith in a power transcendent to self that maturing adults not involved with chemical dependency can gain through a more natural spiritual evolution.

Co-dependents and dependents who have faced their illness, accepted total responsibility for it, and made the necessary

13. Ernest Kurtz, *Not God, A History of Alcoholics Anonymous* (Center City, Minnesota: Hazelden Educational Services, 1980). pp. 175–99.

personal changes to overcome it, find themselves living in a new and totally different world. What would once have been considered onerous problems now become exciting challenges; painful feelings become sources of energy; conflicts become sources of guidance; coincidence become miracles; disturbing thoughts become helpful insights; and burdens become gifts. Once goaded by destructive forces beyond their knowledge or control, they now make free choices out of their knowledge of and faith in themselves and a constructive force greater than themselves. Once trapped in painful isolation, they now walk with God and love others as they love themselves. Their lives have become touched by *grace*.

Co-dependents and dependents do not declare themselves recovered; instead, they call themselves recovering. Not only do dependents know their disease is incurable and that they must be ever vigilant to keep it in remission, but both dependents and co-dependents are engaged upon a journey into wellness that includes working toward increased emotional and spiritual growth life-long. In the process of their continuing recovery, aware of the *amazing grace* in their lives, they declare themselves "grateful." *Grateful for the illness that brought forth such wellness.*

Bibliography

Anderson, Daniel. "The Psychopathology of Denial." *Professional Education* pamphlet. Center City, Minnesota: Hazelden Educational Services, 1981.

Bepko, Claudia with Krestan, JoAnn. *The Responsibility Trap.* New York: The Free Press, A Division of MacMillan, Inc., 1985.

Black, Claudia. *It Will Never Happen To Me.* Denver, Colorado: M.A.C. Printing and Publications Division, 1982.

Buscaglia, Leo F. *Living, Loving and Learning.* New York: Ballantine Books, 1982.

Erikson, Erik. *Childhood and Society.* New York: W. W. Norton and Co., 1950.

Freud, Anna. *The Ego and The Mechanisms of Defense.* London: International Universities Press, 1937.

Krupnick, Louis and Krupnick, Elizabeth. *From Despair to Decision.* Minneapolis, Minnesota: CompCare Publications, 1985.

Kurtz, Ernest. *Not God, A History of Alcoholics Anonymous.* Center City, Minnesota: Hazelden Educational Services, 1980.

Laundergan, J. Clark. *Easy Does It.* Center City, Minnesota: Hazelden Educational Services, 1982.

Peck, M. Scott. *The Road Less Traveled.* New York: Simon and Schuster, 1978.

Vaillant, George E. *Adaptation to Life.* Boston: Little, Brown and Company, 1972.

Vaillant, George E. and Milofsky, Eva S. "The Etiology of Alcoholism: A Prospective Viewpoint," *American Psychologist* 37(5), 1982.

Wegscheider, Sharon. *Another Chance.* Palo Alto, California: Science and Behavior Books, 1981.

Index

About the Author

Ruth Maxwell is the author of *The Booze Battle* and a pioneer in developing services to meet the needs of chemically dependent persons and their families. She has worked in the field as a psychiatric nurse and alcoholism counselor for over fifteen years. In 1980, she founded the Maxwell Institute in Westchester, New York, which has helped to treat thousands of families affected by chemical dependency. Ms. Maxwell has served on the faculty of several universities and is a frequent speaker on chemical dependency in the U.S. and in Europe. She is currently in private practice in New York City and Westchester.